funded today

The Ultimate Guide to Crowdfunding

Discover our PROVEN SYSTEM to quickly raise BIG money for your next BIG idea

By

Zach Smith & Thomas Alvord

Printed in the United States of America
First Printing, 2021

ISBN 978-1-7355728-1-9

Funded Today
717 East 4750 South
South Ogden, UT 84403
FundedToday.com

Edited by Karen Daniels, karendaniels.com

Dedication

To our wives, Courtney Bergen and Melanie Alvord, for their support and patience over the past 5+ years.

To our clients, for their continued trust in us helping bring their "babies" to life.

To our beloved Funded Today team members, who have helped build and made our success.

And finally, to Karen Daniels, our editor, who believed in us and made sure this book came to life.

Contents

Anti-Foreword xix
Introduction 1

Chapter 1: Crowdfunding Demystified Did this Really Just Happen? 3
What is Crowdfunding? 7
Crowdfunding Works 10
Finding the Funds 11
Different Types of Crowdfunding 14
Picking a Crowdfunding Platform 16
Comparing Kickstarter and Indiegogo 16

Chapter 2: Finding a Great Idea that Sells 221
Funded Today's Product Success Formula 22
What other factors make for a good product? 24
Flushing Out a Great Idea 25
6 Tips for Deciding on Your Great Idea 27
Great Ideas are Everywhere 33

Chapter 3: They Really Like You: Get Your Crowd Validation 365
How to Best Utilize Crowd Validation 36

Harness the power of crowd validation: 38
What if the Crowd Doesn't Like Your Idea? 40
What Makes a Crowdfunding Campaign Fail.....44
The Power of the Pivot.......................................47
The Right Mindset is Key 48

Chapter 4: 7 P's of Crowdfunding Success....54
Introducing the 7 P's 54
Product 54
Platform 57
Presentation..63
Promotion 64
Special promotion sub "P's" 64
Price...67
Probability..69
People...70
Summing up the 7 P's 72
Key Takeaways...75

Chapter 5: The Triple F – Friends, Family and Fools 77
The Triple F Strategy 77
How to Implement the Triple F 81
Why You Can't Let Fear Stop You 83

What You Shouldn't Be Worrying About............ 86

Putting the Triple F and Feedback into Action.... 89

Key Takeaways 95

Chapter 6: Setting Up Your Crowdfunding Campaign 97

Elements of a Good Crowdfunding Campaign ... 97

Know the Rules of Your Chosen Platform 99

Kickstarter 100

IndieGoGo 101

Show Me the Money 102

How Much Should Your Funding Goal Be? 102

Kickstarter Goal vs Real Goal 103

The Benefit to Using Your LVG 104

When LVG Isn't Really Applicable............. 106

Setting up Your Crowdfunding Bank Account... 107

Chapter 7: Creating a Video that Converts .. 112

Introducing Our Kickstarter Video Formula....... 112

Component 1:: Product................................... 112

Component 2: Persuasive Script............... 113

Component 3: Visuals and Audio 114

Component 4: You 1145

Your Project Video Outline 116

Video Outline, Part I: Source the problem ..116
Video Outline, Part II: Present the Solution 117
Video Outline, Part III:Why I'm Passionate: 118
Video Outline, Part IV: The Resolution 119
But Wait, There's More 119
The Role of Your Video 120
How Much Should You Spend? 121
Balance is the Key 121
The Shoestring Budget 122
Bringing Your Story to Life 124
The All-Important First 10 Seconds 125
Keep it Short 126
Your Video Crew 126
Video FAQ's 128
That's a Wrap 129
Key Takeaways 129
Video Creation Resources 130

Chapter 8: Developing a Compelling Page...132
How to Make an Unsuccessful Page 132
Warning: Don't Imitate 133
Mistakes to Avoid......................................136
Page Design...137
The Page Structure 139
Page Content 141

Start with the Right Mindset 141
Pitching Lemonade (or Anything) 141
Product Benefits and Features 144
Use Caution if Offering Medical Benefits 145
Your Sales Pitch 146
The Video 147
Images & GIFS 147
A Note on Crew Photos 148
Backer Rewards 149
Actively Manage Your Page 151
Test Everything 152
Conclusion: It's Not About You 153
Key Takeaways 157

Chapter 9: Setting Your Pledge Levels 159
How to Win the Backer 159
Remove Obstacles 160
Obstacle 1: Your Funding Goal 160
Obstacle 2: Your Rewards Structure 161
Your Reward Structure 163
Reward Pricing 164
Describing Your Rewards 166
Stretch Goals 167
Upsells 168

Can a Backer Pledge More Than Once? 170

Prepare Yourself: Backers Will Cancel 172

Reward Yourself 172

Chapter 10: Preparing for Launch Day 177

Your Final Preparations 177

Know Your Platform 175

Plan Your Launch Schedule 176

Your Prototype 177

The BIG M - Marketing 177

Should You Hire an Agency? 178

Marketing Backend Basics 181

Your Email Leads 183

Landing Pages to Increase Email Leads 183

Communicating with Your Email Leads 184

Public Relations (PR) 185

Influencers 186

Reporters 187

And, Finally... 187

Chapter 11: Launch Day 189

Have the Right Mindset 189

Launch Day Final Prep 191

The Private Preview Link 193

The FAQs.. 194

Prepare to Launch 196

Ready to Launch?.. 197

Kickstarter 197

Indiegogo.. 198

Launch Day.. 200

As Soon as You're Live 200

Google Analytics 200

Emailing.. 201

Responding to Comments and Cancelled Pledges 201

A Note About Trolls 202

The Bigger Picture... 203

The Magic Category 207

Kickstarter's "Projects We Love" Category. 208

You Did it! 209

Chapter 12: Mareting - Paid Meida 211

Marketing is Not Magic 211

Pitching Online Products 213

The Single Most Effective Type of Marketing ... 214

Our Best Practices for Paid Media................... 218

Facebook.. 218

Your Ad Set 219

Your Ads 220
The Custom Audience 222
Metrics..223
Click-Through Rate 223
Earnings Per Visitor (EPV) 225
And, Finally... 227
Key Takeaways 228

Chapter 13: Marketing Your Campaign - Press 231
The Odd Kid on the Block 231
Things You Should Know 232
Uniqueness Counts 233
PR Leads to Validation - not direct pledges234
How to Get Started 236
Crowdfunding PR 237
Go for Conversions, Not Greatness 238
Timing...239
Where to Pitch 240
Be Persistent 242
Our Secret Strategy 242
The Snowball Effect 245
Tracking Press Impact...............................247
Is it Too Late for Press? 248

Parting Words of Advice 248
Key Takeaways 249

Chapter 14: Marketing Your Campaign – Other Traffic Methods 251

The Single Best Marketing Strategy We Use ... 251

Why Even Do Cross Collaborations? 253

Best Strategy for Cross Collaborations............. 253

Understanding Conversions 254

Dealing with Naysayers 256

The Kickstarter Community.............................. 257

Getting Other Campaigns to Collaborate.......... 259

How to Do Great Updates................................ 260
6 Tips for Effective Updates:............................ 260

Conclusion: Cross Collaborations DO NOT Hurt Your Campaign... 262

Key Takeaways 263

Chapter 15: Prelaunch Community Building and Email Lead Generation 265

The Pareto Principle 265

The Crowdfunding Success Matrix 267

How the Success Matrix Works................. 268

Outer Darkness - Quadrant 4: “Bad” Product “Bad” Marketing....................................... 269

Black Hole - Quadrant 3: "Bad" Product Good Marketing 270
Shooting Star - Quadrant 2: Good Product Bad Marketing 271
Supernova - Quadrant 1: Good Product Good Marketing. 271
The Importance of Recognizing Your Quadrant 272
Pre-Launch Marketing 273
Target Groups for Pre-launch Marketing 274
Personal Contacts 274
Business Contacts 275
Social-Media Fans 275
Influencers 276
Reporters 276
Utilizing Email 277
Email Leads 277
Email Leads: Landing Pages 278
Email Leads: Communication 279
"Organic" Enticements 280
Key Takeaways 281

Chapter 16: Analyzing Your Campaign 2863
Your Google Analytics Primer 286
The Google Analytics Menu 286
Traffic Sources 287

Learn More 290

Chapter 17: Creating a Campaign that Won't Get Banned 2921
Voluntarily Relaunch 292
Campaign Suspension 293
Involuntary Relaunch Checklist 298

1. Determine reason for the cancellation.... 298
2. Appeal the decision. 300
3. Contact your Backers. 301
4. Preempt the Cancellation 302
5. Reconsider the platform you're on 302
6. Remobilize your Backers 303
7. Resume your Marketing. 303

Conclusion 304
Key Takeaways 3044

Chapter 18: Delivering on Your Campaign 3087
Manufacturing Overview 308
"I've Got a Prototype!" 308
Finding a Good Manufacturer 309
Scalability 309
Use of Existing Molds 309
Location Analysis 310
Your Next Steps 311
Production: FAQs 313

Key Takeaways 319

Chapter 19. Building a Company Post Campaign 321
3 Lessons from Kickstarter 321
1. Kickstarter as a place for validation. 321
2. Be Committed to Success. 323
3. You Get Better with Practice, So Be Patient. Your Next Campaign Will Likely Be Better. 324
Post Crowdfunding - Getting Started 325
Your USP - Unique Selling Proposition 327
Price Point & Cost Per Acquisition 329
Customer Lifetime Value Point 330
Cross Sells & Upsells 333
Your Strategy & Multiple Channels 334
Embrace Your Email List 338
A Note on Ownership 339
Your Brand 341
Conclusion 342
Key Takeaways 343
Bonus Section: That Legal Stuff 344
Patent 345
Trademark 346
Copyright 347
The Law Won't Make You Money 347
What We Recommend You Do: 352

Incorporate 352
Summary 356

Chapter 20: Crowdfunding a Version 2.0 of Your Product and Building a Long Term Business through Multiple Crowdfunding Campaigns 358
Multiple Crowdfunding Campaigns 358
Crowdfunding as a Business Strategy 358
Using Indiegogo InDemand 361
The On-Off Strategy 364
Secret Perks 366
Shark Tank & Investors 367
Key Takeaways 369

Chapter 21: Relaunching Your Campaign if You Don't Hit Your Goal… 371
If at First You Don't Succeed… 371
The Tragic Tale of the Edsel........................... 372
What Can We Learn from This? 374
Preparing to Relaunch 375
Remobilize Your Backers 377
Recommit to Yourself, Your Success 377

A Final Note 380
Additional Resources 383
About the Authors 3901

Anti-Foreword

Can we get real with you for a sec?

We hate forewords. We also hate fluff and theory.

Everything you will read in this book is proven, actionable advice. These are the strategies, techniques, and methods we have used to raise over $300 million for over 2,000 new startups across the globe.

So, let's get down to business. And if you already have an idea, and if you want to take an expedited approach to validate your concept, skip straight to Chapter 4.

(And yes, we love our moms, and everyone else who influenced us, too).

Introduction

If you're reading this book, it's probably because you have an idea. Not just one of those fleeting notions you came up with while sitting around with friends and said, "wouldn't it be great if X existed?" and your buddies wholeheartedly agreed.

Instead, what you have is a solid concept that you've been mulling over – maybe just since last week, or possibly for years. It might be a product that solves a problem, or addresses a challenge faced by a lot a people. Perhaps it's a new twist on something that exists - a better mousetrap, if you will. Whatever it is, you're pretty sure your idea could be big. Really big.

You've run your idea by anyone and everyone that would listen, and have resoundingly gotten positive responses letting you know your product is truly something unique. People want your product. They need it. More importantly, people have told you they would pay to get their hands on it.

That's got you thinking about how to make your big idea a reality. But where to start? It can be a daunting, complex, and overwhelming effort to bring your product to market.

Or, maybe it doesn't have to be.

What if there was a simplified path to bring your product to market and build a successful business around it?

Well, there is. And it's called crowdfunding!

We know crowdfunding works because we've helped thousands of regular people, like you, with great product ideas raise over $329 million dollars. In our more than 20 years of combined experience, we've conceived and launched wildly-successful crowdfunding campaigns that have made many of our clients into millionaires.

Here's the deal. We can help you live the entrepreneurial life you've dreamed about. You don't have to give up equity. There's no beating on the doors of banks or venture capitalists. You don't have to look to family and friends for an investment or loan. We are sharing our crowdfunding expertise with you to make your dream a reality.

In this book you'll learn:

- What crowdfunding is (and isn't)
- Everything needed to successfully use crowdfunding to get your product to the masses
- What successful crowdfunding efforts look like through dozens of real-life examples
- Learn from the missteps of others, and what not to do
- How to build a business around your crowdfunded product

This book is your guide. Your advisor. Your mentor. And your ticket to success.

Your journey starts right now!

1

Crowdfunding Demystified: Did This Really Just Happen?

***Whether you think you can or you can't, you're probably right.* Henry Ford**

"I need $100,000 and you only have 100 hours to get it for me."

We were intimidated. Even a little scared.

Just a few days prior, we had finished raising $115,111 in 35 days for a new product in a similar space.

But this one was different. We only had 100 hours. Essentially 4 days. AND we needed to raise nearly as much money in those 100 hours as we had done in 35 days!

Between the two of us, we had more than two decades of experience marketing companies from Utah to Dubai, launching new products and brands for start-ups as well as established businesses, and consulting on U.S Presidential campaigns as well as for Fortune 500 companies.

However, we had *never* experienced a business situation like this.

And while we had all that vast business experience with startups, crowdfunding was completely new to us. We had no clue what to expect.

Our client, Harry, had an entrepreneurial dream. He had a brand-new startup and had just launched on Kickstarter.com, hoping to raise $300,000 to bring his new idea to life. Unfortunately, over the previous 40 days he had raised just shy of $200,000, well short of his goal by $100,000.

And it got worse:

If he didn't raise an additional $100,000 in the next 100 hours, he was going to lose all of the money he had already raised!

Those were the rules. That's how Kickstarter operates. It's all-or-nothing. Dreams made; dreams dashed. You have to hit the goal you set beforehand, or you don't receive any of the money.

Looking back, he should have set a lower dollar goal to begin with. But he had set it at $300,000, and after his campaign went live, he couldn't change it.

What were we going to do?

Harry reached out to us for a reason. He had seen us raise lots of money for other businesses and startups.

And the challenge got even more complicated. The deal Harry wanted us to take was all or nothing. He wanted us to front the entire marketing bill (all the money that would be required to run online ads). In short, he wanted us to take all of the risk by putting this ad spend on our own credit card.

PLUS, he would only pay us if we raised at least $300,000, pushing him past his crowdfunding goal. If we didn't, he would have no money to pay us.

The risk was huge. The reward, even larger... if we succeeded. IF.

Even for us, the task seemed undoable. So, we spoke with Harry and told him we would have to pass. We were marketing and business professionals but had never faced a time crunch like this. And never with our own money on the line.

Harry wasn't fazed. He insisted we proceed. He said he knew we would be able to do it.

Hah! Easy for him to say!

But then he upped the ante. He agreed to pay us even more money than he initially offered if we hit his $300,000 goal or better. The potential reward became even greater. Now was our shot. How could we turn down this opportunity, no matter how challenging it seemed?

And so, we went for it!

And guess what? The money came steamrolling in.

It was as if we had discovered a formula for printing cash! And a mere 100 hours later Harry's new invention had $325,208 in funding.

Did this really just happen?

That's when we realized we were onto something even bigger than we had imagined. With even more potential than all of our previous business endeavors.

Over the years, we had picked up skills, tactics, and marketing approaches that were designed to raise lots of money for all kinds of different businesses. These skills had not only helped new startups, but as we recognize now looking back, could also be applied to this new and exciting world called **Crowdfunding**.

Those real-world experiences and approaches, and the successful strategies we've learned, form the foundation for this book.

We all know that good ideas can come from anywhere. It doesn't matter your level of education, what you do for a living, your gender, or your socioeconomic class.

But not everyone has the financial means, resources, or connections to take things from a concept to an actual product or business. Maybe you're working a full-time job, and spending all your spare time at night or on the weekends developing your product. Perhaps you've cobbled together a prototype, but need cash to take your product to the next level and make it a reality.

No worries, there's a way to make it happen!

Crowdfunding can power your amazing journey. We love crowdfunding. Mostly because we've now witnessed and participated in thousands of projects that have collectively raised more than $329 million. Our years of hard-won experience working with inventors, innovators, and people with great ideas have proven that anyone can go from an idea to a real product using crowdfunding.

We love helping make these dreams come true. And we want to share our expertise to make you successful, too!

What is Crowdfunding?

You may have heard about crowdfunding. Or perhaps, you're not familiar with the word, but have an understanding of the concept. Let's explain. At its' core, crowdfunding is the collective effort of a large number of individuals who network and pool small amounts of capital to finance a new or existing business venture. Each project is set for a goal amount of money and a fixed time frame. Each day is counted down and the money raised is tallied up for visitors to follow its success - your success!

The term crowdfunding is relatively new to mainstream vocabulary. According to Wordspy.com, the earliest recorded use of the word was in August of 2006[11].

But the concept of crowdfunding long predates documented use of the word. Through the ages, many of the arts - music, books, paintings - were financed by having masses of people invest in projects to bring them to fruition.

In fact, one of the first crowdfunding projects in American history may be Joseph Pulitzer. He went to the masses via the newspapers, and got a couple bucks

---

[1] (n.d.). crowdfunding - Word Spy. Retrieved October 14, 2019, from https://www.wordspy.com/words/crowdfunding.asp

from thousands of people, enough to fund the base of the Statue of Liberty[2].

The concept itself stems from the wisdom of the crowds. This means that large groups of people are collectively smarter than individual experts when it comes to problem-solving. In fact, the ancient Greek philosopher, Aristotle, presented the theory of collective judgment in his work *Politics*. He used a potluck dinner as an example, explaining that a group of individuals may come together to create a more satisfying feast for a group as a whole than what one individual might provide.

What that means for you is that there is a long and rich (and delicious!) history of large groups of people coming together to support and invest in the ideas of others to bring them to life.

Reasons vary for supporting the efforts of others to produce *something* - be it a film, a musical endeavor, or a product. Here are some of the reasons people might have to support the effort of others:

- People may have an altruistic intent. They simply want to provide philanthropic support for something they believe is needed, or something that makes the world a better place.

- Some backers may want bragging rights by association to claim they had a part in making this "thing" become a reality - especially if they think it will be a big hit.

---

2. "The Statue of Liberty and America's crowdfunding pioneer - BBC." 25 Apr. 2013, https://www.bbc.com/news/magazine-21932675. Accessed 13 Nov. 2019.

- Others, still, may see a product as something they can't live without, and therefore, participation in financing the product will make it come to life.

All these reasons work in your favor. Having the backing of the masses can not only provide financial means for you, but it proves that what you're offering resonates with people. They like it. They see your vision. And they are willing to buy into it - literally.

This book, **Funded Today - How to Launch Your Next Big Idea**, focuses on how to get a lot of people to fund your idea, your product. We are not talking about the efforts of pure donation for a charitable cause using a platform such as GoFundMe.com. Those types of giving/donation platforms are meant to help a person or group or entity in need - usually because of a tragic occurrence. Often, if there are victims of fire or natural disaster, or someone is battling a medical problem, a GoFundMe campaign is started to offer relief and financial support.

While that is certainly a form of crowdfunding, the intent of this book hones in on the most effective way to use rewards-based crowdfunding as a way to raise money for a product and build a company. In other words, using crowdfunding to fund your entrepreneurial dream.

Money is easier to make than you think!

Crowdfunding Works

The path to raising money for a product via crowdfunding has captured the attention of millions.

The truth is in the numbers:

- The number of crowdfunding campaigns is expected to reach 216,200 by 2022 - Statista (where?)
- The transaction value for crowdfunding is expected to show an annual growth rate (CAGR 2018-2022) of 10.4% by 2022 - Statista.
- Between Kickstarter and Indiegogo, (the two popular platforms for raising funds for new products), roughly $1 billion is given to new campaigns each year. (Source: **Funded Today** internal data).

Now, let's take a look at one of the most successful crowdfunding campaigns of all time: The Coolest Cooler.

In August of 2014 the product raised more than $13 million, and had more than 62,000 backers. That amount raised was a jaw-dropping 26,570% over the amount of the company's goal.

Seriously? It's a cooler. Coolers have been around for decades. But the inventor dreamed of reinventing a basic item with innovative features he wanted when he spent fun time outdoors. So, the Coolest Cooler has a built-in blender for conveniently making cocktails outdoors, removable Bluetooth speakers, a waterproof USB charger, advanced storage systems, LED lights, a bottle opener, and so much more. This struck a chord with others - 62,345 others to be exact. The Coolest Cooler is the complete redesign of what a cooler can be.

There are tons of successful crowdfunding projects to read about and learn from. It's important to realize that a particular product's success is not necessarily linked to the total amount of money raised. Not all products need millions to launch. For example, have you ever heard of a PopSocket?

The PopSocket campaign "only" raised $18,591[3], **but then went on to gather more than $168 million in annual revenue.**[4]

Pretty great, right?

Finding the Funds

The Coolest Cooler is just one of thousands of crowdfunding success stories. And, as the PopSocket illustrates, not everyone has initially raised millions of dollars, but many have still been very successful after their initial crowdfunding campaign. Most entrepreneurs using crowdfunding have more modest goals. Nevertheless, the internet has made crowdfunding easier and given a wider - even global - reach to anyone that has an idea and wants to raise the money to make their idea a reality. It doesn't matter if you need to raise $1 million or $50,000: crowdfunding can power your success.

---

[3] "PopSockets iPhone Case: It Pops, Props, Kicks ... - Kickstarter." 8 Jan. 2012, https://www.kickstarter.com/projects/1250439912/popsockets-iphone-case-it-pops-props-kicks-and-cli. Accessed 13 Nov. 2019.

[4] "PopSockets - Boulder, CO - Inc.com." https://www.inc.com/profile/popsockets. Accessed 13 Nov. 2019.

Previously, if you had an idea for a product, you had a variety of ways you could finance your idea. However, nearly all of them were a hard road, and often required massive tradeoffs.

Here are some of the alternatives to crowdfunding and some of the pitfalls:

- Raise money from friends and family. It's nice that those closest to you believe in your passion. However, it could make for tense family relations if something doesn't work out.
- Try to secure a small business loan. These are typically hard to get, especially if you haven't got a product yet. And since you're trying to get the loan in order to build a prototype or finance the project, it turns into the chicken and the egg conundrum.
- Use whatever nest egg you've saved. This option could put you at risk of losing your retirement or your children's college fund, leaving you with no fall back financial cushion.
- Take out a second mortgage. If things don't pan out, you might end up homeless and put your family at risk.
- Navigate the complex network of venture capitalists to find an investor. Even if you secure an investment, it will require you to give up equity in your business, and possibly even lose overall control of it.

So, yes, there are different ways to finance an idea. But most come with a substantial downside and a host of challenges. The biggest problem with most of the options listed above is that you MUST have product (or at least proof of concept or a prototype) prior to seeking nearly all of these financial paths.

Enter: crowdfunding.

The benefits to rewards-based crowdfunding are numerous. Here are just a few.

- When you crowdfund, you often don't need to have a completed product. In fact, you can start a crowdfunding campaign to raise money for an idea for a product without actually having the product. Of course, you have to be up front and explicit about the state of your invention. And fortunately for you, crowdfunding kind of already has this built in. This makes it easier to explain and outline your progress as you seek out investments via crowdfunding to create your product. The good news is that this means there's no upfront cost for you to hire a manufacturing firm to begin producing the product before getting the money.

- You don't have to give up equity in your business. As we mentioned, other fundraising options force you to give up a percentage of your company (if you even have a company at that point). This often means that, right off the bat, you are not in total control of things. You don't want to put decisions about product features, pricing, marketing, and hiring employees in the hands of someone who has invested cash but doesn't have the passion and sweat equity you've already invested.

- Crowdfunding also enables you to control every aspect of the fundraising process. You're not standing in front of suit-wearing venture capitalists who are set on getting a specific return on their investment. Instead, you are "pitching" this to regular folks, who probably relate to where you're coming from, and are eager to actually buy your product when it becomes available. This is solid proof that you have a market. That there is a viable opportunity for you to make money.

Different Types of Crowdfunding

There are several types of crowdfunding. We're going to lay out the most popular types here and explain what type works best in which situations, and also how you can effectively set up these various types of campaigns. And most importantly, we'll get into details in subsequent chapters on reward-based crowdfunding, which will be the focus of this book.

1. **Donation**
2. **Equity**
3. **Debt/Lending**
4. **Reward**

Donation. With donation-based crowdfunding, a person gives money or a resource to support a cause. This is like we described earlier with GoFundMe.com. These donation-based efforts often help people or organizations in need. Nothing is given in return to the donor. It's all about altruism and feeling good, while contributing to someone in an effort to offer support and relief.

Equity-based crowdfunding. Equity-based crowdfunding enables those providing financial support to gets shares (or a percentage) of the company that is raising funds. This often motivates those making an investment to further promote a crowdfunding campaign. Because the more successful the company is in raising funds, the better it is for them as a minority owner. If the company gains traction and achieves success after the crowdfunding efforts, these investors/owners can receive dividend checks. An example of an equity-based crowdfunding platform is MicroVentures.

Within equity-based crowdfunding is real estate crowdfunding. Real estate crowdfunding could be considered a sub niche of equity crowdfunding, or could be its own category. In either case, investors put in money for shares of equity in real estate. Typically, these are open only to accredited investors. Popular platforms for real estate crowdfunding are RealtyShares, CrowdStreet, and RealCrowd, but there are many others.

Debt-based crowdfunding. If you simply want to borrow money from the crowd, you might employ a debt-based crowdfunding strategy. This is where you essentially are asking people to contribute, but you have a legal obligation to repay the loan at set intervals and with a predetermined interest rate. The most popular platform for debt crowdfunding is LendingClub.

Reward-based crowdfunding. Reward-based crowdfunding gives the investor a reward or perk in exchange for their financial backing. There are often different levels of rewards, depending on the amount given. For example, you could set a goal that you need to raise $5,000 to make and manufacture a new wallet. If somebody pledges or contributes $20 they would receive one wallet, $35 for two wallets, and $45 for three wallets. The most popular platforms for rewards-based crowdfunding are Kickstarter.com, and Indiegogo.com. This book will focus on reward-based crowdfunding, because reward-based crowdfunding is the primary type of crowdfunding Funded Today has utilized to help raise over $329 million dollars for more than 3,000 entrepreneurs across the world.

Picking a Crowdfunding Platform

What makes crowdfunding work is the online platforms that power your campaign. There are two main crowdfunding platforms for rewards-based crowdfunding: Kickstarter and Indiegogo. At their core, they both function in similar ways.

Generally speaking, here's how crowdfunding platforms work:

1. You apply to get your product listed on the platform.
2. Once approved, you set the length of the campaign and all the details, including your goal of how much you'd like to raise.
3. People going to the site see the campaigns and decide if they want to back *your* campaign.

Those are the very basics. And while each of the platforms function the same at the core, there are definite differences.
Where Kickstarter and Indiegogo differ is in terms of performance and scope.

Comparing Kickstarter and Indiegogo

In our professional opinion, if you're trying to decide between Kickstarter and Indiegogo, **the answer is 100% Kickstarter.**

Kickstarter outperforms Indiegogo on every objective measure that matters. Namely, raising money for your campaign.

There is no doubt in our mind that if you are launching a crowdfunding campaign, and trying to decide between Kickstarter vs. Indiegogo, your best option is Kickstarter.

The reason we can say that with total confidence is because our company, **Funded Today** has worked with (as of this writing) 2,506 Kickstarter campaigns, and 382 Indiegogo campaigns. That's 2,888 campaigns in total, with 87% of our campaigns on Kickstarter, and 13% of our campaigns on Indiegogo. Of those 2,888 live campaigns that ended, we followed 230 of them to Indiegogo InDemand. We've also worked with 60 additional InDemand campaigns that we never helped while they were live. Currently (October 2019) we have 27 live campaigns running and dozens more that are preparing to launch.

We have more actual experience working with both Kickstarter and Indiegogo than anyone else. We know Kickstarter and Indiegogo inside and out. In fact, at **Funded Today** we have run more marketing to Kickstarter and Indiegogo than anyone else in the entire world.

Nobody has worked on as many Kickstarter and Indiegogo campaigns as Funded Today, and no one else has spent as much money driving traffic to Kickstarter and Indiegogo as Funded Today.
In addition to our experience, we also have more Kickstarter and Indiegogo stats and data than anyone else - except Kickstarter and Indiegogo themselves.

Funded Today tracks every Kickstarter and Indiegogo campaign, and every hour updates how many pledges each campaign has, how many backers each campaign has, along with many other statistics. We have years and years of stats and data on each and every campaign.

In addition to tracking the public data on every Kickstarter and Indiegogo campaign, we have detailed data on 2,091 campaigns. Looking at just the stats and data we have from Google Analytics in our database, we have 2,245,752 rows of data, tracking every visit, and every pledge, and every referral source, for every campaign we have worked on. Additionally, our custom link shortener, called fnd.to, which we run all our marketing, has tracked 75,242,578 visits. Our data includes over 374,000 Kickstarter campaigns totaling $3.6 billion in pledges, and over 303,000 Indiegogo campaigns totaling $1.2 billion in pledges.

When we dive into the Kickstarter vs. Indiegogo stats, the data doesn't lie. And the bottom line is that you are going to raise the most money on Kickstarter.

- The average amount raised on Kickstarter is 2.35 times higher than on Indiegogo. Specifically, the average pledge amount on Kickstarter is $9,835, whereas the average pledge amount on Indiegogo is only $4,182[5].
- The probability of raising $10,000 on Kickstarter is 14%, whereas on Indiegogo it is only 5%. That's based off of the historical data for Kickstarter and Indiegogo.

---

[5] "Kickstarter vs Indiegogo - Which is Better? | Funded Today." https://www.funded.today/blog/kickstarter-vs-indiegogo-which-is-better. Accessed 13 Nov. 2019.

- If you are aiming for higher amounts, the probability of raising $100,000 on Kickstarter is 1.5%, whereas on Indiegogo it is only .4%.
- Want to shoot for $1 million? Your chances are .08% on Kickstarter, but only .03% on Indiegogo.
- Looking at campaigns that raise $10,000+, you are 3 to 5 times more likely to hit that amount on Kickstarter than on Indiegogo.

Additionally, we have worked with dozens of campaigns that were both on Kickstarter and Indiegogo at the same time. Everything about the campaigns and ads were identical (product, graphics, videos, etc.). The ONLY difference is the platform.

Notwithstanding the fact that EVERYTHING was exactly the same, the conversion rate was always lower on Indiegogo. Even our ad click thru rates, for the exact same ad, perform worse when the destination is Indiegogo instead of Kickstarter.

People are more likely to click on your ad and buy your product if they see Kickstarter instead of Indiegogo.

We believe it's because Kickstarter regulates their community and campaigns a lot more than Indiegogo. Thus, Kickstarter has a stronger brand reputation, and greater public trust. You associate your product and receive validation from Kickstarter by virtue of the fact that you are on Kickstarter. It's not every campaign that gets to be on Kickstarter. You must be approved.

However, when it comes to customer support, Indiegogo hands down wins here. Kickstarter's customer support is not good. To their credit, it has improved over the years, but it is still lacking. Good luck trying to talk to someone at Kickstarter either before or after your campaign launches. If you do, you often have to wait up to a few days to receive an email back, which is typically just from a generic email address at Kickstarter.

And while Indiegogo will likely try to entice you to launch on its platform by promising you some extra promotions, most people - including us - would rather have a campaign that raises 3 to 4 times the amount with lackluster customer support than a campaign that has great customer support but raises less.

Both platforms charge fees - 5%, plus credit card processing fees. This means the issue of fees is irrelevant and shouldn't be part of your platform choice.

One last factor to consider is whether Kickstarter will let you launch on their platform. If you are creating a product, Kickstarter requires a prototype. If you don't have a prototype, you won't be able to launch on their platform. This is a double-edged sword. They have this policy for a reason. Kickstarter knows that having a prototype greatly increases the chances you will be able to deliver on your product. However, sometimes you need to crowdfund to get the funds just to do the prototype.

Indiegogo will let you be in the pre-prototype stage and still launch your campaign. If you don't have a prototype, this isn't so much a choice between Kickstarter vs. Indiegogo, as you only have one option at this point.

Now that you have some basic, foundational knowledge, let's dig in to the specifics of running a crowdfunding campaign. Now the fun begins!

2

Finding A Great Idea That Sells

The person who says it cannot be done should not interrupt the person doing it.
Chinese Proverb

Everyone has a jacket.

Everyone needs a jacket.

The concept of a jacket has been around for ages. And it's pretty simple. It covers you up, keeps you warm, probably has pockets, and maybe a hood. But one couple had a great idea and decided they were going to invent a jacket that was so much more.

The BauBax Travel Jacket was born out of the desire to create a jacket that would make it easier to accommodate people's gadgets, and quickly give them access to those much-needed items that make travel easier and more comfortable.

The BauBax jacket has 15 different features, including a neck pillow, eye mask, gloves, earphone holders, a built-in pen, and plenty of dedicated pockets to fit passports, drinks, and yes, even a tablet.

The BauBax made a splash on Kickstarter back in 2015. It reached its $20,000 goal in less than five hours and went on to raise more than $9.2 million by the time the campaign had ended. This was the 6th Most Funded Product of all-time on Kickstarter.

In short, BauBax struck a chord with hundreds of thousands of people, and was proven to be a great product idea.

But how do you know if *your* idea is a good one?

Rather than just imagining that it is, or guessing, we can help you determine the feasibility of success before you put in large amounts of time and money and go public with your product. So, if you already have an idea, use the following information to determine how your product might do. (And if you're still in the 'thinking about it' stage, we suggest you come up with at least ten ideas before pursuing one.)

Funded Today's Product Success Formula

After years of seeing thousands of products and helping people raise millions of dollars, at **Funded Today** we have found some common elements to the products that achieved success through crowdfunding. In other words, we know what works and what doesn't. And we have created several formulas for success, based on our hard-earned experience.

One of those formulas, that we've proven out, and that resonates with the entire crowdfunding experience, is:

"Ubiquity + Tech/Innovative/Cool + Compelling Story = Huge Chance for Success".

Time and time again, we've seen this formula prove to be a big winner. Now, let's break the formula down:

Ubiquity - Think about something that everyone needs or uses. This is a product with mass appeal. While there is also room for a niche product that targets a very specific segment of the population or small distinct group of potential users, mass appeal is a winner. For example, we all wear jackets.

Tech - This doesn't mean that something is a tech product in the traditional sense, such as a new smartphone, app, or smart device, and you don't need to be a Silicon Valley programmer or a technology geek to create a product that leverages tech to bring something new to the table. People love tech. But, we'd like to add that it's not a requirement that your product be techy for it to succeed - creating a new market often aides in chances of success as well. The BauBax fits the mold for "techy" because it takes the traditional jacket and adds in all kinds of features that no other jacket had before. This is what we mean by techy.

Innovative - This is relatively straightforward. In the context of the formula, innovative means that you have an idea for a product with added features, or a new twist, that takes that product to a different level. The Coolest Cooler that we mentioned in Chapter 1 is an example of this. It's a cooler, but the added features make it so much more innovative and appealing.

Cool - This part of the equation is a little bit more of an X-factor, and harder to define. People may have a hard time verbalizing what is cool to them, but they know it when they see it. Cool can be a combination of factors - design, marketing, features, functionality, etc. - that give a product that extra "wow" factor, and make it a must-have for people. In some cases, people may view the product as a status symbol (Think the Apple Watch), or something that makes them stand out as unique.

Compelling Story - Most people want to back not only a product, but the people behind the product. So, if you can talk about how the idea for the product came about, or why you felt that there was a need for such a product, people will buy into it. The compelling story, or the chill factor story, which is basically a story with the founder of a product that is inspiring or brings awe, or that imbues additional trust into that product.

Check this study out - researchers took some wine, just some standard generic wine, and they gave it to people in a generic bottle and asked them "How does this wine taste?" People said, "Oh! It tastes awful, it's horrible." But then, the researchers took that exact same wine and offered the exact same people, who had just tasted the other wine, the same wine and put it in another bottle. They put it in a very fancy bottle, said that the wine was old and refined and amazing, and they had those same people taste it. The people said "This tastes absolutely amazing!" The only difference was the story behind that wine. So, when you have a story behind your product, it literally imbues your product with additional merit and value, outside of whatever is already intrinsically there.

What other factors make for a good product?

We are going to cover these factors in detail in **Chapter 4: The 7 P's of Crowdfunding Success.** But, for now, think about your product, or big idea, and keep asking yourself these 6 questions:

1. **What makes my product unique?** Your product has to be different or special.

2. **Does my product solve a problem or offer a new benefit?** What does your product do better than other products already on the market?

3. **Will people actually give me cash for it?** This is the, "Here's my money, I want in" step.

4. **Is the product "techy" or cool?** Tech products, or those with a coolness factor, sell well.

5. **How big is the market for your product?** Is there the potential that a large number of people will need or want your product?

6. **Is your product dependent on other products?** If your product is dependent on the buyer owning something else, how will this affect your potential market?

Successful products offer the consumer something new and exciting that makes them want to have it. Don't be afraid to change your product if you decide it doesn't offer enough of the factors that make for a successful crowdfunding project.

Flushing Out a Great Idea

Get Familiar with Crowdfunding Projects that have Proven Successful

It is well worth your time to study different projects on Kickstarter and Indiegogo. Your goal is to gain a general understanding on what projects have worked, and which ones have not worked. A great question to ask yourself is: "What types of projects raise the most money on Kickstarter?"

Successful Projects - by Category

At Funded Today we have analyzed what projects are most effective. In terms of the Kickstarter categories, currently, the top 4 categories with the most pledges (as of October 2019[6]) are:

- Games – $1.12 billion
- Design – $1.02 billion
- Technology – $868.78 million
- Film & Video – $456.04 million

If you're thinking about creating a product to launch on Kickstarter so you can raise money, those are the top 4 categories you might want to consider.

Successful Projects - by Individual Project

Another way to look at what kinds of projects raise the most money on Kickstarter is by browsing the projects. You can do that here: https://www.kickstarter.com/discover

On that page you can filter projects by category, amount raised, keyword(s), and a handful of other useful criteria. For example, if you wanted to launch a new sock line, or luggage company, or wallet design, you could see historically how much those types of projects have raised on Kickstarter. Browsing individual projects

---

[6] "Kickstarter Stats." 5 Nov. 2019, https://www.kickstarter.com/help/stats. Accessed 13 Nov. 2019

enables you to see what has raised a lot of money on Kickstarter, and what has not.

6 Tips for Deciding on Your Great Idea

Start at the Beginning

If you want to produce a successful product for Crowdfunding, you have to be invested in what Crowdfunding is. This means, don't launch a product on Kickstarter or Indiegogo if you've never backed a product yourself. Go back a product for $1 or $5, and learn about the process. Look at five, 10, or even 20 different products, and then see what these products have in common, and how they are different. This is important because crowdfunding is quite different than E-commerce.

Getting firsthand knowledge of the Crowdfunding process is key, because if you haven't been down that road and you're telling and wanting people to go down that road for you, then how are you going to be able to ask them to do that when you haven't done it yourself? Don't be a hypocrite. You want to start your new business out right. So, practice what you preach. When you want thousands of people to back your own campaign, being involved yourself creates credibility and supports the notion that you're part of the Crowdfunding community. In short, show that you're willing to support others, and that will make others want to support you. Reciprocity.

When you're in search of your next big idea and you're going through Kickstarter projects, you can ask yourself, "How can this technology apply to something else that's ubiquitous?" The Kickstarter project Onsen saw all kinds of successful past Kickstarter projects involving silver-infused socks and shirts, but never a towel that had antimicrobial properties infused with silver. So, Onsen took a traditional bath towel and infused it with silver. By looking up successful features of other Kickstarter projects, they created a towel that raised hundreds of thousands of dollars. You can apply this same process time and time again with all of the hundreds of thousands of other inventions that have already succeeded on Kickstarter.

Tip 1: You don't always need to build a better mousetrap; you just need to build what somebody wants right now.

There are many examples of this done with common items. For instance, travel pillows. Travel pillows and travel products are very, very common on Crowdfunding. As you look at these types of products, you'll see that there have been a few that have revolutionized the game and changed the design, the look, and the feel of travel pillows. As examples, BullRest, FaceCradle and Woollip all took a product that sells millions of units every year in airports and online, and they changed the way that it looks. then, they launched a Crowdfunding campaign with a new twist on an extremely common item.

Tip 2: As they say, timing is everything.

The timing of your idea is crucial compared to what your competitors have done, and how well they've executed their idea. If you're second to the game, you need to be certain about what you are doing different or better than what's been done before.

If you are going to go create another wallet, it better be revolutionary. By this point, there's been hundreds of wallets launched on Kickstarter and Indiegogo. And if you're going to go create Smart Luggage, it better be something people have never seen before. You can't say this is going to do better because it does all the same things that prior successful Smart Luggage projects did...ie. that it charges faster, it wheels better, it spins better, it's got more compartments, etc. - those are cool - but they are not new. They're not innovative anymore. People have already seen it, and therefore, it doesn't resonate with them as strongly as it needs to in order to become successful.

Tip 3: Consider products that are new to Kickstarter, not new to the world.

Keep in mind that a product which is new on Kickstarter does not mean it has to be new to the whole world. New can mean new to Crowdfunding, because again, the crowdfunding ecosystem is a very niche community. Backers support the Creators on Kickstarter or Indiegogo because they want them to be successful and they want to be among the first supporters, the earliest adopters, for a new invention or business. That's why certain people can back hundreds, or thousands, of projects in a year! And as crazy as that might sound, that actually happens. In fact, they even have a name for these types of backers: Superbackers. And you were going to want them to support your project as well. They are amazing when treated properly.

DanForce is a tactical flashlight. DanForce was so successful on Crowdfunding because they took an idea that is very common with projects on Kickstarter: **tactical**. Tactical bags, tactical knives, tactical etcetera, are popular. DanForce thought, "Okay what's a product that's in the tactical space that hasn't been launched on Crowdfunding before?" There are hundreds of options on Amazon for tactical flashlights. But tactical flashlights had not been introduced on Crowdfunding, and so that's how they raised over six figures. All because they introduced something **new to Crowdfunding**.

Tip 4: Platform matters.

As we discussed in Chapter 1 in the "Finding the Right Platform" section, the same product might do better on one platform than another. Go to Kickstarter or Indiegogo and look at the data. On Kickstarter (you get a little more data) there is a community tab. It will show you the number of backers on a campaign, as well as whether they are first time backers, or repeat backers. And on many campaigns, 80% to 90% of the backers are repeat backers.

See where your product fits in, and whether similar products are backed by repeat backers – those are potential backers for your project, too.

Tip 5: Look for a product's Hit Factor.

What do we mean by this Hit Factor? The Hit Factor is used in spaces like sports where people can look at a young athlete, for instance, and predict if they are going to be a great athlete later on in their career. We see products as having hit factors, as well. When your product is being made, or produced, does it have the Hit Factor?

Look at a product and ask yourself:

- "Would I use this product myself?"
- "Could I see my friends and family buying this product?"
- "Am I proud or embarrassed to tell people about this product?"
- "How might people react when I tell them about this product?"
- "When I share this project on Facebook, Twitter, or Instagram, how many likes, comments, and shares do I get? How do those likes, comments,

and shares compare to my typical posts on social media?"

If you can compare your product to your competitor's product and say, "Yes, this is a better product, this does accomplish what I was meaning to create," then you've done it. That's the Hit Factor that you need to capture in the presentation of your product.

Tip 6: Know yourself and your budget.

Gone are the days when you can release an inadequately produced prototype that doesn't really meet all of your end requirements, and still have success. You need to come to the table with a product that is ready to sell.

You're going to need a working prototype that not only encompasses the "Hit Factor," but that also looks the part. A working prototype that looks like a $10 product will probably mean that it's going to raise no more than $10. If your product does not look like a million-dollar product, then it will not become one from Crowdfunding. So, don't take shortcuts, because by doing so, you're neglecting to set yourself up for success from the very beginning.

Well then, what do you do if you are budget-conscious and you feel like you want to raise a million dollars, but you don't have $50,000 to go build an awesome prototype… or you don't want to take such a huge risk?

Remember this - "Scared Money Doesn't Make Money."

If you want to go big, you have to go big in the production, and you have to go big in the presentation. If you want or need to take a more cautious approach, that's fine. Know what you're capable of, and work to your strengths. But also look to who you can partner with. There are a lot of different ways to create prototypes, to partner up with people who are ready and willing to take a greater risk. You can partner up with individuals who have done the process before and have connections to factories in China, or other places overseas, who can do your prototyping at a cheaper price. And if you need recommendations or connections, just reach out to us via email and we will happily make those introductions for you.

But if you are new to the crowdfunding game, and you don't have a huge budget, but you have a bunch of ideas, begin with your product invention that has the fewest barriers to start. Just know that others are looking to get into crowdfunding too, so you can bet your bottom dollar that if your product is a success, a lot of people are going to jump on that and create a lot of competing products. But that's okay, because after your first successful product, you will have some capital for your next idea, so you won't need that rich uncle, or relative, or anybody to give you a bunch of money to start your idea. You will have created that seed money through that entrepreneurial leap of faith on your first idea. Or, if your first idea fails, you can do so with your second idea, your third idea, and so forth- until you finally find success.

So, begin with the idea that most sets you up to succeed, while being capital-conscious as you select from the many good ideas you may have.

Great Ideas are Everywhere

Everyone has ideas. It's the challenge of acting on them that stops most people.

That's part of what makes platforms like Kickstarter so exciting. Every project on that platform is an idea that was brought to life through action. We love Rewards-Based Crowdfunding! It's an amazing thing to be able to look at hundreds of thousands of people who have done it before and say, "Okay, I want to create a towel" and then you type in "towel," and you see all of the towels that have already launched on Kickstarter. "I want to create a wallet," and you see the hundreds of wallets- or, "I want to do smart luggage," and you see the hundreds of different types smart luggage that have previously successfully launched on Kickstarter. And then, you take those ideas "horizontally" a bit, and you create something slightly different using the same ideas and technology that they already used to raise millions. You really can't do that anywhere else - at least not with the amount of transparency, details and statistics that those comments and community tabs on Kickstarter provide.

This clearly shows that your great idea doesn't have to be wholly unique. You can become very, very successful with somebody else's idea (from another niche), and you don't have to have the idea from the ground up. Somebody could get you to Point B, and then you can take it to C, D and E.

You don't have to be the person to get it off the ground, just take it into the sky.

And remember, success is a subjective term. Raising $100,000 or just $30,000, could be the start you need to create a multimillion-dollar company. It's not always the biggest projects that are the most successful in the long run. The biggest project on Kickstarter was "Pebble Time" – there were millions of dollars raised by that campaign - and they're no longer in existence today. And some of the projects that raised $50,000 are around today, and are still thriving. PopSockets, as you might recall, raised just under $19,000 originally in 2012, and yet in 2018, they had gross revenues of nearly $170 million! So, keep your head-up if you don't raise a million dollars the first time around, because that's not the benchmark of success.

Make your great idea a product that you like, that you have an interest in, that you would use yourself, and at the end of the day you'll be happy with yourself going forward selling thousands of units, and helping the make the world just a little bit of a better place.

3

They Really Like You: Get Your Crowd Validation

Success is stumbling from failure to failure, with no loss of enthusiasm. **Winston Churchill**

You've no doubt experienced those moments when a new product hits the market and you think, "who would buy that?" or "why would anyone need that?" Why? Why? Why? And you're left shaking your head.

Chances are good that the product wasn't tested in the market prior to being available to the public. There was no market validation or real-world feedback - meaning the inventor or creator didn't see if anyone actually liked or wanted the product. They were operating in a vacuum.

And this leads us directly to one of the biggest benefits of crowdfunding, other than the obvious of raising money:

With crowdfunding you have a chance to see if people are actually interested in the product you're offering.

People vote with their money, so you find out directly if there is a viable market. Having a successful crowdfunding campaign means that people like and want your product. They give you money by contributing to your project.

On the other hand, an unsuccessful campaign can mean just the opposite. Sure, there are a lot of factors that go into a crowdfunding project that influence its success. But the bottom line is always about the amount of money, and the number of backers.

The beauty of crowdfunding is that everything is trackable because it's online. The crowdfunding platforms track who clicked on the campaign, how many people looked at it and passed, how many people converted from simply looking to contributing, and much more. This data can be invaluable to you as you move forward.

In future chapters we go in-depth on how you can create a campaign that ensures maximum results and success. At this point, just know that crowdfunding is the only platform that lets you get validation or rejection from the marketplace. Without spending huge amounts of money up front, you are able to gauge interest before your product is released. And that's invaluable.

Just remember that this process is only valuable so long as you're willing to accept honest feedback from the marketplace.

How to Best Utilize Crowd Validation

As an example of how not to be, let's look at a potential client who came to us some time ago - let's call him John. John was a textbook example of making all the missteps when it came to crowd validation. He came to us at **Funded Today** with a product he was intensely passionate about. He was convinced it was the next big thing. But... we weren't. So, we asked him a lot of hard questions. However, his ego and overwhelming confidence got in the way. He was boastful, defensive, and overall insistent that we simply 'didn't get it.'

He made big claims about his four years of research and development. But in all of his research time, not once did he think at ask people around him - friends, family, peers - whether they thought his product was a good idea! Can you believe it? He missed the simplest step of all. And, if he had followed our process, he would have known this wasn't a product anyone wanted, or that similar products already existed. His product was not revolutionary, or even evolutionary. But, he didn't want truthful feedback. And that's always a big mistake. We must constantly try to detach ourselves from our "babies" (our inventions) in order to seek after the truth of what the market is saying. That's not to say we should not be emotionally invested in our big ideas. Rather, we need to balance out our emotions with the facts of cold-hard crowd validation, too.

John's passion, while admirable on some levels, got in the way. Being passionate about what you're doing is part and parcel of moving forward. At **Funded Today** we always applaud passion. It drives and fuels you and can help you overcome challenges. And, it can enable you to get beyond detractors. However, in John's case, his passion and unwillingness to see the truth was wrapped up in too many emotions that blinded him to reality. We passed on working with him, and his idea never did succeed.

It's one thing to attempt to prove naysayers wrong. But it's unwise to completely ignore, or not even solicit, feedback. Taking negative feedback and finding ways to use those suggestions in a constructive way is what helps you deliver a product people want to buy.

Then, there was Timberline Slider Belts (which offered limitless adjustment options for a personal, custom fitting belt every time). The creator, Don Wilder, launched a crowdfunding project which didn't raise a lot of money. Basically, his campaign was a failure. Don found that the crowd didn't validate his product. They didn't want it because there were other options of belts available, and his product did not stand out as something entirely new or unique to Kickstarter. It was a hard realization for Don (knowing that people didn't want his product now, or maybe ever), but he took the feedback gracefully.

And here's the difference between Don and John- Don didn't get mad. He took his emotions out of the equation. Undeterred, he pivoted, and within a few months he created a new product. We helped Don Wilder ditch his worm, that product which was never going to fly (The Timberline Belt), and find a caterpillar (Apex Laptop Stand), which became a $400,000+ Kickstarter high-flying butterfly!

That's what acting on honest feedback can do for your business. Yes, passion is necessary, but it's important to think about business as more of an equation - when you have all the right elements, everything adds up - and that equals validation (and money) for your next big idea.

Key elements to harness the power of crowd validation:

- **Eliminate Emotion** - It's important to step back and take the emotion out of things. Look at everything from a business perspective. We understand that inventors think of their products as their babies. No one wants to be told their baby is ugly. But you can't take things personally. You need to look at the big picture, and think about what you are trying to achieve. Ultimately, your goal should be to deliver a product that people want, which makes you money, and allows you to create a sustainable business.

- **Let Data Drive Decisions** - Getting feedback, conducting market research, or looking at the data from a crowdfunding campaign (whether positive or negative) should dictate your decisions. The more informed you are, the better choices you will make. If only a handful of people back your crowdfunding campaign and you fell short of your initial fundraising goal, that's an indicator that you may need to rethink or re-tool your product.

- **Don't Fear Feedback** - Don't be like stubborn John. Feedback is a necessary part of the process. Don't be shy about asking those around you (friends, family, co-workers, neighbors, the guy who runs the local market, or anyone who will listen) about your product. You should *want* to know people's thoughts and opinions (good or bad) on your invention. Encourage everyone and anyone to provide constructive criticism. This will allow you to refine your product, and possibly even unearth new features people desire. Maybe they have something to add that you hadn't thought about. You can't get better without feedback.

- **Pivot and Pursue** - If all the feedback is negative, maybe it's time to reassess. Having an idea that doesn't resonate with people doesn't make you a failure. Consider negative feedback one of those necessary setbacks on the road to success. Setbacks provide you with an opportunity to reevaluate and determine if making changes will work. Or maybe, it's time to completely scrap your first idea and move on to another.

Remember, the goal is to get your product out there. That means having a sizable number of people who will want to purchase your product when it's available. Determining that without using crowdfunding as the vehicle to test the waters is expensive and nearly impossible. (And as we wrote earlier, as far as we know, John never did get a successful crowdfunding campaign off the ground).

What if the Crowd Doesn't Like Your Idea?

So, what happens when you launch a campaign and your idea tanks? Everybody worries about this. Everybody is scared about it because it's your baby that you put out into the world and now everyone insists that your baby is ugly. Ouch.

That's a problem, right?

Yes and no. There is more to Crowdfunding than raising money. You're also launching a crowdfunding project to validate your product idea. If it's a homerun, you can run with it. But if your project is a failure, or if it's struggling, or, if it's just not doing nearly as well as you would like, you can pivot to a new idea and keep going until you hit remarkable success.

We all have ideas we think are so amazing the world is going to suddenly stop and take notice. And when this doesn't happen, know this: you are not alone!

Thomas Alvord, co-founder and chairman of Funded Today talks about this in "Failure, Pivoting, and Success", our 4th podcast episode[7].

> *I remember when I was in my Grad Program. I sat down with one of my professors, I had this new idea I was working on, not Funded Today, it was something else at the time. I was so excited about it. I just knew this was going to be revolutionary, right? It was literally going to change the world. I was talking with my professor and after we spoke he said, "You know what? Just a heads up - this idea might not work. It might not be as big as you're thinking".*
>
> *A lot of people think they have the next big idea, and really, they don't. I remember at the time I responded to my professor and said, 'Yeah, that probably is true for other people and for other ideas, but that's not the case with me. I know my idea is different. This is going to be huge'. I was offended and actually taken aback.*
>
> *I just knew this idea was going to be so massive. Huge. Well after four years of pushing it and pushing it and pushing it I finally came to the realization that it wasn't a good idea, there wasn't a market for it, companies didn't want this product, there wasn't a need for it.*

---

[7] (n.d.). Failure, Pivoting, and Success | The Funded Today Podcast. Retrieved October 14, 2019, from https://www.funded.today/podcast/failure-pivoting-and-success

The point is, any one of us can get so invested in an idea that we can't hear what anyone else is saying about it. One of the things, psychologically, that you need to understand, is that **your idea might fail.**

AND THAT'S PERFECTLY OKAY!

Be committed to success, not to any one idea.

When you are too entrenched about a single idea to keep moving forward on your path to success, we call it 'entre myopia.' That's because as entrepreneurs we can get myopic, unable to have the complete vision necessary to allow our ideas to blossom more fully.

And we're not saying your idea isn't revolutionary. But we have found that most often the people who do have ideas that revolutionize the world usually weren't thinking that would happen when they first started.

We can give many examples of people who were more wedded to their idea than to success. One of the first Kickstarter projects we worked on at Funded Today was a "metal wallet." We ran some marketing, but it wasn't working. And in those early days we had not yet developed the finesse to ease people into the fact that their idea wasn't panning out. So, we told the metal wallet client that his idea wasn't a good one because our marketing wasn't converting. He got so upset he started cussing and yelling. He told us flat out that he was the next Steve Jobs. There were even some hang-ups and slam-the-phone down episodes in there! You see, there have been a lot of successful wallet projects on Kickstarter. And if this guy had been more open to input, he could have played around with other wallet ideas, pivoted just slightly, and maybe ultimately even found success for his wallet invention variation. Unfortunately, he was committed to his image, and the "idea of success," his vision that he was Steve Jobs incarnate, rather than what success actually is.

Certainly, like with everything else in life, there are exceptions and maybe you will change the world right out of the gate. But in most cases, life-changing ideas kind of just happen.

In fact, our business, **Funded Today**, is an example of that. When we started **Funded Today**, we weren't even expecting what happened next. And now, we're pulling over 8 figures in revenue every year. We didn't set out planning on building such a successful company, but because we had a great idea, we tested our idea out gradually, soliciting feedback along the way, executing on our vision, and pivoting and making changes along the way. Ultimately, we built an amazing company that we are still very proud of today.

To be a success, you must be able to pivot, adapt, and change your ideas and plans into what actually might change the world.

Winston Churchill, one of the greatest public figures of all time, perhaps said it best, "Success is stumbling from failure to failure with no loss of enthusiasm."

What Makes a Crowdfunding Campaign Fail Even if the Idea is Brilliant?

Now, what if you have a great idea, as evidenced by the input and response you've received from everyone you talked to before launch, but you still fail? Initially, everyone wanted your product. Everyone said they would put money in. And yet, you're now live and your campaign is failing. What next?

A wonderful example of this comes from one of **Funded Today's** clients, Aaron Johnson, of ShotBox 2.0.

When ShotBox 2.0 first came to **Funded Today**, Aaron had raised about $8,000, and he wasn't going to hit his funding goal of $15,000 (and as we've talked about earlier, on Kickstarter, if you don't hit your minimum funding goal, you don't get any of your other money that you raised). So, Aaron wasn't even going to get the $8,000 he did raise.

ShotBox 2.0 is a product you can use as a type of pop-up tent, where inside you place a product. Then, you just take out your smartphone, or your DSLR camera, and snap a picture. In short, it is a small, portable "ShotBox" where you can take high-quality photographs of your products.

Interestingly enough, all of the strategies **Funded Today** uses to market campaigns weren't working well, either. So, we put on our detective cap and we examined everything a little closer, Soon, we noticed a lot of stuff wrong with Aaron's video and his project page design - things that weren't effectively selling his amazing product.

Specifically, and ironically, even though Aaron's product was meant to be used to create beautiful product image shots of other products, it wasn't doing that for itself Furthermore, his video and reward structure were confusing. All of the different presentation elements were simply not doing a good job of showing off this product.

Fortunately, Aaron agreed with everything our analysis revealed. He was humble, listened to our input, and in less than two weeks we turned his entire campaign around. We shot a new video, cleaned up the entire Kickstarter page, restructured the rewards, and relaunched. These fixes resulted in a $184,791 raised. And now Aaron has raised hundreds of thousands of dollars and most recently had a very nice spot on the TV show HSN where he sold thousands more ShotBox 2.0's to a global audience.

Sweet, right?

All this to say, just because your crowdfunding campaign fails, it doesn't mean that your idea is bad. Sometimes there might just be something wrong with your project presentation (video or page design).

So, let's say you have 200 hundred people lined up, cash-in-hand, ready and committed to give you $100 for your product when you launch.

And you launch, but none of them decide to back your project. What do you do then?

This was the position ShotBox 2.0 was in. So, this is what we did. We created a survey and we messaged all 200 of those friends, family, and others. The very first question we asked was, "Would you like to own this product? Why or why not?" Then, to gather more feedback, we asked follow-up questions like these: Why didn't you back this project? If you did back this project, what level did you back it at? How did you feel when watching this video product? What was your experience as you went through the page? Please share any questions you still have about the product. Are there any other backer options or rewards you'd like to see? Is there anything else you'd like to say about this project?

Every one of these questions were free response because we wanted as much user feedback from backers and prospective backers and people who said they were going to purchase (but did not) as possible. Then we took all that information, compiled it, and looked for common themes. Only then did we change the page design and video to match what these people were saying. All those little tweaks and edits that came from the solicitation of user and backer feedback made all the difference.

Learning from important feedback does not only apply to crowdfunding. Unless you've been living on an island, most people have heard of Barack Obama. What most people might not realize is that he ran for the "US House of Representatives" in 2000, losing the vote 60% to 30%. Even though he lost, he learned from those mistakes, and ran for the Senate in 2004 and won. The rest is history. We can go on and on with examples like this, but the point is, campaigns have been lost, people have learned, *some* people have changed based on feedback received, and those people are the ones who went on to achieve great success.

Don't ever define yourself by a project or campaign. Whether it's good or whether it's bad does not define you.

We've also seen projects where the creator was successful, raising millions of dollars, and then launched another project that totally flops. You never know how an idea is going to perform until you test it in the market. No one can divine what is going to work and what's not.

In this way, crowdfunding is not different than any other type of business. Look at the Venture Capitalist. If they have one out of ten ideas that succeed, that's a homerun for them. They're happy. They understand 50% or more of the deals they put money into are going to flop. And that's AFTER they have put in their due diligence and researched these new and inventions extensively. 50% or more STILL FAIL! And these are the people vetting new businesses and new ideas. They are in the business of doing this, yet even they can't predict 100% accurately.

The bottom line is that you and NO ONE ELSE actually knows how a product will do until that new idea is put to the market and tested. And rewards-based Crowdfunding allows you to learn and apply all of these principles on a lean startup budget. And that's the beauty of crowdfunding. It does this better than anything else.

The Power of the Pivot

If you fail, that's okay. It doesn't matter. You just can't be so committed to your idea, or so in love with your brilliant mind, that you ignore reality. A true entrepreneur is going to realize that you launch a project to see how it does. If it doesn't work, you go to something else.

This is very hard to accomplish if you are "entre-myopic" - focused on the vision of this one product that you feel can't change. Being focused on a thing rather than success summarizes what many entrepreneurs get stuck in. If you want to be a successful entrepreneur, expand your vision.

Rewards-based Crowdfunding, whether using the platform of Kickstarter or Indiegogo, is, in our opinion, the very best way to get your product out to the market to see if you can get that product validation in order to gauge potential success. And if you don't get product validation, be ready to recognize early failure and pivot. Remember when we mentioned "ShotBox 2.0" where we were seven to ten days into the campaign before we realized that it was not going to succeed? We had to pivot and change, and then two weeks later, with everything cleaned up, we launched again. And, the rest is history. $200,000+ raised. A successful HSN appearance. Most importantly, a thriving and successful business.

Pivoting and change can happen very fast, just like Aaron Johnson of ShotBox 2.0 experienced. The faster you recognize failure (at any level) and separate the emotional elements entre-myopia creates from the hard data, the statistics, and the facts- the greater the likelihood your speed towards success accelerates.

The best advice we can give a young entrepreneur?

Be in love, be passionate and excited because that's what makes entrepreneurship so great. Then use that passion to pursue evidence rather than the emotional elements of what's inside your mind, or vision. That's the fastest path to success.

The Right Mindset is Key

Your commitment to success needs to carry across the duration of the life of your product, your business, or your services. In other words, this commitment cannot stop at the end of your very first crowdfunding project. We see too many crowdfunding projects raise money but then after their Kickstarter or Indiegogo project, they're just running a one-product-E-Commerce "business" that doesn't work, doesn't convert, and is not able to drive traffic at a profitable ROI. If this is you, you're not going to be in business for very long.

The most successful entrepreneurs are always looking to see where they can pivot and grow. Markets change and decline. When a previously successful product finds itself in a changed market that doesn't support it, it doesn't make sense to continue to pursue that idea.

This doesn't just apply to new entrepreneurs and start-ups. To succeed, even the largest companies have to realize that everything is an evolution, always changing, growing, and morphing. Take a look at some of the biggest companies that are out there. Did you know that 90% of the Fortune 500 companies in 1955 are now out of business? It's true! The ones who survive and stay alive, even at the Fortune 500 levels, typically grow through acquisitions, pivoting, and changing. They're usually building new things internally and they're not staying in a single niche or their starter industry. GE is much more than an incandescent light bulb nowadays. They grow to maintain revenue streams. Fortune 100 and Fortune 500 Companies are on top of it getting inspiration from new "Nascent Markets" and tapping into those through acquisitions. Like you, they have to be willing to pivot and to make those changes.

The right mindset allows you to fail, and even to fail fast. Perhaps there's no better illustration of this principle than that of Brooklyn Dodgers hall-of-famer Jackie Robinson. There's a famous photograph of Jackie Robinson on third base, attempting to steal home-plate. The pitcher still has the ball in his hand. He hasn't even made the pitch to the catcher yet. The batter is looking to swing, and here's Jackie on third-base, probably 75% of the way to home-plate, getting ready to slide in for the win! That's the type of mindset you need to have.

Always remember that one failure does not mean that you yourself are a failure.

There are so many examples of this. One of the most famous crowdfunding entrepreneur examples is Hiral Sanghavi. His "BauBax" raised $9.2 million on Kickstarter ($12 to $13 million raised when you add in Indiegogo InDemand). But we bet you haven't heard of the "Wireless Charging Apparel", because that didn't raise any money. Hirai canceled the campaign. Same exact guy, same exact mindset, same exact everything, but his idea of Wireless Charging Apparel didn't ever raise a single dollar. In fact, he actually lost a considerable amount of money that he spent on video, page design, and marketing that was ultimately of no avail for this crowdfunding project.

Success does not indicate future success, failure does not indicate future failure, and one failure does not mean you're going to be an ongoing failure.

Be committed to success, not just *your* idea of success.

What's important about this is that you can be at the bottom, feel broken, be mentally demolished, and have ten failed ideas. However, with literally just one new idea, you can become a millionaire.

Perry Marshall, one of the most expensive business strategists in the world[8] and one of Thomas' mentors, has talked about two people that had written him, who were completely broke. One was even living out of his car. And just a few months later, both of them were on the path to make over one million dollars per year. That's how powerful a successful business can be.

You can make more money in business than doing almost anything else. The point is this: if you find the right idea, not only can you change your life, you can change the world.

As Thomas shared in Funded Today's first podcast[9], he was dirt poor even though he had a Law Degree and a Master's Degree.

> *"I was listening to Perry Marshall's inspiring messages. I was literally going door-to-door selling coupons just to make thirty bucks a piece. but I remember listening and thinking, "That's going to be me. I might have been wrong with thinking my first idea was going to be the ticket but I was right thinking I'm going to be like those two broke guys. I'm going to be a millionaire someday."*

All of us have those moments when we need to pick ourselves up and try something new.

We know talking about failure can seem a bit gloomy. And yes, you want to hit a homerun every single time

---

[8] (n.d.). Perry Marshall Bio - Who is Perry Marshall? | Perry Marshall. Retrieved October 14, 2019, from https://www.perrymarshall.com/bio/

[9] "Funded Today's Origin Story | The Funded Today Podcast." https://www.funded.today/podcast/origin-story. Accessed 15 Oct. 2019.

you step-up to the plate. Or if baseball isn't your thing, to borrow for other sports metaphors, you want to net that three-pointer, or score that goal. But sometimes it doesn't work out that way, and that's more than okay. It's all part of the excitement of being an entrepreneur, and you should never let failure, or anything for that matter, define you or stop you. Don't settle for limitation.

Steve Jobs said it best:

"When you grow up you tend to get told the world is the way it is and your life is just to live your life inside the world. Try not to bash into the walls too much. Try to have a nice family life, have fun, save a little money.

That's a very limited life. Life can be much broader once you discover one simple fact, and that is — everything around you that you call life, was made up by people who were no smarter than you. And you can change it, you can influence it, you can build your own things that other people can use."[10]

---

[10] (n.d.). Quote by Steve Jobs: "When you grow up you tend to get told .... Retrieved October 14, 2019, from https://www.goodreads.com/quotes/653020-when-you-grow-up-you-tend-to-get-told-that

4

The 7 P's of Crowdfunding Success

Imagination is more important than knowledge.
Albert Einstein

Crowdfunding, as we know it today, via platforms such as IndieGoGo (started in 2008) and Kickstarter (started in 2009), is quite new.

And yes, we totally get that the idea of participating in something so cutting-edge and exciting makes the thought of creating a crowdfunded project very appealing. However, no matter how gifted you are as an entrepreneur, there are certain key elements you need to consider and incorporate to get your crowdfunding project funded and off the ground.

At Funded Today we call those elements "The 7 P's of Crowdfunding Success."

And no, we haven't just thrown these ideas together to sound clever. The 7 P's are based on our rigorous testing process, and we've applied the 7 P's to thousands of projects. We've developed and refined a validation program that is HIGHLY effective, and very rarely inaccurate.

Introducing the 7 P's of Crowdfunding Success

For all our crowdfunding projects, we strive to achieve statistical significance. We let the data speak to how capable a project is of achieving a positive ROI (return on investment) and continuing to raise money. We apply numerous techniques and elements, including the 7 P's, to all our projects to maximize the potential for success.

The 7 P's of crowdfunding success tell you WHY, or WHY NOT, a project/campaign gets funded or ultimately fails.

The 7 P's are:

1. **Product**
2. **Platform**
3. **Presentation**
4. **Promotion**
5. **Price**
6. **Probability**
7. **People**

1. Product

Every crowdfunding project begins with, of course, the product.

Your product ***has to be good***.

Even the greatest campaign in the world won't salvage a bad product and promoting a product that the market simply does not want, robs you of money.

So, how then do you know if your product is "good?" We mentioned some of this in ***Chapter 2: Finding a Great Idea that Sells***, and here it is in more detail, as promised.

When you are flushing out your product ideas, ask yourself the following questions:

1. **Why is my product unique?**
   Can you buy a very similar product in a store? Your product must be a product that consumers can't buy at Macys, Target, Amazon, or Wal-Mart. Your product has to be different and special.

2. **What problem does my product solve, or what benefit does it offer?**
   Ideally, your product should give people an added benefit that no other product offers. Even if there are many similar products already on the market, what is it about yours that no other product offers? Does your product offer a solution to a problem? Does it prevent the problem entirely? How does it do this better than other products already on the market?

3. **Will my family, friends, and others actually give me cash for it?**
   This is that step beyond, "Hey, that's a great idea." This is the, "Here's my checkbook, I want in" step. What will people actually put money in for? Often, your friends and family are going to tell you what an "amazing idea" you have. But to see if they are actually supportive, you have to "get real" with them.

   Ask for the sell directly like this: "That's awesome you think my new invention is such a great idea!

Now just to be clear, it's going to cost $135. So, can I count on you to back my project when I launch this coming month?"

By asking this type of follow-up question, you are going to get real feedback. And if your friends and family tell you they won't support you, it's important to go back and get feedback from them as to why they don't want to purchase. This will help you before you even launch so you can make the necessary changes to create something that everybody is going to want to purchase.

And remember, part of your research on this needs to include other crowdfunding campaigns to see if similar products have sold. And, if so, how much did those similar projects raise? What do the Kickstarter comments say about this product and what do the Facebook ads comments say about this product? By searching through this valuable, transparent, third-party content, you will learn a lot.

4. **Is your product "techy" or cool?**
   Certainly, your product doesn't need to be techy or cool for you to make money. But no one can deny that tech products, or those with a coolness factor, sell well. If you can find a consumer product that has widespread use, and make it smart, it has the potential to raise a lot of money on Kickstarter. Some examples include:

   - Watch + Tech = Pebble Time ($20 million raised)
   - Cooler + Tech = Coolest Cooler ($13 million raised)

- Luggage + Tech = Trunkster ($1.4 million raised)
- Meat Thermometer + Tech = Meater ($1.2 million raised)
- Wallet + Tech = Woolet ($332,000 raised)

5. **How big is the market for your product?** Does your product have mass appeal? Is there the potential that a large number of people will need or want your product? We talked about this in Chapter 1 and we cannot emphasize enough the importance of a product that will be used by large numbers of people. And obviously, the bigger your market, the greater your chances that more people buy your product, and the more money you stand to make.

6. **Is my product dependent on other products?** For example, the Pebble Watch band depends on owning a Pebble, and OrbiPrime depends on owning a VR headset. If your product is dependent on the consumer owning something else, you need to understand how this will affect your potential market. You also need to know how big that parent market is, and what percentage of those users will want your product.

2. Platform

First consider whether crowdfunding is even the right platform to launch your new business or idea. For example, if you want to start a landscaping company, that might very well be a great idea. But it's NOT a good idea for crowdfunding. That's mostly because it's too localized, so it doesn't have mass appeal. Plus, scalability for that type of business comes with expensive infrastructure costs, so it is not as practical for the platforms of Kickstarter or Indiegogo.

Once you decide your product or idea is a good fit for a crowdfunding platform, then you need to determine which crowdfunding platform is the best for you. There are many to choose from. But the two top players are Kickstarter and Indiegogo.

Kickstarter
Currently the hottest crowdfunding site. Kickstarter is a global community built around creativity and creative projects. Since its launch on April 28, 2009, 17 million people have backed a project, $4.6 billion has been pledged, and 171,383 projects have been successfully funded[11]. Kickstarter accepts all major kinds of creative projects but not for causes or awareness campaigns. And for more in depth learning, we've included a link to Kickstarter's rules at the end of this chapter too[12].

Indiegogo
At Indiegogo, you can jump start any project, and the rules are a little bit looser than Kickstarter's. The Indiegogo community has helped bring more than 800,000 innovative ideas to life since 2008, with more than 9 million backers representing 235 countries and territories[13].

To determine which crowdfunding site is the best one for you, do thorough research. Find out which platform performed well for products similar to yours.

---

[11] "About — Kickstarter." https://www.kickstarter.com/about. Accessed 14 Oct. 2019.

[12] "Our Rules — Kickstarter." https://www.kickstarter.com/rules. Accessed 12 Nov. 2019.

[13] "About Us - Indiegogo." https://www.indiegogo.com/about/our-story. Accessed 14 Oct. 2019.

You can search Kickstarter and Indiegogo projects for examples to give you an idea of products that do well on each platform.

To help get you started, here are some of the categories you may want to research:

- Art
- Comics
- Crafts
- Dance
- Design
- Fashion
- Film & Video
- Food
- Games
- Journalism
- Music
- Photography
- Publishing
- Technology
- Theater

So, which platform should you choose for launching your crowdfunding project?

The answer might surprise you.

We've tracked data for over five years between Kickstarter and Indiegogo. We have over $5 billion in pledges across different campaigns and across the platforms. We have over 700,000 campaigns between Kickstarter and Indiegogo.

In other words, we have tons of data and our analysis is objective. And when it comes to the numbers – which don't lie – you will see Kickstarter is better than Indiegogo.

At Funded Today we are all about the numbers, not theory. We believe in client or customer lifetime value, and we don't have any personal preference on who we like better, Kickstarter or Indiegogo.

As of this writing Indiegogo had 3,749 live campaigns, with $3.6 million in live pledges - the average pledge therefore was $960 per campaign.

Kickstarter has had 2,681 live campaigns with $15.4 million in live pledges - average pledge per campaign $5,749. (This data will vary, of course, based on the data and the date ranges that you're using).

Kickstarter also dominates traffic. There are 16.9 million visitors on Indiegogo on any given month, and on Kickstarter there's 36.7 million.

If more people are coming to your website, that means more possibilities for people to pledge for more campaigns.

When it comes to stats, Kickstarter is definitively, and without fail, the choice.

As an example, let's look at Samsara, a luggage company. Indiegogo excels at customer service and support. Samsara was hooked, they really wanted to go on Indiegogo, which they did. Their project completely failed. In fact, it failed big time, so they canceled it and hid it from their website. Samsara then relaunched on Kickstarter, and raised roughly $300,000.

That's just one example of all of the hundreds of campaigns we worked with that started on Indiegogo, failed, only to go onto Kickstarter and succeed.

Even when we make the Indiegogo page exactly the same as the Kickstarter page- with the same images, same pledge levels, same amount, and with the exact same paid media efforts (even down to the exact same image), the Indiegogo page or the Indiegogo InDemand page will convert three or four times worse than the Kickstarter campaign.

Don't get us wrong. We love Indiegogo. They are an amazing company, but we still cannot run campaigns on Indiegogo, at least to start, because the numbers and metrics definitively prove Kickstarter is superior at this time.

IndieGoGo has way better customer support. They will call you, they will talk on the phone with you, they have salespeople, they have a customer support team, they have account managers. If they get behind your idea, they can get really excited - they may even feature you in their newsletter, which can raise thousands of dollars or even tens of thousands, in just one email newsletter blast, for the right product.

BUT even with all those wonderful great things, and even with Kickstarter doing nothing to actively support your project, you'll still raise far less on IndieGoGo. Keep in mind also, that some of those IndieGoGo perks come with strings attached. For instance, they'll offer you certain things only if you raise, say, $30,000 first. So, if you raise that 30K, they will do as they promised. But if you don't raise it, then you didn't do your part for the contract and therefore they don't have to do their part.

On Kickstarter if you just do what we recommend in this book, you don't even need those Indiegogo perks, or any perks or added outside help, to still be successful.

There are other differences, as well. On Indiegogo, just like on any other webpage basically in the entire world, you can place a Facebook conversion pixel, meaning that if you're running Facebook Ads and somebody makes a purchase, you can know somebody made a purchase from that ad. Kickstarter, on the other hand, even after many years of existence, still doesn't let you place a Facebook pixel which can make tracking things more difficult.

Kickstarter also has a very strict trust and safety team. Their trust and safety team evaluates campaigns before you launch, and throughout the launch of your campaign, and they will suspend things that they believe are rip-offs, not new, not going to be able to happen.

Indiegogo is a little more lenient. But because they are more lenient, and because they help creators more, this actually has hurt them in terms of their conversion rate and the ability to raise money because backers, the people who give money, don't support Indiegogo the way they do Kickstarter, because the public trust and reputation of Kickstarter is simply greater.

So, to sum things up: Kickstarter dominates Indiegogo in every metric that matters to you as a creator, and the only reason you should launch on Indiegogo is if, for whatever reason, Kickstarter won't allow your campaign to launch on their platform. And if you launch on Kickstarter first, you can still transition to Indiegogo InDemand after your successful Kickstarter, anyway. And that's the best of both worlds, and our recommendation for 99% of the projects we see.

3. Presentation

You might have the best idea in the world but if your crowdfunding project has a poor presentation, you are certainly not doing yourself any favors. When we talk about presentation, we are including the video and the page design of your crowdfunding project. To create an effective presentation, at the bare minimum, you need to consider these factors:

- The quality of the video
- The appeal of the page
- The visual attractiveness of the page
- How well your presentation sells the product
- How the product will be used by its' primary demographic and target audience
- Incorporating use cases of all the different scenarios showing how someone might use the product
- Highlighting all the product benefits and not just talking about the features
- Making sure all the video and messaging is emotionally compelling
- Setting clear and motivating reward levels to entice potential backers

We'll dive deeper into the specifics of creating a compelling presentation in **Chapter 8: Developing a Compelling Page**, but right now what you need to know is that presentation comes down to one thing…

you must create a sales page/landing page that makes people want to buy your product.

4. Promotion

You need to promote your product to make people aware of it. This is not a "Field of Dreams" movie scenario, where if you build it, they will come. You need to spread the word yourself.

You can hire an agency (such as **Funded Today**), or you can do it yourself. Any promotion you do needs to take into account what the marketing has been up to this point.

And after years of doing this, we've determined what needs to be included to create a phenomenal crowdfunding promotion, and now we're going to share those secrets with you.

Our special promotion sub "P's" - paid media, press and partnerships.

Paid Media
It boils down to this - you have to spend money anywhere you can to make money. The best places to spend your money, after spending millions of our own, is through paid media. And when we talk about paid media, we're largely referring to Facebook ads. Why "only" Facebook to start? That's easy! Through Facebook ads, you can breakdown your ideal demographics, targeting BILLIONS of potential customers, and then segmenting those Facebook users down to the exact ideal customer you are hoping will buy your product. And if your product is really successful, only after testing things on Facebook, we have found some success with Instagram's paid media options, Google's paid search and display ads, and YouTube's video ads and overlays. But before you try anything else with paid media, start with Facebook. And before you

even launch, you should be building an email list of potential customers. In order to really be able to scale a campaign, you're going to need to dial in your paid media efforts before anything else. The campaigns that raise millions of dollars spent thousands, if not tens of thousands, of dollars just on Facebook ads. If your Facebook ads email lead generation efforts of promotion aren't effective, don't even bother with our next two sub P's of Promotion: Press and Partnerships.

Press

Working with Press is simple, but not easy. For effective press you need to create a unique angle with a great story, and then be able to tell the Press (in a non-salesy way) why they should write about you and your product.

It's important to remember that the media is bombarded daily with press releases and calls. That's why you need to stand out by clearly communicating why and how your product is different.

Your goal: to get an article featured in a major press outlet that is then syndicated across hundreds of other websites to generate massive publicity. To achieve this, consistency is key. The first email you send to a journalist is likely to be ignored. You need to be diligent and dedicated in your follow-up. You need to be creative and candid in your pitches. And you can't give up after just a few attempts. You need to try to convince the Press, media, and journalists alike to believe in your product as much as you yourself do.

Partnerships

Partnering with others who are excited about, and want to help promote your crowdfunding project, gives you access to massive customer email lists. But how? You need to offer your partners great incentives. Partnerships can be with anybody, because it's about building relationships and leveraging connections in a win-win way. But the most important partnerships are with companies who have products or services that are similar, but not directly competing with, the new invention you are trying to bring to market. Those are the partnerships where you want to spend the most energy, because the types of customers found within those companies are going to be most likely to purchase your product as well.

Testing is the key factor in determining which aspects from above are actually working. The objective is to aim for an average minimum ratio of 1:3, which simply translates to this:

For every $1 you spend on any promotion, you need to make $3, minimum.

At **Funded Today**, to determine what's working and what's not, we use the $1 spent should equal $3 made, and other metrics, alongside the Earnings Per View (EPV*) metric:

EPV, or Earnings Per View, is a metric we use to determine how many backers/pledges there are for every 100 or 1,000 visitors/page a project/campaign receives.

If 100 visitors visited a page or viewed a product
And 10 of those purchased, that would mean 10/100 or .10 or 10%
So, for every 1 visitor you are "earning" 10 cents.

10% = The Conversion Rate and $0.10 = The Earnings Per View (EPV)

5. Price

Price is not just a number and determining the right price is often very difficult for Crowdfunders. You must set a reasonable price right from the start.

Certainly, as you go about setting up your promotion, you need to set an initial price of your product, and at the right price entry point too. However, price is something that should shift as you test it during your promotion stage.

Price questions:

- How do you know if your price is too high or too low?
- Are your pledge levels set up properly?
- Are there early bird pledge levels?
- Do you have different pledge levels for people who want to buy more than one of your product?
- Are the pledge levels clear and understandable?

Generally speaking, we recommend pricing your product as high as possible to begin. If Backers love your product and purchase in droves, wonderful! You are going to have amazing profit margins right from the get-go and you may even be able to test charging even more. Our Client Katherine Krug, of BetterBack fame, tried this approach on her first Kickstarter project to great success. Initially, she priced her product at $75. She got backers, but not as many as she liked, and not at a very good EPV. Then she dropped her price to $50 and the rest was history. She was able to build, ship and fulfill on her product for about $8. So, even by dropping her initial price $25, from $75 to $50, she was still very profitable. She went on to raise over $1.2 million on that Kickstarter project, and followed that momentum up with a successful TV appearance on Shark Tank. Now, she has a thriving company with multiple successful Kickstarter launches to the tune of millions more raised from crowdfunding alone. You can always lower your price, so long as you have built in comfortable margins initially in your planning stage. Just remember that if you "price yourself out of the game" before you even begin, you run the risk of offending prospective backers, even before you price drop.

For example, let's suppose you have a product which has minor modifications to it. In other words, it's not exactly the same as other similar products on the market. You decide to offer a crowdfunding early bird special for $100. However, a quick Google search turns up many similar products priced at $99 or below.

That's a problem. Long gone are the days when people can't easily compare prices. In this example, your price at $100 is going to feel too expensive. There's a perception element to the way you price your product as well. If a potential backer looks at your product and thinks, "Hey, that's a $25-$30 gizmo, max," and then they scroll down to view your rewards and the least expensive option is $100 minimum for them to back your product - your project won't attract too many backers either.

So, if manufacturing and fulfillment costs dictate that you price your product at $100, then your presentation and stand-out benefits HAVE to convey, "This is a $100 product." Or better still, "This is a $200 product, but we are only charging $100 for it."

But what if you find out that you simply can't competitively price your product and still make a reasonable profit? Pivot, disband and invent something new, or move on to your next adventure.

Remember, this is business, not personal. A failed project does not represent you in any facet of the world. Mistakes are key to our growth.

The bottom line?

Even a worthy product/service won't sell if it's too costly. It's better for pricing to err on the high side (and correct downward) than on the low side (and correct upward). It's important to show people that they need to pledge NOW in order to avoid paying more

However, determining your pricing doesn't stop once you have your entry price. After setting the initial price and selecting the platform, you can do A/B Split Tests on price, during the promotion stage. We will explain more about what A/B Split Tests are later on, but in a nutshell, it's comparing two versions of something, while keeping all other variables exactly the same (aside from the one you are testing) to see which performs better.

A/B Split Tests are how we determine the absolute best price point for great conversions and crowdfunding success.

6. Probability

The previous Ps, for the most part, are relatively concrete. When we talk about the 6th P, Probability, though, it's harder to quantify. It can still have just as much impact on the success of your project as any of the other Ps.

- Will people think your product can really come to fruition?

- Is your creation a product with a lofty undertaking and, if so, will consumers still believe in your product?

As an example of probability let's look at **ORBI Prime: The First 360 Video Recording Eyewear**[14]. People struggled with the idea of this project:

Supposedly effortless, intuitive, and durable, ORBI Prime is designed to let anyone create incredible 360° videos and images.

What about this product made people struggle with it?

Many thought ORBI Prime was just NOT realistic. In other words, they didn't think the probability of creating something like that was high enough to justify backing OrbiPrime. The fact that people perceive that does not mean that it can't be done. It just means that you'll have to overcome that factor in your presentation and promotion.

When consumers are predisposed to not believe in your product - even if it's a great product and you can deliver - that clearly makes it much harder to get the funding you need.

7. People

Even if you've gone through all the steps above, and believe you have all your P's in a row, there is still one last P for you to understand and examine:

---

[14] "ORBI Prime: The First 360 Video Recording Eyewear ...." https://www.indiegogo.com/projects/orbi-prime-the-first-360-video-recording-eyewear. Accessed 15 Oct. 2019.

The people behind your product.

You need to take an honest look at your team. Do the people you have behind your product, including yourself, lend credibility to your potential on delivering on what you're promising to your backers? In other words, knowing the strengths and weaknesses of your team, can you deliver what you say you are going to deliver, and are consumers going to believe that?

If we go back to the example of ORBI Prime, one of the issues is that prospective/would-be backers did NOT fully trust the people behind the product to be able to deliver, or they thought that the ORBI team simply couldn't pull it off.

Why?

ORBI Prime had a SMALL team, and even HUGE companies like Google have failed when it comes to products of similar nature, like the Google Glass, for instance. Google Glass was a similar product, with a huge company behind it, and EVEN GOOGLE had all sorts of issues.

Potential backers must trust you (and your team) as the creator. This is one of the things about rewards-based crowdfunding that makes it different than other forms of E-commerce. Usually with E-commerce, when you go to buy a product online, you don't see the face of the creator. Maybe you can find an "About Page" where you get a glimpse, but that's about it. With crowdfunding, 98% of the time the PEOPLE behind the product are front and center because you have a Kickstarter video, or an Indiegogo video, and you're saying here's who I am, here's what I'm creating, here's why you should trust me - let's make this a reality together.

One great example about this that always sticks in our minds is the crowdfunding campaign called "Ukulele", which ran a couple years back out of the UK. It raised over $2 million[15]. The creators of "Ukulele" were some of the people who used to work on the video game "Donkey Kong." So right out of the gate, it doesn't even really matter what they say or don't say, potential backers are thinking, "Hey, I grew up playing 'Donkey Kong!' These are the guys that used to work on 'Donkey Kong', and they're creating this new game. 100%, I'm in!"

If you have expertise in what you're doing or experience you want to display, show people that on your project page as part of your Presentation P. Show them that you are the creator and you have something amazing and substantial because of who you are.

This is the KLT factor -
Know
Like
Trust

If you can get your Prospective Backers to feel this way about you and your people behind your product, it will make a substantial positive impact on your campaign.

Summing up the 7 P's

And just when you thought we were done with the "P's" there is one more vital P - Perception.

---

[15] "The 7 P's for Crowdfunding Success | The Funded Today ...." https://www.funded.today/podcast/the-ps-for-crowdfunding-success. Accessed 16 Oct. 2019.

Each of the 7 P's really has two elements to them: The actual fact of the 7 P's and the PERCEPTION of the 7 P's.

Perception.

Let's pause for a moment to talk about perception. You can have a presentation that highlights your product as having X value, but you can CHANGE your presentation, and the PERCEPTION of your whole product will change.

Even though your PRODUCT might not change, when you PRESENT it differently, the perception of your product's value will change in the minds of your customers/backers.

You know from personal experience that the way you perceive something changes based on how you're feeling. Suppose you are just starting out in business, and you make $300 in one week.

You say excitedly - "I made $300!"

But what if you made $1100 the week before. Then you might state in a somewhat down tone… "I only made $300."

The $300 hasn't changed, but your perception on how good that $300 is has changed.

In crowdfunding, perception primarily comes down to the FIRST P of PRODUCT. For instance, when you look at a product such as LunoWear, you know you are backing generations of watchmakers. As the campaign says:

"4 generations of watchmaking, from great-grandfather to son, bring 100 years of watchmaking history."[16]

Talk about an awesome initial perception of a product! The story resonated so much, in fact, that it was often raising $50,000 or more in a day. That's the power of a good story that pairs and synchronizes well with a great product! In turn, that adds immensely to the perceived value of your product.

Or, go back to our earlier example in this book, the wine bottle - same wine, different bottle, different reactions. The bottle looked fancier, so people actually said the wine tasted better.

Product + Presentation = Perception

When you are strong on all your P's, you are going to have a successful crowdfunding project. You are going to profit. As are your backers, and buyers who get all those awesome benefits. And if you're underutilizing **even one** "P", your chances for success diminish drastically.

- Product.
- Platform.
- Presentation.
- Promotion.
- Price
- Probability.
- People.
- Perception.

And all these P's lead to the best P of all - PROFIT.

[16] "All Natural Wood And Leather Watches | Indiegogo." https://www.indiegogo.com/projects/all-natural-wood-and-leather-watches. Accessed 16 Oct. 2019.

Your Crowdfunding Success equation looks something like this: Potential + 7Ps = Profit

Key Takeaways

- The most vital factor in your crowdfunding campaign's success (or failure) is always your product or service. Strive to offer a worthy one.

- Even a worthy product/service won't sell if it's too costly. It's better for pricing to err on the high side (and correct downward) than on the low side (and correct upward). It's important to show people that they need to pledge NOW in order to avoid paying more.

- Although your product/service is vital, YOU serve as the supporting factor, and backers need to feel that you are likable, passionate, and competent- enough so that they can trust you to fulfill your promises to them.

- Some projects are ill-suited for rewards-based crowdfunding, while the rest will raise funds more easily on Kickstarter than on Indiegogo.

- An effective presentation can multiply success, and your media (video and page) is more important than your marketing.

- Promotion involves reaching out to the best audiences while effectively persuading them to come view your presentation. Crowdfunding marketing techniques may include advertisements, cross-promotions, affiliate marketing, and/or public relations.

- Potential backers are more likely to pledge when they feel confident that your campaign will succeed, which is why success breeds success in crowdfunding.

5

The Triple F - Friends, Family and Fools

The supreme accomplishment
is to blur the line between work and play.
Arnold J. Toynbee

To put it bluntly, if your mom and your best friend don't want to buy your product, it's unlikely others will either.

Okay, so your own mom will probably support your efforts. But you get the point. You need to get some initial feedback to determine if you have a product that people actually want, or need, **and most importantly, <u>that they'll pay for.</u>**

In **Chapter 2: Finding a Great Idea that sells**, we talked about the importance of validating your product. Now we are going to dive deeper into our proven strategy to further validate your product.

The Triple F Strategy

The single most important step you can take before launching

Our proven Triple F strategy is the single most important step you can take before launching your crowdfunding project. We can't stress enough how imperative it is to employ the Triple F.

The basic premise of the Triple F is pretty simple:

You need to get at least 100 of your friends, family and fools (that's what we are calling your random connections that aren't friends of family) to commit to back your crowdfunding campaign on the day it launches.

By doing the Triple F, you are not only validating the product, but jumpstarting your fundraising efforts on Day 1.

Let's start with the validation component.

More often than not, we see inventors with ideas who have not asked anyone for feedback. It's baffling. When you are committed to success, you want to know what people think of your idea.

Most people don't actively solicit feedback out of fear people will have negative things to say, or not be interested. But as we previously discussed, feedback can let you know if you're going down the wrong path entirely. And if that's what you discover, it's okay. It allows you to pivot and come up with another idea, or retool the existing product.

We know no one likes rejection. You've probably spent countless hours working through all aspects of your product, and to be told that people don't like it is hard to hear. But this is truly where the rubber meets the road - the pivotal time when you can get honest feedback and possible suggestions that will allow you to incorporate features to make your product better, and more attractive to a wider audience, exponentially improving its' chances for success.

Effective entrepreneurs - and you are an entrepreneur if you create a product and want to sell it - are willing to ask the hard questions, because they are committed to success rather than just a single idea.

Think about it. Many huge global brands and respected companies have launched a new product and failed. Ideas are a dime a dozen. It's all about execution, and successful execution is not unique to large companies. You can create a successful execution as well.

Using the Triple F Method, we've seen campaigns raise $50,000 or more in the first 24 hours. Because you are getting at least 100 people to commit to support your campaign on the day it launches, you not only get the money from those backers, but you get additional positive benefits.

A deluge of backers at the start of a crowdfunding project launch boosts your rankings on Kickstarter in a variety of important categories on the platform, including the New, Trending, and Magic categories. Those boosted rankings yield further benefits, because the more people who see your project, the more organic search love you'll receive.

In our experience, getting an initial crowdfunding jolt of $10,000 in pledges might get you another $5,000 to $20,000 from organic pledges with Kickstarter.

Let's pause for a moment to talk about the Kickstarter algorithm. The reason a project with an initial boost in rankings makes more money is because once a project ranks higher, it takes advantage of the snowball effect. We like to say that Kickstarter is a paradoxical vehicle, meaning that to get the snowball effect, you first need to start rolling the snowball down the hill yourself, with your own crowd. In order to get THE crowd, you first bring YOUR crowd.

When you raise a ton of money and bring hundreds of backers to your project upon launch, you have the added benefit of attracting more press, receiving additional exposure and internal promotion from Kickstarter, and helping craft a more compelling narrative for your campaign. This helps ensure that others will be more interested in supporting your project, too.

Kickstarter's algorithm is also slightly weighted towards total number of backers over total funds raised. So, if a project on Kickstarter were to raise $10,000 from 20 backers and your project were to only raise $5,000, but from 100 backers, your project is going to rank higher than the $10,000 project. Remember, ranking higher in Kickstarter's New, Trending (Popular), and Magic categories will help you make up the $5,000 difference between your project and the hypothetical $10,000 project, because of the additional exposure those higher rankings will provide your campaign.

Employing the Triple F Method is also important to use, because for some projects, the money generated on the first day might be close to all they receive for the entire campaign. For projects attempting to raise a small amount - like $5,000 - the Triple F can help you reach or exceed that goal on day one.

Often product creators are only seeking to raise a small amount of money. Not every campaign sets lofty six-figure goals. The smaller fundraising goals might be based on simply wanting enough money to finalize some aspect of the product, secure manufacturing, or whatever you determine your need to be.

In a future chapter, we'll dive into setting up fundraising goals and the specifics about what makes sense for your product.

Regardless of the amount you are trying to raise, the Triple F Method is your best bet to kick off your crowdfunding efforts with a bang. It's like the old adage, "nothing draws a crowd like a crowd."

How to Implement the Triple F

Get started by using **Funded Today's** Triple F spreadsheet that looks like this:

Name	Email	Phone	Status	Pledge Amount	Notes
John Doe	johndoe@gmail.com	(555) 555.5555	Commited	$150.00	He said he'll pledge $150 on launch. I'll email him and follow-up.
Jane Doe	janedoe@gmail.com	(555) 555.5555	Commited	$100.00	She said she'll pledge $100 on launch. I'll email her and follow-up.
Johnny Doe	johnnydoe@gmail.com	(555) 555.5555	Commited	$50.00	He said he'll pledge $50 on launch. I'll email him and follow-up.

We have one already built for you and it's free. Here's the url: fnd.to/fffsheet.

You then enter all the names, phone numbers, and email addresses of everyone you can think of within your circle. These are family, friends, and other people in your immediate circle as well as beyond.

We've even created a YouTube video with an explanation on how to use this prelaunch outreach list.

You can find that supplemental training video here: fnd.to/fffvideo

Once you have 200 or more people entered into your worksheet, begin to reach out to each of them individually. You can send a mass email, but if you're asking for their commitment and their money, you probably want to make it a bit more personal and reach out to them on a one-on-one basis.

When contacting your Triple F network, you need to explicitly ask each of them:

"Will you commit to support my crowdfunding campaign on the day it launches and give me (pledge) $X for my new invention?"

Be sure to tell them the specific date of your project launch if you already know, and if not, circle back to them when you do know to give them the date and time. Let them know that you expect them to go to Kickstarter and make their pledge. Provide your Kickstarter preview link, have them set up an account, and ask them to click the click the "Notify me on launch" reminder button, as well. Help them get familiarized with Kickstarter's website, too. Essentially, you need to give them all the information *they* need, to do what *you* need them to do.

By implementing this process, you already have a group of people that will help boost your project directly out of the gate. So, if you get 50 people to pledge $100 on the first day of the launch, you already have $5,000 to help fuel your efforts. If you're overall fundraising goal is $10,000 over the entire length of the campaign, then you're already halfway there on day one!

Again, The Triple F is one of the most important steps you MUST take before launching to ensure your success.

Though the Triple F strategy might seem simple, it's exceptionally powerful. We've seen entrepreneurs who implement the Triple F strategy raise $100,000 in the first 48 hours of their campaign. And it's primarily because of their friends, family and what we call "fools" (which we mean in the friendliest way) - those people who are throwing in money just because, or from a desire to help out.

Why You Can't Let Fear Stop You

The fear of getting rejected has made many entrepreneurs fail. We've had plenty of clients who hire us only after their product is already launched and failing. By and large, the main reason they initially failed is because they didn't bother to ask people if they would buy their product (i.e. Employ the Triple F Method) before launching. We had a client with a pretty successful business, but this particular product was struggling. He had done four years of research and development, and in all that time, he never even bothered to ask people if the new product he was creating was actually something people would want.

To us, this was just baffling - the equivalent of shooting yourself in the foot, and then wondering why you have a limp.

Here's the thing - even if you ask your friends, family, or colleagues about your product and they say, "cool idea," it doesn't mean anything if you never ask them to support your project and put their money where their mouth is.

Maybe they want to buy the product... or maybe they don't.

But you don't know until you ask them.

That is what the Triple F is all about: creating a list of 100+ people who, on the day you launch, are going to support your campaign.

You must ask them!

> "Hey Mom, I'm trying to get 100 people who will support my campaign on the day I launch. Here's what the project is, and I'm going to have these different pledge levels where you'll receive these rewards for your pledge. May I get your commitment that you'll make a pledge of $$?"

They might say "yes, or no, or uh, I don't know. I don't think I would use it." But you have to ask to know.

Entrepreneurs can be so easily misled. Let's get psychological for a second here. You're afraid to ask the important questions because it might lead to your baby, your product, your new idea, being rejected.

Here's one way to avoid that pitfall, and this is something we practice personally at **Funded Today.**

Ask yourself this one question: "What's the worst that can happen?" And then play out those worst-case scenarios in your mind- let your mind run free.

"Well, if my best friend says 'no, I won't give you $100 for that idea. I think it sucks. It's a terrible idea. Why did you even invent this?' Then, you simply ask yourself: What's the worst that can happen if they say that?"

In this hypothetical example, perhaps you determine if you're still going to be friends or not. Or, what if no one likes your idea? Then you just have to come up with a new idea. That's okay. No big deal.

We've got you covered. Go back to **Chapter 2: Finding a Great Idea that Sells**.

Really, the worst that can happen when you ask the hard questions is not actually that bad. Nobody's going to die.

You have to ask the hard questions if you want to get the answers to figure out whether or not you have a good idea or not, and it's WAY better to figure this out BEFORE you invest months or years and money on an idea that is not going to work. Remember, be committed to your success, and not your idea itself.

Here's the reality: ideas don't matter at all, it's what you do with them that matters. We've said that before, and we will say it again, because we tend to forget. There are ideas that can work that will totally change the world, but sometimes even those ideas are not properly executed, or even acted upon at all. And there are less-substantial ideas out there that someone acts effectively on, and those do change the world.

The right actions, not ideas, are what matter.

What You Shouldn't Be Worrying About

So many people want to come to us and say, "Hey, I've got this NDA (non-disclosure agreement). Will you sign this NDA? Otherwise, I can't tell you about my idea."

Our response is nearly always the same, "Wow, we are wasting all this time with legal things way before they are necessary."

Don't get us wrong. There are some good things with legal and things you want to take care of. And you should absolutely consult an attorney and talk about those sorts of things. First, take action, get feedback, figure out whether something makes sense or not before you spend your hard-earned money and precious time on things that may not matter. Work smarter, not harder.

Don't waste so much time worrying about all of these things that don't even matter, because you haven't made any money, so nobody really wants to copy your idea. It's all about execution. Ideas are a dime a dozen. Everybody's got the next big idea, the next great thing, the next Facebook, which is suddenly is going to raise a billion dollars.

So when potential clients come to **Funded Today** asking us to sign all this stuff, because they just know this idea is going to work and be big, and we ask them how they know it's going to work, 9 out of 10 times - no joke - they haven't even asked anybody what they think of their idea!

9 out of 10 times. Wow! Right? 90%.

In fact, we even find that some people haven't even asked themselves if they would back their own idea. Do you like your own idea? Did you invent your product to solve a need that makes your life better? If you didn't do that, you might be in the wrong space right off the bat.

Get validation.

There's that word again, that we talked about right from the beginning. Validation. The best way we know of to get validation for your next big idea is using the Triple F Method.

This is, in fact, the whole concept of rewards-based crowdfunding. You can launch a campaign and validate if people are interested in your idea, your creation, your new venture, before you actually go and mass produce it and spend all this time building out the product.

You do the Triple F so you can get that upfront feedback, even when it's hard, because, as we talked about above, you don't usually want the feedback mentally and psychologically. However, in practice, you need that feedback more than anything, so you don't work for years on an idea that you can learn isn't going to fly in just days after employing the Triple F Method.

Maybe this is an idea that's been in your head for 15 or 20 years, and you've never taken any action because you've been too scared to make the ask. The Triple F is one of the easiest ways to make the ask in a friendly environment, because it's your friends and your family. Yes, it's a double-edged sword. On the one hand, it's about raising the money. On the other hand, it's about validating. So even if you launch and you fail, you know you're not a failure and it's just this particular product failed and is not going to be a good fit. Then, you can quickly move on or pivot (based upon the feedback from your friends, family, and "fools") to your next new product attempt.

We have raised hundreds of millions of dollars for thousands of campaigns now, and full disclosure, yes, there are campaigns that fail that we work with. That's fine. That doesn't mean we're a failure. We're not emotionally attached to the ideas we attempt to raise money for; rather, we're emotionally attached to success, so we pivot and we adapt and change, and then we ultimately find success.

You can have this same approach. Success might not come on your first idea, it might not be on your next idea; it might not come on the 10th idea, but perhaps on your 11th idea. You raise a million dollars once, and your past 10 "failures" are just dust in the wind.

As we've mentioned, many of the largest, most successful companies, with the brightest people in the world, such as Google or Amazon, launch new products that completely fail. That doesn't mean they're failures, clearly. It's just that there's not a market for that idea, and that's okay. They move on and they go to the next thing, striving for validation as quickly as they can, each and every time.

By using the Triple F Method to quickly launch crowdfunding projects, not only are you able to validate and get immediate feedback on your ideas, you can actually use that feedback. And that's what matters most.

For example, along the way, some of your Triple F network and backers might say, "I like your idea. But I don't think I would use it because of x, y, and z." Well, there you go. Listen for the "but," and what comes after that keyword. If a certain concern or bit of feedback starts to become a common theme, maybe it's something that is more generic in the market that you need to address - as opposed to somebody who may be an outlier, and you know their interests or idiosyncrasies don't really apply. In other words, you don't alter your idea based on the feedback of just a few people. You look for trends in your feedback that tell you what changes are needed.

"I love your new wallet idea. I just wish it had a slot for some cash."

"I love your new wallet idea. I just wish it were just a little bit larger and it came in brown as well as black, because it would match my outfits better."

That's the kind of feedback you're going to get when you go with the Triple F method.

Putting the Triple F and Feedback into Action

Let's talk about how to put Triple F feedback into action, so it's not just some kind of abstract belief.

Let's just start with Mom. That's your easiest and weakest ask, but it makes sense to start there. She's going to probably say yes close to 100% of the time. If she doesn't, that's when you stop. That's when you stop and you say, "Okay, I've got a really bad idea. My Mom is not even going to give me $20."

But if you were to ask Mom about a wallet that you've invented, as an example, here's how that should play out.

Hey Mom, I've invented a new wallet and I want to ask you a few questions. I've sewn up a little prototype. Here's why it's great. Here's why I think it's great. Here's why I invented it. It's going to cost $25 retail. I'm going to sell it for $20 on Kickstarter, as a discount to you and others. Will you give me $20 bucks for it on August 2nd at 11:00 AM? Can I put your name down on a spreadsheet and commit you to give me $20? Will you be one of my backers as soon as I launch?

Imagine if she says, "I will back it, but I don't think I would actually use it."

You should reply: "Oh, okay. Interesting. So why not? I mean, what do you not like it? Wrong color? Or, do you think this just isn't a good idea?"

She may reply, "It's just really bulky. It looks more like a man's wallet. Are you targeting men as well as women? It's not going to fit in my pocket. I guess I could put it in my purse, but I still don't love it."

And you should follow-up again like this: "So, is it the bulk that bothers you the most? Or is it perhaps a different color that would help it appeal to a wider audience, of any gender?"

Your mom then says, "Yeah, I think it's mainly the size. I would have liked to just have more of an everyday wallet, so it can fit in my pocket. This one just looks too bulky."

You ask, "So, do you think if I removed a pocket or two and trimmed it down, would that solve those problems? What if I made it in red, pink, or perhaps yellow as well? Or, what about even light blue?"

Mom continues, "Yeah. I think if you had something besides just a black option, that would work really well for me!"

And now you have some solid feedback to work with! So, you reply, "Okay, perfect. Let me go back to the drawing board, mock something up, and I'll bring it back to you in a couple of days when I have the next little prototype. Thanks so much for your honest feedback, Mom."

Boom. That's a validation. Yes, she rejected the initial prototype, but you got a little bit of important feedback on it.

Now let's say your Mom accepted it. Great. You're doing so well. Now, it's time for Triple F with Dad.

"Hey Dad, I've invented a new wallet! I've sewn up a little prototype. Here's why it's great. Here's why I think it's great. Here's why I invented it. It's going to cost $25 retail. I'm going to sell it for $20 on Kickstarter as a discount to you and others.

Will you give me $20 bucks for it on August 2nd at 11:00 AM? Can I put your name down on a spreadsheet and commit you to give me $20? Will you be one of my backers as soon as I launch?"

And then your dad replies, "Hey bud, this thing IS amazing! It's perfect. I can slip it into my pocket so I don't lose it. I love it. I'll give you $20 for sure. Put my name down."

Perfect, you take out your Triple F Google Sheet and put down Todd Smith, along with his phone number, email, the amount he committed for - $20 - all on your handy dandy Triple F automated worksheet: fnd.to/fffsheet.

Again, utilizing the Triple F strategy is the most important thing you can do if you're going to launch a new product. You should not launch your product until you've spoken with at least 100 people. Feel free to ask way more than that. Use all your network connections, and before you've ever launched you can have a lot of promised money coming in. Pretty exciting, right?

Don't forget the other benefit of the Triple F - that on the day you launch, you will have a flood of pledges, along with previously uncommitted backers, which will boost your rankings on Kickstarter's categories. That is going to give you a lot of organic love from Kickstarter.

If on the day you launch you line up, say, $10,000 worth of pledges, you're probably going to get something more between $5,000 to $20,000. You'll see double that amount from organic pledges, or even more. Yes, it could be less. But generally speaking, you get at least double from organic pledges.

Why is all this so important for some projects? Because, believe it or not, that might be all of the money the campaign generates. Once we even saw a campaign literally raise $150,000 right off the bat, and all of our other marketing somehow did not convert. We sent out a newsletter in our cashback network, which, on a good campaign, could raise you $20,000, $40,000, or even $50,000 – but on this particular campaign it really only raised around $100.

We were baffled. But, do you want to know what the one saving grace was for this project (that ultimately was an amazing success)? You guessed it: The Triple F.

What you do with all this comes down to your strategy and what you want to do. If you really are just trying to validate, do the Triple F so you can have a strong launch. Then, if you're not able to raise money with your other marketing, you might reconsider whether you want to keep running the campaign, or cancel it.

If you just need $X amount, the Triple F can be your very best bet. Then, you might be able to look at things and think, "Okay, my product is $50. I'm going to go get 100 people. I'm going to ask all of my friends and family and see if I can bring this baby to life."

There was a kid who submitted his project on our website, applying for our services. He was only looking for around $750 to go build some smart home items. He was just 14 or 15 at the time so he didn't know 100 people offhand he could ask; he hadn't yet made the network connections necessary for the Triple F Method, due simply to more limited life experience.

Since we love entrepreneurship, we trained him on the Triple F Method, and had him apply the strategy through his neighbors, going door-to-door. The pitch was simple: "Hey, I'm just trying to get 50 people who will each put in $100. If I can get 99 other people, would you be willing to put in $50?" Again, that's the power of the Triple F. If this young entrepreneur can do it, you have no excuses. You can do it too.

Crowdfunding is not like the famous movie Field of Dreams. If you build it, they won't come. Once upon a time, it was more like that, but not anymore. So, if you want the crowd to come, you need to first bring your own crowd. How do you bring the crowd?

Yes, no doubt you can fill in the blank by now: The Triple F.

Only when you bring the crowd, will the Kickstarter crowd come.

And since Kickstarter has millions and millions of visits a month, you want that crowd to come. You want to trend, and maybe become the project of the day.

To take the best advantage of your crowdfunding platform of choice, you have to do all your work first. Just like if you're an insurance agent. You start with your friends and ask them who they're using for their insurance. Then, you try to get them a better deal, and follow up by asking them which of their friends and family would be a good fit for your invention too.

You have the Internet. You have Kickstarter, the platform. It's all very powerful and exhilarating.

Honestly, every time we talk about the Triple F Method, we get so excited, we cannot even sleep. No joke. Why? Because it works. We know it works. Grassroots efforts often lead to big things. If you apply the strategy, you will too.

The Triple F, and every strategy we are presenting to you in this book, works. They are battle-tested and project-proven. Their success is evident.

We don't want to spend time on something that doesn't work any more than you do. It's the 80/20 principle - where can you spend 20% of your time doing something that will generate 80% of your results?

This principle says get a few of your friends and family onboard, and then Kickstarter will help to bring the rest.

Now, you might be thinking that you don't have time to reach out to all of these people. In reality, you don't have the time to *not* do it! Otherwise, you're chasing something you haven't even validated, wasting your time because you "didn't have the time" to do the prep work.

Quite frankly, it's a copout if you say you don't have time to go do the Triple F. Whether you're a 14 year old kid, or the Billion Dollar Company that's going to Kickstarter to kickstart a new idea, or the established business going to test out a new marketplace. If you don't have time to solicit good feedback to make your pitch, then why are you even doing this?

In addition to bringing your crowd, so the crowd from Kickstarter will see your project, this whole process will give you social proof. Once your campaign has hit its goal, that additional social proof means that ads you're running and press you're landing are usually going to have a higher conversion rate.

Some of our best ads we've created are for projects that got funded in 24 hours with hundreds of Triple F supporters. The ad writes itself: "Hey, these people have already backed it. What are you waiting for?"

And that only happens if you've done your homework upfront.

The Triple F.

Key Takeaways

- Ideas don't matter without action.

- Don't wait until your crowdfunding project launches before you try to determine if anyone actually wants to buy your product. Instead, overcome doubt and fear, and test the market.

- Your family, friends, and other personal contacts can not only provide "safe" feedback about your ideas, but also pledge to enhance your campaign's first-day success, which leads to even more success.

- "An entrepreneur should be committed to success, and not to their idea." Never fear to fail, and learn and improve from that until you achieve success.

6

Setting Up Your Crowdfunding Campaign

These mountains [that] you are carrying, you were only meant to climb. Najwa Zebian

The Elements of a Good Crowdfunding Campaign

No matter how great your product is, without the right factors in place, your campaign will suffer.

There are many things that go into setting up an effective and successful crowdfunding campaign. We are going to be breaking down many of the elements in their own chapters, but for now, let's get acquainted with the general factors you need to be aware of.

1. The Best Platform for Your Product (detailed in Chapter 1)
2. A Proper Funding Goal: This Chapter
3. Setting Up Your Bank Account: This Chapter
4. An Effective Product Video: Chapter 7 - Creating a Video that Converts
5. Memorable Campaign Page: Chapter 8 - Developing a Compelling Page

6. Good Pledge Levels: Chapter 9 - Setting Your Pledge Levels
7. Google Analytics: Chapter 15 - Analyzing Your Campaign

To start, here are 6 Key Factors to remember as you develop your crowdfunding campaign:

Key 1: A crowdfunding campaign can be simple, and still very successful. Think, "less is more."

Key 2: Any element that is front facing (the customer sees) should be tailored to fit your niche. This includes using the right language and phrasing to help you establish rapport and credibility; strengthening your ethos.

Key 3: Presenting features is good, but presenting benefits is better (especially avoiding bad things more than obtaining good things) is better, and conveying both is best. Think "feature your benefits" if you really want to encapsulate this point.

Key 4: Appealing to reason is good, but appealing to emotion (through music or imagery or conflict) is better, and appealing to both the heart and mind, is best. This is your pathos rhetoric; appealing to your audience's emotions.

Key 5: Immediately grab audience attention with a "hook," capturing interest and persuading prospective backers it's worth their time to continue reading, listening, or watching.

Key 6: Compelling images matter - don't skimp here.

Before you develop any of your good crowdfunding campaign elements, ask yourself these questions:

- Why is this product different/special/unique?
- Is there something about your product, some benefit, that makes it wholly special?
- Would you buy this product? Will your family and friends actually give you cash for it?
- Is your product "techy," cool, or unique in another way?
- Will a lot of people need or want this product, and its' benefits?

Hopefully, you can answer these questions positively, and confidently.

Know the Rules of Your Chosen Platform

The last thing you want is to end up with a campaign that is not accepted or banned. So, once you've decided on your platform (see **Chapter 1: Introduction to Crowdfunding**), we suggest you become familiar with the rules and regulations of that platform. This is by no means a comprehensive list, but will give you a general idea.

Kickstarter

On the Kickstarter platform you can have a project that falls within any of the following categories[17]:

- Arts
- Comics & Illustration
- Design & Tech
- Film
- Food & Craft
- Games
- Music
- Publishing

And here are the 5 rules every Kickstarter project must follow[18]:

1. Projects must create something to share with others.

2. Projects must be honest and clearly presented.

3. Prototype demonstration should reflect a product's current state, and should not include any CGI or special effects to demonstrate functionality that does not yet exist. If a project requires software and hardware integration, creators are required to show that functionality and any dependency clearly, or disclose that it has not yet been developed.

---

[17] "Start a project - Kickstarter." https://www.kickstarter.com/learn. Accessed 23 Oct. 2019.

[18] "Our Rules — Kickstarter." https://www.kickstarter.com/rules. Accessed 23 Oct. 2019.

4. Misleading imagery includes photorealistic renderings and heavily edited or manipulated images or videos; anything that could give backers a false impression of a product's current stage of development.

5. Projects can't fundraise for charity.

6. Projects can't offer equity.

7. Projects can't involve prohibited items.

IndieGoGo

For Indiegogo, here are the general guidelines for types of projects that are allowed[19]:

- For-profit campaigns
- Campaigns benefitting nonprofit organizations or nonprofit beneficiaries
- Campaigns for products
- Anything within "Community Projects" that is not a personal cause
- Educational campaigns in the Tech and Innovation category

And here is a list of their overarching categories[20]:

- Tech & Innovation
- Creative Works
- Community Projects

---

[19] "Is My Campaign Allowed on Indiegogo? – Indiegogo Help ...." https://support.indiegogo.com/hc/en-us/articles/360000574528-Is-My-Campaign-Allowed-on-Indiegogo-. Accessed 23 Oct. 2019.

[20] "Explore Crowdfunding Campaigns & Unique ... - Indiegogo." https://www.indiegogo.com/explore. Accessed 23 Oct. 2019.

Each platform is different, and each product and campaign is different. To succeed you have to have the important crowdfunding elements done in a way that appeals to your target audience and stays within the guidelines of your chosen platform.

Show Me the Money

Before we jump into the chapters that deep dive into each element you need to consider for a successful crowdfunding campaign, let's talk about the all-important topic - money. After all, though you may be bettering the world with your product or project, it's still nice to make money from it.

Setting up the right funding goal and the right type of account to hold all that hard-earned money is important.

How Much Should Your Funding Goal Be?

One of the questions we get asked most often pertains to people wanting to know what funding amount to set their Kickstarter or Indiegogo goal.

And after running 3000+ crowdfunding projects, we've come up with a simple formula to determine how much your goal should be.

Set your Kickstarter goal to be your Least Viable Goal (LVG).

The LVG is the least amount you need to raise so the fulfillment on your product is viable. Let's say, for example, you want to raise money for a new wallet. Let's also say that to produce, manufacture, and ship 500 of your wallets, it will cost you $4,500.

While $4,500 may be the amount you need to fulfill on your product, it may not be your LVG. Suppose that either you or a family member has $1,000 they could chip in if needed. That means that really your LVG would be $3,500, because to deliver on your product you only need $3,500 from your crowdfunding campaign. The other $1,000 is coming from elsewhere.

In considering your LVG, take into account your production quantity. As the amount increases, you should have lower costs per unit. This will also affect your LVG.

Kickstarter Goal vs Real Goal

"But," you might be thinking, "I don't want to raise $3,500. I want to raise $15,000 or more on my campaign!"

There is a difference between your Kickstarter goal (which we recommend you set at your LVG), and your real goal.

When we work with clients before they launch, we often ask what their Kickstarter goal is as well as what their *real* goal is. The Kickstarter goal is the amount they are setting for their crowdfunding project. The real goal is what they are hoping to raise – the amount at which they will be satisfied and happy with the outcome of the campaign.

Your Kickstarter goal and your real goal are two different things, and they shouldn't be confused or mingled together. If you really hope to raise $15,000 on Kickstarter, that's great. But don't set $15,000 as your Kickstarter goal, unless $15,000 also happens to be the minimum amount you need to raise to fulfill on your product.

The Benefit to Using Your LVG

Here's why.

There are 2 main benefits to setting your Kickstarter goal at your LVG.

- Benefit 1. You may save money. A LOT of it. Often, campaigns don't raise as much as they hoped to raise. Which means that a few days before the campaign is over, they are having friends and family put in contributions of $1,000, $2,500, $5,000, or more just to meet the funding goal so they get the money.

  Kickstarter takes it's cut. Kickstarter takes 5% and credit card processing takes about another 3%. That's a total of 8% being taken, and that adds up if your friends and family are putting in money just to help you out.

  So, if your project has a goal of $50,000, and you raise $40,000 on your own, when friends and family put in another $10,000, you effectively lose 8% on $10,000, which is $800, compared to them giving you the money directly.

  Getting friends and family to put in money right at the end is not uncommon for projects that are close to their goal. You want to avoid this at all costs, especially when that cost is 8%.

- Benefit 2. People prefer winners, not losers. When we first got into crowdfunding, we wondered what would generate more sales: a project that needs a little boost to hit its goal, OR a project that has already passed its goal and shown it will fund?

  In other words, are backers on Kickstarter motivated more to help out the creator with a new business idea that is close, but not quite there? Or are people on Kickstarter more motivated to get behind a successful project?

  We can definitively now say the answer is the latter.

People prefer to back a project when it has already reached 100% of its funding goal.

Why is that the case? It's because backers prefer to put money into a project that they know they will actually receive, because the project has already reached its' funding goal. This means that when your goal on Kickstarter is higher than it actually needs to be, you unnecessarily make it take longer to look like you have reached success. The lower your goal, the quicker it is reached, and the more backers you will receive.

For example, a project that has raised 250% of its funding goal ($250,000 raised with a $100,000 goal), sounds better and more successful than an identical campaign that has raised 41% of the funding goal ($250,000 raised with a $600,000 goal). Even though in both cases the project has raised $250,000, the 250% sounds better.

In short, as we wrote earlier, crowdfunding is paradoxical in the sense that people only believe you are successful once you *are* successful. So, by setting your Kickstarter goal to your LVG, you have a much greater chance of hitting your Real Goal.

When LVG Isn't Really Applicable

To give you the full picture, it's important to know there are scenarios where setting your crowdfunding goal at your LVG isn't necessarily applicable.

Scenario 1: You already have all the funds you need to deliver on your product, but you want to launch on Kickstarter because of the extended reach you'll get for your product. In this case, our recommendation is to set a reasonable goal you are certain you'll hit.

In this case, "reasonable goal" means reasonable in relation to what you are in the process of delivering. For instance, a wallet might have a goal of $2,500, whereas a smart luggage might have a goal of $50,000. Those are reasonable goals in relation to the product you are creating. A goal of $5,000 on a smart luggage invention would seem unreasonable, and that goes against our "Probability" P from our 7 P's for Crowdfunding Success from Chapter 4.

Scenario 2: You only want to create and fulfill on your product if you hit a certain amount. Maybe you are launching a Kickstarter project to validate a new business idea and unless you raise $50,000 on the campaign, under no circumstances do you want to proceed with the creation and fulfillment of that product. In a case like this, set your goal to exactly what you want it to be.

Setting up Your Crowdfunding Bank Account

No matter which crowdfunding platform you have selected, you will need to link your bank account to your crowdfunding project so that you can get paid. This is done on the Funding tab you find in your project's dashboard.

Because you don't receive any money if you don't hit your funding goal, you won't receive any of the funds until the campaign has ended. Kickstarter promises that so long as there are no issues, you will receive your funds 14 business days after your campaign has ended. On Indiegogo, the time period is 15 business days after your campaign has ended.

Beware! Make sure all your bank account details are correct, or it's likely to cause issues with getting your money as quickly as possible.

Here is information Kickstarter gives for how to handle the bank account set-up process[21]:

"The bank account used to set up a project must belong to the person who verifies their identity as the project creator – the person running the project. If the funds are intended to be transferred to a company bank account (or an account belonging to a legal entity), then the bank account on file must be able to be accessed by the person who has verified their identity as the person behind the project.

---

[21] "What type of bank account can I use to set up my project ...." 25 Sep. 2019, https://help.kickstarter.com/hc/en-us/articles/115005136114-What-type-of-bank-account-can-I-use-to-set-up-my-project-. Accessed 24 Oct. 2019.

The bank account must support direct deposit (for U.S. bank accounts, this means that the bank account needs to be ACH compliant). Typically, accounts matching these specifications are *checking* accounts. Accordingly, **our payments processor, Stripe, only supports checking accounts at this time**. If you have questions about whether or not your bank account is set up for these types of transactions, we recommend checking with your financial institution.

Please note that we are not able to offer PayPal, Square, or other similar third party services as viable methods for payments collection or payout transfers at this time."

Indiegogo's banking information[22]:

"You will be required to complete the bank form found on the Funding tab of your campaign prior to launching. If the bank form is not completed, you will not be able to launch your campaign.

If you are raising money for someone else, we ask that you enter their bank account information or add them to your campaign team as an editor so they have access to enter their bank account information. This way we can ensure that the funds raised can be sent to them directly.

Indiegogo is not able to verify the accuracy of the bank information you provide. To ensure accuracy of the information you provide us, please confirm the relevant details with your bank, before entering your Bank

---

[22] "How to Set Up a Bank Account – Indiegogo Help Center." https://support.indiegogo.com/hc/en-us/articles/202916298-How-to-Set-Up-a-Bank-Account. Accessed 24 Oct. 2019.

account information into the Bank Form on your campaign.

Be sure to select the correct country option for both your bank country and where you legally reside when first creating your campaign. These fields cannot be changed, see here for more information. Once you select your funding type (Individual, Business or Nonprofit) this field cannot be updated.

You can use a personal or business checking account. Please ensure you discuss receiving funds from Indiegogo with your bank to ensure your account is set up to receive them. Indiegogo is not responsible for customers' inability to receive funds due to limitations in place by their bank.

Indiegogo is not able to disburse funds to virtual bank accounts or third-party money sending services such as PayPal, Payoneer, Venmo etc."

Setting up your bank account link with your crowdfunding project is relatively straightforward. To read all the details for each platform, please use the links we provide in the footnotes.

Now, let's move on to creating great project elements for your campaign so you can maximize your funding potential.

Fun Fact:

Did you know that Funded Today has raised more than $300M USD for 3,214 projects around the world?

7

Creating a Video that Converts

***Don't fear failure. Not failure, but low aim, is the crime. In great attempts it is glorious even to fail.* Bruce Lee**

Here we go!

One of our favorite topics - THE VIDEO. This chapter will give you a lot of key information and tips to help you create a video that draws people in and converts them into buyers. So, grab your caffeinated beverage, kick back, and dive in.

Your crowdfunding project video is, essentially, the sales pitch of your campaign. To get sales, you need a great sales pitch. We've seen plenty of products do extremely well on Kickstarter, with only basic photography but a killer sales pitch. Pristine imagery is not necessary, though it definitely adds a professional touch.

You need to show potential backers they can use your product and convince them they want or need what you're offering, too. The purpose of your video is to present your product in a way that people will see themselves using it, and evoke an emotion in them so they'll take action right by hit the "back" button to support your campaign.

NOTE: ***Your Kickstarter video can only raise what you give it the power to raise. Don't fall prey to thinking your product is so awesome that it will sell itself.***

Introducing Funded Today's Kickstarter Video Formula

Awesome Product + Persuasive Script + Clear Visuals & Audios + You + ??? = A Compelling Crowdfunding Video

You may be wondering about those unknown "???"

Because every product, campaign, and creator is unique, your video should be unique too. This means there is not an exact Kickstarter video formula that will work for every campaign. However, with all of the four known components - Product, Persuasive Script, Clear Visuals and Audios, as well as the fifth component, You, incorporated properly, your video will be off to a great start.

Component 1: The Product

This Kickstarter video formula won't work unless the star of the video, your product, is something customers want. A very important question (as we've mentioned before) to ask yourself from the start is this: Would I, myself, want to back this project? If so, why? If not, why not?

How universal is your idea/product/service? Is it something everybody needs? The goal is to excite as many people as possible about your product. If you expect others to back your campaign, start by deciding if you would back it yourself. Then spread the question to a wide range of people.

If it turns out that your product is something hardly anybody needs or wants, the video can't perform as well as it could otherwise. In other words, even the best video can't compensate for a poor product.

Kickstarter Video Formula Component 2: Persuasive Script

The script is the most effective way to persuade your backers. And before jumping right into the script, first create an outline you can build upon and perfect. A Kickstarter video without a good outline is like a body with a bunch of broken bones. It's still a body, but it won't get you anywhere.

There have been countless campaigns on Kickstarter that have amazing footage, yet the campaigns failed. Why? They didn't have the "bones" of the Kickstarter video outline in place to build the foundation for a compelling script.

The script is the most important part of the Kickstarter Video Formula. If your script is poorly written or nonexistent, it won't matter if your Kickstarter video looks like a million bucks.

As a brief overview for your video:

- Begin creating the idea for your script by locating the problem(s) your target audience has that your product solves.

- Let that problem really sink in, and explain the impact it has on your prospective backers' daily lives.
- Once you've reminded your potential backers of the reason for their headache, it's time for you to come to the rescue with the cure to their pain. What are the solutions your product has to offer?
- Last, make sure you ask for the sale. Did you know that 85% of sales interactions end without the salesperson asking for the sale[23]? Don't let this be you after all your hard work. Asking for the sale in your Kickstarter video script can be short and simple, but make sure it's there. Consider it your "call to action."

If you have the budget, it's always better to have a professional write your script. We make it sound easy in the brief outline above, but it takes great discipline and skill to write compelling, clear sales scripts.

Kickstarter Video Formula Component 3: The Visuals and Audio

Crystal-clear sound, compelling footage, and controlled lighting are all elements needed to add a professional touch to our Kickstarter Video Formula. True, many past Kickstarters have succeeded with low-quality footage, especially when they are a scrappy startup. But those times they are a changin'. Stepping up your quality will improve your company image and ethos, and help you stand out among the thousands of other projects live on Kickstarter and IndieGoGo during your own launch. You

---

[23] "How to Dissect the Kickstarter Video Outline into 4 parts ...." https://www.funded.today/blog/how-to-dissect-the-kickstarter-video-outline-into-4-parts. Accessed 13 Nov. 2019.

can easily achieve these goals with the right equipment.

1. Professional video camera. Your phone by itself is not good enough to achieve the desired professional quality. Neither are most low-end digital cameras. Image clarity is crucial if you want to impress potential backers and keep them fixated on your video and product. Bad quality video detracts from your product and sets a bad expectation for the quality of your actual product.

2. Lighting. Natural, diffused lighting is an inexpensive path to quality if you know how to use it correctly; It's just not always available. That's why it's good to have high-quality lighting equipment on hand. Having improved in recent years, LED lighting can be a great, inexpensive option when it comes to Kickstarter video lighting equipment.

3. Microphone. The sound in your Kickstarter video is almost more important than the imagery. High-quality microphone equipment is key to capture the clear and rich sound needed for a professional-sounding video.

Kickstarter Video Formula Component 4: You

Your backers aren't just investing in the product. They are backing your product, your cause, and your company - in other words they are backing you, and most importantly YOU and YOUR DREAM. Your Kickstarter video is a great chance to show your potential backers what makes your product and your company so special.

There are endless ways to do this. So be creative, and have fun.

If your campaign has a captivating emotional, and/or moving story, share it. You can capture this on camera, or even with a voice-over while showing other powerful imagery.

One word of caution: be careful when using humor. While humor may seem like a great way to entertain in a video, it is also very tricky to use correctly and can end up hurting your campaign. Most of the time humor is not even necessary to attract backers to fund your Kickstarter or Indiegogo campaign.

Your Crowdfunding Project Video Outline

An effective crowdfunding video is not something you can produce in the spur of the moment, like you would with a social media post. Let's talk about how to develop a solid video outline.

Campaign Video Outline, Part I: Source the problem

First, you must have a good hook. Your audience needs an emotional, personal, and highly targeted mental hook that will capture their minds and keep them on your project page. Begin by using your strongest material first.

David Ogilvy, an advertising executive says, "When you advertise fire extinguishers, open with the fire."

Start out by locating the key problem(s) your primary audience has. The more universal the problem, the better. Even though you probably have a target market in mind, you don't want to close doors to others who might be interested. Keep it broad.

Spend enough time on the key problem(s) to let that problem really sink in, and explain the impact that problem has on their daily lives. Make your audience think and realize, "Oh, yeah, I'd love a fix for this."

Campaign Video Outline, Part II: Present the Solution

Now that you have reminded your potential backers of the reason for their headache, it's time for you to come to the rescue with the cure to their problem. **What are the solutions your product has to offer?**

Here is a tip:

When you are ready to capture footage for your video, feature an actor interacting with your product and demonstrating how it solves the audience's problem(s). This will build credibility for your product because your viewers will be able to see that your product actually works. If you have a product that syncs with an app, try to show someone using the app to show how the product and app work together. The more you can show rather than tell, the better. Give them irrefutable proof that your product works.

This part of the video outline is also the time to show off what makes your campaign so special. Why will your prospective backers need your product instead of something else already out on the market?

If you know of any objections and counter-arguments, overcome them. For instance, if the price is "too high", explain why it's not. Highlight the features, quality, and benefits that give your product value. Objections can often be countered with further information and clarification.

Campaign Video Outline, Part III: This is Why I Am Passionate:

Viewers rarely care about your story until they decide whether or not they are interested in your product. Now that you have their attention, you can deepen their commitment and interest level in your business with your story.

Remember - backers are not always just pledging to get a product. They are also backing you!

One of our referral partners, CrowdOx, sent out a survey to 50 repeat backers. Their findings were enlightening. 78% wanted to be part of something cool, 52% actually needed the product, 37% wanted a discount from retail, and 33% wanted an exclusive product or to be an early adopter[24].

Do you have a cool story? Share it. 78% of backers want to be part of it.

---

[24] "How to Dissect the Kickstarter Video Outline into 4 parts ...." https://www.funded.today/blog/how-to-dissect-the-kickstarter-video-outline-into-4-parts. Accessed 13 Nov. 2019.

You can also opt to include your story in your page design. Just like with your video, sell your product first on your page template, and then share your story. One of our favorite stories is from a watch product we marketed. The story was simple, yet beautiful and compelling. "72 year-old watchmaker passes on legacy of watchmaking to grandchildren." Do you see how this story encompasses so much more than "just another watch invention" on Kickstarter?

Campaign Video Outline, Part IV: The Resolution

The most basic, yet often overlooked aspect, in projects of this nature is asking for the sale. Too many people have a good video but forget to ask people to "buy."

Don't let this be you after all your hard work. Again, asking for the sale in your video script can be short and simple, BUT MAKE SURE IT'S THERE.

Your goal should be to get backers to say "Yes, I need that!" and then back your campaign immediately, without delay. You can't expect backers to answer yes to backing your project if they were never even asked.

Campaign Video Outline: But Wait, There's More

If this outline sounds too simple, you are correct. We are just scratching the surface of everything you will want to know about creating an effective Kickstarter video outline.

You can do all of the research by yourself, or you can hire us, **Funded Today**, the world's leading crowdfunding marketing agency who already knows how to put together a kicka** video outline. We also understand how to bring that video to life with compelling imagery and expert video editing skills. We would honestly have to write even more books to discuss all the skills and finesse that goes into making that happen.

The Role of Your Video in the Crowdfunding Environment

Crowdfunding is different than the retail environment, because with crowdfunding projects you're talking about a product that doesn't even exist yet, so people can't feel or touch it. Therefore, your video really has to resonate with people so they can understand what they're even potentially backing or purchasing.

Crowdfunding platforms like Kickstarter and Indiegogo are really a unique space, because rarely do project creators have the opportunity to reach out to potential backers before there is an actual finished product. Potential backers will listen to your pitch (the video) for one or two minutes max (often only for 30 seconds or less), or they'll pay attention throughout the whole thing if you do your video right and it has no distractions.

Distractions are things like bad audio, or a shaky camera, or other elements that visually make your product look bad. Distractions can make people not want to back your product. When your video is good with no distractions, people can focus on the product you're presenting, and this leads to better conversion rates.

Without a video, your backers will really have a hard time envisioning themselves using your product. So, the purpose of the video is to get people to be familiar with your story, with your product, and with you. When done right, doing founder statements and other personable segments in your video can bump up your standing for people who want to back your project.

How Much Should You Spend?

Balance is the Key

We sometimes hear from Clients who indicate they want an iPhone **commercial** look for the price of an iPhone **phone**. In essence, they want their video to look like an Apple commercial. Well, Apple spends millions of dollars making commercials. Of course, we'd all like our product to have a video commercial like that. But there is always a price for value. And an iPhone level value is definitely outside most people's budgets.

Most often you are on a crowdfunding platform because you are trying to raise money to create a business or company. So, it's likely you don't have a lot of money on the front end. That being said, certainly putting some money into your video and marketing, or on your page, can convert into more money for you on the back end.

The amount you ultimately spend has to be a balance between the quality you want, the budget you have, and the vision you are trying to fulfill. That's why we can't say what your video will cost right away. At Funded Today, we approach this by talking with creators beforehand, so we all understand the important factors. Only then can we give a personalized bid - which means incorporating what you want while factoring in realistic budgetary constraints.

Since we promised to not beat around the bush and shoot straight with you, we know you probably want a ballpark number. $10,000 is therefore a good starting figure if you want to give yourself the best shot at raising

6 figures, while $20,000 can get you a video that anyone would be proud of.

And you can certainly spend a lot more. For example, Hiral Sanghavi, the creator of The BauBax Travel Jacket, spent $50,000 to $80,000 on his first project, and another $50,000 to $60,000 for his BauBax Travel Jacket 2.0 creation. His first project raised around $9.2 million on Kickstarter, and then a couple million more on Indiegogo's InDemand platform. His second one raised around $3 million on Kickstarter. That's an example of why we say your video can only raise what you give it the power to raise. If you want to raise a lot of money, you should put a little bit of money into your video upfront.

Every video is going to be different, every product is different, every story is different, every creator is different, and that's why it's really important to have a real conversation with real experts about your video, and learn what can be done and for what price.

Never forget - your presentation always trumps your promotion (i.e. marketing) when it comes to our 7 P's for Crowdfunding Success (Chapter 4). No amount of great promotion will fix a bad presentation, but a great presentation, with the same great promotion, often makes all the difference.

The Shoestring Budget

What if you really only have a shoestring budget, and you've already spent everything on R&D or manufacturing?

Hopefully you're reading this book before you've gone that far, so we can say: **don't get yourself into that position!**

There is no reason to over-analyze, because the power of a crowdfunding campaign is that you can get product validation before you sink all your money into your new invention. So, you don't need to put in nearly as much money to do your prototyping and your manufacturing when you go the crowdfunding route.

What you do need to do is tell the story of your product and bring it to life, because there is a chance that as good of a story as you tell, as good of an idea as you have, nobody may want it. Whether nobody wants it because they don't like it, or because the timing isn't right, or for some other reason, you want to find this out before you've spent all you have on R&D or manufacturing, otherwise, you'll be in a real financial bind.

Taking all of this into account, let's say you need to create your project video on a really small budget. If this sounds like you, you absolutely have to make your video count.

The first thing to do is get your story down. Write your video script, and then read it to at least 10 other people. After sharing your script with these people, ask them, "Does my script for my video seem cool? Does it make sense? Does it grab you?"

Just like you did with the Triple F, get people's feedback before you even begin filming your video. Get as much feedback as you can, from everyone that you can- and yes, if possible, even people you don't know.

Here's how to approach this feedback cycle: "Hi, do you have two minutes? I'm trying to create a Kickstarter video and I'd love to tell you what I'm doing so I can get honest feedback from people like you. Would you mind helping me out?"

This is a very good practice before you create anything - a webpage, a video, whatever. Go talk face-to-face with people and see what their common objections are, find out what questions they have, what they like and don't like about it. This practice gives you a much better chance of creating something successful, because you've essentially talked to a focus group.

After you've asked and received all this feedback, use it as you start to tackle your video. In fact we recommend this no matter what your budget - you need to get into the mind of the consumer, and unless you have those discussions, and unless you have the sales pitch right, you're never going to get that information.

Bringing Your Story to Life

It's vital that your video message is done in a way that engages immediately. There is a story of the product, or the story of how the founders got here - either way it has to be a story that evokes emotion to the viewer.

To be clear - it's not enough to tell a story - you have to **have** a story. If you're just telling a story, maybe you can trick some people, but if it isn't real, if you don't actually have that story, deep down you're not going to hit that emotional element that makes people resonate with getting behind a creator - to want to help bring a new idea to life.

Human beings are emotional. Emotion causes us to decide what to buy, how we vote, and to decide how we settle an issue. So, when we speak about triggering emotion in your video we're not talking about big emotions – not trying to inspire tears, or anger, or other extreme reactions. Effective emotional appeal are very subtle and nuanced.

Then the question becomes, what emotions do you want to evoke, and what can you include in your video to evoke those emotions?

One method that makes for a good story, good marketing, and can evoke emotions, is conflict. The greater the conflict, the greater the emotion.

As an example of this, let's go back to the PurTrek example. The creator's basic conflict is that he wanted to have a simpler way to go backpacking, but the bigger conflict of his was that he wanted to have a better time with his family. So, the small conflict of just carrying too much stuff, or having a heavy backpack, is a very practical conflict. But, the next step in the conflict is wanting that more enjoyable experience in nature with his family. When you can bring those nuanced levels into your video, that's when people really believe what you're saying - it takes your video to the next level.

The All-Important First 10 Seconds

The first 10 seconds of a video is a golden time – meaning if you don't connect with your audience by the end of those 10 seconds, they likely will not watch the entire video. So you need to start off strong, have a good compelling pitch, show that conflict, or show something that makes people interested in watching.

Your call to action does not come until the end of your video, so if you lose people's interest in the beginning, they don't get to that take-action part, and that's a problem. You won't get backers.

We are a fast-paced, instant-gratification-based society, in no small part because of technology. We can have just about anything we want with one click. People want it NOW, without having to invest too much time - think of this as technology induced ADD. This comes into play with your video. You must hook that potential backer in those first five to ten seconds, and then you better keep them hooked throughout the video.

So, get your unique selling proposition that solves a personal problem from a story in your life. Get why that matters to the watcher, and get that set up as quickly as you can in your video.

Keep it Short

Once you have your video script, cut it down. We promise you, it's too long. Cut it in half, cut it in to thirds.

As the creator, you don't want to leave out any little tiny detail. You'll want to have your product and all the features no matter how insignificant. But here's the thing: some details of your product are better shown on the page, so save video time, save space, save your audience's time- so they get to that call to action.

For any detail you feel you want in your video, ask yourself if that detail could just be on the page as an image, or in a list of features.

Cut it down, and then cut it down some more. Only then are you finally ready to pick up a camera.

Your Video Crew

If you're not hiring professionals, at the very least find someone who knows how to use a camera. You can rent a good camera. For sure do not try and do this yourself if you have no background in video or film.

You can post on Facebook - “Hey do any of you, my friends, have media experience? Who is a good videographer? Who can help me? I've got everything done; this isn't going to take you very much time. I've got the script, the storyboard, the story, everything is right here ready to go. Who can come help me for a couple hours? By the way, if you help me, I'll buy you dinner.”

Absolutely call in favors. Even if you don't want to spend a decent amount of money to hire a full creative service (like us), put some money into your video. Most film crew members have a day rate. Make sure they're comfortable, make sure that you're paying them right. You want them to be happy, so they do good work for you.

A note on sound: if there's dialogue in your video, you need a separate recording device.

Find the best locations for filming.

Everybody has a network - leverage that network!

You also need a film editor. There is timing and angles and all sorts of details that you won't know about if it's not your area of expertise. So, get someone who knows how to edit to put it together. Videos that are edited by amateurs often have wasted space and wasted time. A video that should really be a minute and ten seconds is two minutes. Again, that's not what you want to do. The longer your video, the less likely your audience will watch all the way through.

You will need music. There are a lot of music sites where you can license music for only around $50 to $100.

If you have a voiceover - maybe you don't have the best voice for this - there are some voice over people on Fiverr[25] that you can check out. Or, maybe you have a friend that you think could be on the radio because their voice is just so good.

Hire actors to demonstrate your product in the video, and make sure they look happy to be using your product. This may sound obvious, but sometimes creators forget to show potential customers how the product will benefit a real human being. It builds credibility for your product and shows your backers applications in which the product can be used.
A visual demonstration is great education. If you only have a prototype, that is fine. The more it looks and functions like the final product, the better.

Video FAQ's

1. Should you, as the creator, be in the video? If you can, yes.

2. How long should the video be? Under two minutes.

3. How much video budget do I need for a video if I want to raise $100,000 or more for my product? In most cases, $15,000 minimum.

4. How long does it take to make my video if I hire Funded Today right now? Generally, a month after you've approved the script we will write for you.

5. How long does it take to write a script generally? For us, between three to five days.

---

[25] "Fiverr." https://www.fiverr.com/. Accessed 30 Oct. 2019.

6. Okay, so, if I hired you at the first of the month, I might be launching within the first week or two of the next month? If everything was just right on schedule and you didn't hold anything up as the creator, then yes, it can happen that quick.

That's a Wrap

Your video can be the most important thing you do for your crowdfunding project. Your video can be the difference between getting funded, and having to re-launch in another month or two. Put that in perspective when you are debating on budget. Do what's best for your product, and for your campaign.

If it's something that you want us to help you with, we are happy to do so. Funded Today is one of the only crowdfunding video production companies with the experience of helping thousands of campaigns.

Key Takeaways

- The most important part of campaign videography is good scriptwriting, which can start when you honestly compose your true story. Practice sharing your story with others, and obtain as much honest feedback about your story as possible in order to perfect it—and, by perfecting it before filming it, you can avoid expensive revisions.

- The purpose of a campaign video is to initially hook viewers - right away.

- Tell an engaging and true story (without distractions) within 1-2 minutes, that elicits emotion through conflicts that are ultimately resolved by the product being offered. Also, introduce the creator if possible, and finally, present a strong call to action that motivates viewers to pledge.

- Effective presentation (especially through campaign videography) is even more important than effective promotion, because bringing traffic to a campaign page is pointless if that traffic doesn't convert readily into pledgers.

Video Creation Resources

If you decide you absolutely want to do your video yourself, we have a lot of material. Please see our Resource Section at the end of this book for specific links if you want more information.

8

Developing a Compelling Page

Be who you are and say what you feel, because those who mind don't matter and those who matter won't mind. Theodore Geisel-Dr. Seuss

When you begin work on your crowdfunding project page, always keep in mind that the goal is to appeal to your backers' hearts and minds. There is one thing you can do to ensure your success: include lots of kitten images!

Just kidding - sort of. Well, unless you're creating a cat product. You do, however, need to appeal to the hearts and minds of potential backers. In this chapter we are going to give you tips and instructions on creating a compelling crowdfunding project page to give you the greatest chance of reaching your goal. As we emphasized in previous chapters, getting feedback along the way greatly improves your chances for success.

Don't hesitate to seek input and suggestions from people you know who are part of your target audience. **Before we talk about what does work, let's talk about what does not work**.

How to Make an Unsuccessful Presentation Page

As an example of what doesn't work, let's talk about new watch products. We have designed dozens of pages for watch campaigns, and feel we can pull up just about any watch page on Kickstarter that hasn't met their funding and we'll see this exact formula:

- First, they start by claiming they've discovered a new lifestyle, but there is no mention of product specs or any concrete information.

- The page spends tons of time explaining to everybody what a visionary the creator is – often in 1000 words or more.

- Coupled with this, are several 50 megabyte animated GIFs to capture the reader's interest.

- Then, they've copied the structure from the top third of a million-dollar campaign page, and pasted those components on top of whatever is on their page.

- And, of course, the profile picture is really large - and posted several times throughout the page with Big Kahuna written right under the photo.

- Only then is there a mention of rewards, the pricing, and your plan to deliver this to backers in a timely manner - and even then, these points are skimmed over as quickly as possible.

- Finally, there is a reminder to everybody that you're going to change the world together.

Warning: Don't Imitate a Million Dollar Campaign

Beyond the elements mentioned above, another way to hurt your project is to decide to imitate someone else's successful campaign.

Too often, creators look at campaigns that have raised hundreds of thousands of dollars, or even millions of dollars, on Kickstarter or Indiegogo, and then they believe they can imitate those campaigns and make-up something that doesn't have the right story, or that doesn't have the right motivation behind it. In essence, they are trying to emulate success but it's not real or genuine to their product or themselves. That is simply not going to work.

Don't get us wrong - imitating elements of success can be good. But you have to know what to imitate, and how to make it your own. A few years ago, there was a campaign for a jacket, and they were attempting to imitate the "BauBax Travel Jacket." They thought they were copying the structure of the BauBax campaign when they had each of the different features, why the features were awesome, etc.

By all accounts, the project looked like they were copying the structure of BauBax. However, when you looked at it more closely, you could see it was different because BauBax would always talk about the benefits of each of their different features, while this other campaign literally was saying "hey, here's this feature, here's another feature, and, oh, lest we forget, here's this other feature." They didn't understand the difference between a feature and a benefit. They were not explaining why their features were good; they were just listing them out.

Copying success can be good and can be useful but you have to know what you're doing.

In other words, you can't just go look at the million-dollar campaigns and copy them. You need to know the nuances of what they did, and why they did it, to really imitate that success, if that's what you're attempting to do. You need to study them.

The other vital aspect to be aware of when you want to use previously successful elements is that you really cannot make projections based upon how much a campaign raised. You need to know what their actual profit was, how efficient their campaign was, what their cost for conversion was, along with many other metrics, to determine if they were successful. In other words, just because a project appears to be successful doesn't mean that it actually was, because so many other elements make up success.

An example that comes to mind is "Bluesmart." This was a huge Indiegogo smart luggage campaign that initially raised millions through rewards-based crowdfunding. Ultimately, and sadly, they ended up declaring bankruptcy.[26]

This is something we talk about at Funded Today all the time - just because a campaign posts $1 million, $2 million, $10 million or even $20 million, does not mean they will be ultimately successful. Go back to our previous chapter example featuring the "Coolest Cooler." This project also raised a ton of money, and still

---

[26] "Bluesmart shuts down after airlines ban smart luggage - The ...." 1 May. 2018, https://www.theverge.com/2018/5/1/17306410/smart-luggage-ban-bluesmart-shutdown-refunds. Accessed 22 Oct. 2019.

hasn't been able to find a way to deliver to all of their backers, and is in a lot of financial trouble because they did not properly take into account shipping and prototyping costs, as well as other factors.

All this to say, when you're looking to borrow from success, don't only go by the total dollars a campaign raises. Scanning for the most funded campaigns is instinctively going to be a bad move for you to base your own presentation on.

Repeat after us – just because something worked for a million-dollar campaign does not mean it will work for you.

Every project has a different business agenda and different social conventions than yours.

Many million-dollar campaigns have been launched by reputable brands and creators who target people, and then they already have a Kickstarter account and followers. One that comes to mind is the "Nomatic Backpack." They do a new Kickstarter project generally once every fiscal quarter. We get a lot of clients saying, "We want to look like Nomatic." Not a good idea.

Nomatic has a design that is almost unchanged since they first launched. You can see the price, the reward that they're giving is going up and down. What they are doing is not based on any sort of objective fact. They're just doing what they did the first time, since it worked, so they continue doing it without testing that design. Nomatic also has a very loyal customer/backer following that you yourself will first have to earn by creating a wonderful new invention and then delivering on your promises to your backers.

Testing is what allows us to know what is actually working vs. what we think will work. We will talk more about this in a later chapter, too.

Mistakes to Avoid

Don't ask your viewers for their money before you sell them on your idea. It's almost always more effective to sell your project to people before asking them to fund it, rather than asking people for money and then trying to explain to them why they should give it to you.

Don't Assume Knowledge

If you have an existing fan base outside of Kickstarter and/or Indiegogo, or if you are upgrading a previous crowdfunding project, then it's best to assume that potential backers know nothing about your previous work. Chances are good they won't bother to search for it on their own.

Some projects include charitable aspects. We've noticed that charitable features can potentially help sales, but are normally less-effective selling-points than others. Your "sales pitch" should always focus upon your product's benefits, rather than on corporate philanthropy; otherwise, people will probably donate directly to that cause without buying anything from you.

After you've "sold" them, don't forget to ask them for their money! Some campaigns make the mistake of never asking for money at all. This is also usually counterproductive. So, anytime you believe that you've sufficiently persuaded someone they should buy something, always remember to explicitly ask them to do so. This can be done by including simple calls to action as clickable buttons on your crowdfunding page. Make it easy and accessible to them.

Some entrepreneurs also find it helpful to educate page-viewers about crowdfunding itself, how it constitutes a great new way to shop that eliminates needless middlemen so that consumers can buy innovative new products directly from producers at wholesale prices. If you feel your project may attract a lot of attention from people who have never backed a project before, this strategy may be especially beneficial for you.

Page Design

Now that you know what *not* to do, let's talk about what you should do.

Your crowdfunding project will have many moving parts. Your Page Design is, in part, what ties all those parts together into a dynamic and effective campaign.

As you begin developing your presentation page (your lemonade stand), there are two important elements we want you to keep in mind:

1. People detest marketers. Many studies show that as soon as you start typing in anything that looks like marketing, such as "our thing is the greatest thing under the sun and everyone should unite under us," people immediately turn away from that. Readers want to get the important information without feeling hassled.

2. Don't worry about your "brand." You don't have one yet. We find that many people new to crowdfunding put too much emphasis on the idea of "their brand." The reality is, offering a product does not make you a brand. This is important because we don't want you to get hung up on the idea of a brand while you are developing your presentation page. We get a lot of Funded Today clients who say "I don't want to hurt

my brand so please do not do such and such when you design my project page for me." Once you raise a considerable amount of money over a period of time (not in just one project), then maybe you'll have a brand.

We all like the idea of brands. Influencer and marketing expert Neil Patel wrote an article[27] talking about the power of branding, explaining that strong branding is the primary reason why people go to Nike.com, Starbucks, or wherever else. So, we know the lure of a brand. But you don't have that brand power initially when you're trying to launch your startup on Kickstarter or Indiegogo. You might think of this phase as the beginning of building your brand but that's not your goal - your goal should be to drive traffic, and to drive sales (backers). That is your focus.

You will, ultimately, also be creating ads that link to your presentation page. It is the job of your ads to incite and evoke curiosity in your prospective backers. The job of your page design - coupled with the reward structure, the video, the ad copy, and the story - is to convince that curious clicker to become part of your tribe by backing your campaign.

So, it's not so much about sleekness and polish, it's about your value proposition and what you're doing and offering. We are not saying it's okay to make your page look bad, we are saying focus on what matters more than actual design elements. You can have a gorgeous page with no quality content, and get no results.

For example, go look at the very first "Pebble Watch Campaign." You'll see that the video was not good at all.

---

[27] "Neil Patel." https://neilpatel.com/. Accessed 1 Nov. 2019.

But it didn't matter, because the value proposition and what they were doing was far more substantial than any design elements. We recognize the irony here. You do need to have a good design, but don't let a design get in your way. Find a balance.

Don't just aim for pretty and glossy - the goal is a page that converts.

The Page Structure

The most effective crowdfunding pages generally start by presenting a strong, articulate, and heartfelt case-in-a-nutshell- in just a few short sentences. You want this "sales pitch" to render your viewers both impressed, and willing (ideally, even eager) to know more.

Then the remainder of your page-space should be used to elaborate section-by-section upon various aspects of that initial sales pitch, as well as proactively resolving any concerns that might influence page-viewers to hesitate in pledging.

The total quantity of information on your page isn't nearly as important as how skillfully that information is both structured and conveyed. People value their own time. So, it's vital to help potential pledgers to find what they need as efficiently as possible as they scroll down your page from top to (hopefully) bottom.

That means your more-important selling-points need to be placed higher on the page, and your less-important ones lower - especially on Kickstarter, where lower content may initially be hidden from visitors unless they click the "show full project description" button.

As you create your page think: "As long as you keep scrolling down my page, I'll keep giving you reasons to back my project." This can help you stay with compelling information about your story, your product, and its' benefits.

Though you want to aim for short, clear statements, you also need to avoid being too concise, because that can leave your prospective backers with unanswered questions. Their response to that is either losing interest in your project, or needlessly flooding your comments section with questions.

Also, be aware that images sometimes communicate more efficiently, or effectively, than text, and sometimes an image that incorporates text is your best bet. Try and come up with images that can help to clearly explain relatively complex concepts, rather than relying on wordy explanations.

Just as in your video, your page should begin with a strong "hook" to engage viewers both emotionally and mentally. Gradually you "reel them in" with your sales pitch, keeping in mind that they may not go through your entire page before deciding whether to back you, or not. Selling is primarily emotional, but mental appeal shouldn't be ignored, either - so, when selling your project, your page and video should, ideally, appeal not only to viewers' hearts (through fitting music and lifestyle imagery and such), which is vital, but also to their minds (through highlighting various great features, plus how those features will specifically benefit their lives).

Even if your product has complex features, your page (and video) should never be complex. So, stay firmly focused on the basics of what you're trying to communicate. Your presentation page should remain both evenly-paced without ever feeling rushed.

Page Content

Now it's time to start writing your content. To get started here are some general content tips:

- Sound confident, not desperate
- Show your product in action, if possible
- Show people enjoying your product
- Focus on your product, not philanthropy (charity)
- Include instructions on how to pledge
- Place "back us now" buttons throughout your project page, as well as at the end

Start with the Right Mindset

Let's begin with a simple thought experiment.

Pitching Lemonade (or Anything)

Imagine trying to sell a product or service without making any effort whatsoever to pitch it. For example, opening a minimalistic lemonade stand with nothing more than a big absolutely-plain sign that simply reads "LEMONADE for 25¢." This would inform any passers-by what they're being offered, and nothing else. With that minimal offer alone, your stand might still sell a little lemonade to thirsty pedestrians, or to people who desire to be kind to its vendor.

But… it probably won't sell very much. This is because people don't buy things just in response to becoming aware that those things exist. They buy things because they feel a clear incentive-based desire to do so, and such incentives are not conveyed through simple information alone. The information must be accompanied by persuasion, or else people will need to find their own incentives to act. On a sweltering day, an especially thirsty runner might easily find his/her own desire to buy lemonade for a quarter-dollar (or more). But most people won't bother to actively hunt for motives to spend their money. The motives must hunt them.

You may have heard that the best products sell themselves. Yes, there's truth to this. If you produce a lemonade that naturally looks so delicious that observers can't help but drool, for example, and that tastes so delicious that half the people who drink it will naturally want to tell their neighbors and friends about it, then you might not need to say much about it.

But such products ARE RARE. And, even when your product is so amazing that it can "speak for itself," it can only "toot its own horn" so loudly. It will ALWAYS get heard a lot better with help - not only from satisfied buyers, which is priceless - but also from the seller who's offering it.

Why shouldn't you, as a creator, assume an active role in presenting your own creation? And, if you're going to spend your time presenting your product anyway, then why not do so as effectively as possible?

So, how might you help a good lemonade deal to "sell itself" even better, from your hypothetical stand?

You might start by rewriting your simple sign to present the same offer in a much more appealing manner.

Something like: "Ice-Cold Freshly-Squeezed All-Natural Lemonade for Only 25¢" (assuming that this is honest), using a bold, yet attractive, font, and perhaps incorporating a bit of red ink to help catch people's eyes. You could show those passing by fresh lemons ready to squeeze, along with putting lemon slices in their lemonade. This helps emphasize how freshly-squeezed and all-natural your particular blend of lemonade is. Presentation is key.

You might also add some small, highly-readable plaques about how lemon juice or hydration improves health. Incentives to drink the juice in the first place.

Then, you could spruce-up your plain stand with some appealing summertime decor, play some popular upbeat music in the background, and extend a canopy to provide visitors with some welcome shade from the heat (or even a fan blowing cool air), all of which would encourage people to both pause and linger, making your stand seem popular.

If your stand is in a touristy area, then you might even post an easy-to-read map.

Rather than sit patiently behind your stand awaiting customers to approach you, you could, instead, actively engage passers-by in conversation. You could ask them if they'd like to stop to refresh themselves, and assure them what a great lemonade you've prepared for them to drink. You could tell them how much other people have been enjoying it (assuming that this is true). Or better yet, you could take your stand on the road and create a mobile version where you bring your lemonade directly to where your customers are.

If you can genuinely present yourself to potential customers as a competent and trustworthy and likeable lemonade vendor, who has their best interests at heart, then they'll be even more likely to want to transact business with you.

Each of these factors would almost certainly increase people's motivation to buy your lemonade. For each factor, neither the lemonade nor its price (unless you need more money for all of this extra paraphernalia), would change at all from when your stand simply offered "LEMONADE for 25¢." But people's feelings about buying it could improve dramatically and as we know, emotions are primarily what drive sales, although reason can also contribute.

These simple lemonade-stand techniques are among the same ones that professional salespeople and marketers typically learn for pitching offers to prospective buyers - from using good "hooks" to capture people's attention, to explaining how a product's features will benefit their audience's lives, to closing sales with rousing calls to action.

Product Benefits and Features

If you haven't already done so, now is the time to compose an exhaustive list of your product's selling-points, plus its potential drawbacks. Prioritize these items. Then make sure that this ordered list is reflected in your page, including in its video. Selling points like "it may save your life" should generally rank higher than selling points like "it comes in a variety of colors."

You can use ad copy and images that illuminate, in tempting and powerful ways, the benefits and features of what you are offering.

It's good to show features, but it's better to show benefits, and it's best to show both – and to focus especially on the benefits of avoiding bad things rather than obtaining good things.

If there are products similar to yours, it may help to provide a chart that compares your product to the other product(s), showing very clearly why your product is better than any alternatives (organic lemons!).

In pitching your project's benefits, the general rule is that although telling people things is good, showing them, in addition to telling them, is often significantly better.

For each selling point you make, you might consider ways that you can effectively show that selling point in action, such as with an image.

For example, if your product is super-strong, then perhaps show it holding up a massive weight. Or, if it's exceptionally durable, then show it being mangled or crushed in some powerful manner, but then springing back to its former shape without any damage. This is what we mean when we talk about featuring and proving your benefits.

Use Caution if Offering Medical Benefits

If your product has medical benefits, then you need to present these with caution. This is because both Kickstarter and Indiegogo prohibit projects that are explicitly intended to cure or treat disease. However, if you carefully avoid claiming that your product will do such things for people, then you can still get your campaign approved, and perhaps even funded. Our past client Rezzimax TUNER[28] provides an excellent example of how to carefully present medical products in ways that KS/IGG will allow.

Other content that should generally rank high includes "social proof," such as any awards that your project has won, plus a graphical list of news sources that have

---

[28] "Rezzimax Tuner | Indiegogo." 23 Aug. 2017, https://www.indiegogo.com/projects/rezzimax-tuner. Accessed 5 Nov. 2019.

featured this campaign, along with any persuasive "authoritative" statements about it that can be quoted from newscasters, celebrities, experts, or ordinary people who resemble its target audience.

Content that should generally be placed near your page's bottom includes social-media sharing buttons or links. In between any of this content, you may place periodic call-to-action buttons urging your readers to fund your project. Make these accessible and common; you don't want your readers *searching* for the button to pitch in, lest they give up.

Your Sales Pitch

Your webpage's "sales pitch" should ideally convey confidence without arrogance. Stay away from conveying a sense of worry or desperation that it's worth supporting- don't beg. Showing genuine passion about your work is good. You might also do well to incorporate classic principles of persuasion into your presentation, such as:

- Showcasing yourself and your product in a likable manner (especially through both emphasizing similarities with other people, and praising them)
- Noting reciprocity between your products and others' pledges
- Citing authoritative quotations in favor of pledging (which is especially helpful for people who don't find projects quite as relevant to them personally)
- Noting that other people (especially those who resemble your target audience) are already pledging and conveying urgency/scarcity in your offer.

If you practice selling your project to people repeatedly in spoken conversation, that experience will help you to know how to effectively "pitch" your product in writing. You might also want to invite feedback from your target audience on social-media to determine what benefits they want from your product. Consider using the same words that they use in your sales pitch, since using their terms helps build rapport with your audience.

The Video

You've obviously picked up by now that you should definitely include a video, which is key to your campaign's success. Your video's cover image (which is your campaign's "thumbnail" image), should boldly attract people's attention to itself, through both color and contrasting text. For those who watch your video, it should quickly present your product's benefits to them in a manner that's both attractive and persuasive, without their needing to spend any effort trying to figure out what they're being shown.

You may even consider using closed captions in your video, because many people watch videos without sound. Your video's "play" button will appear at its center, so please compose your image to accommodate this button. You might even want to compose multiple thumbnail images for your project, and then rotate those images regularly during your campaign to help it to stay "fresh."

Images & GIFS

GIFs are a powerful and relatively new way to quickly show your product's features and benefits in action. If your product includes selling points that can't be conveyed directly through audiovisual means, such as great flavor, then convey those points as close-to-directly as possible, such as by showing other people experiencing them and reacting to them. In general, it's helpful to show imagery of people enjoying using your product.

Because viewers are being invited to pledge for a product that doesn't exist yet, (and might never exist), except perhaps as a prototype, it would be helpful for your page to present that product as tangibly as possible to your potential backers. This helps them feel more confident in pledging.

A Note on Crew Photos

You don't have to include photos of you, the creator, if you're not comfortable. However, we've noticed that many effective crowdfunding campaigns will skillfully feature not only a great product at a great price, but also the creators. Backers generally feel more comfortable pledging to innovators whom they feel are both competent and trustworthy. Remember our 7 P of People? They also feel more comfortable transacting business with people who aren't complete strangers to them.

Your team is not nearly as important as what you're offering, but they can serve as a contributing factor in encouraging pledges, especially with creators who are likable due to their passions, character, dreams, and intentions, and who have a good true story they want to join in their own small way. Having a team means that you have hired people to handle certain aspects of the project better than you could yourself. That increases the perceived probability of the campaign successfully delivering, and it makes people more likely to back you.

One of our successful wristwatch projects, LunoWear Watches, that we've mentioned before, did very well by featuring a grandfather passing along his watchmaking legacy to his grandsons. Many viewers felt motivated to pledge in support of that cause.

Similarly, large companies like Apple and Google, have prospered greatly, not only because they produce exceptionally-good products, but also because their founders have enjoyed such good reputations. This motivates customers to want to support them in such tasks as lauding dreamers, standing up boldly to "Big Brother" monopolies, valuing the policy "don't be evil" over increasing their profits, and transforming our society for the better through investing their profits into various innovative projects.

So, it may help your profits to sell yourself along with your product through honest storytelling, images, and quotations that present you accurately, and at your best. This gives potential backers multiple reasons to feel confident about transacting business with you.

Along those same lines, we've also noticed that ads featuring images of innovators interacting with their creations, whether serious or silly, stylish or plain, are often among the best ads, in terms of drawing traffic to crowdfunding pages.

Backer Rewards

This section is about general aspects of the pledge levels you are going to offer. For details on how to decide about backer rewards to offer, check out the details in **Chapter 9: Setting Your Pledge Levels.**

Your page's story may also include simple, but effective, reward graphics that present comparative prices at a glance for "early-bird" backers, other backers, and retail buyers. This conveys a sense of urgency to pledge *now*, which drives up sales.

For the rewards themselves, in your page's right column, it's generally best to keep your reward structure simple.

Place your core product FIRST in your list of reward options. Then add more-expensive reward options that include bulk discounts, or added accessories. Limit your total reward options to 5-10 at most, and present each reward both clearly and concisely.

For some variations of your product, such as color, you don't need to create a unique reward for each variation. Instead, you can allow backers to provide remaining details later, in a post-campaign survey.

NOTE: You can continue to add new rewards after your campaign has launched, and each backer can select only one reward per campaign.

Reward availability should start low, because scarcity encourages sales. After your campaign starts, you should increase reward availability as needed, so that your rewards remain scarce without ever running out (unless you want them to do so).

For those who like your project enough to not only back it, but also publicize it to their associates, it can help to include social-media sharing buttons or links. Make sure that those buttons or links don't distract potential backers from pledging, though.

Actively Manage Your Page

Too often, creators who are doing their first crowdfunding project don't ever bother to change their page as their campaign evolves. But, you need to actively manage your page. Don't think, "I have my video, I have my copy, I have my images, so I'm done." Don't ever let a day go by where you're not actively reviewing and managing your page.

Throughout your entire campaign, you should be making pivots, tweaks, and edits. When you begin your project, you may have little to no social proof. So, as that begins to develop, and as your backers and others make awesome comments, weave those things into your existing content.

Curiously, success even multiplies itself! Although some potential backers will pledge to a project in any case, other potential backers require varying degrees of "social proof" to persuade them that a project is worth their support. So, whenever they see other backers rapidly pledging to a given project, hastening it toward (or, better yet, beyond) its' goal, they'll be much more likely to pledge, too. You want to always strive to have up-to-date numbers and information for those upcoming new backers.

Don't make tweaks "just because" - you should be testing different aspects of your page to see what works best for conversions. We go into details of analyzing your campaign, what's working and what's not, in Chapter 16. For now, know you should be looking at different metrics to determine conversion rate and what resonates most with your prospective backers.

Test Everything

The most successful ecommerce sites are always testing different versions of pages to maximize conversion. Many use what is called A/B split testing, where you are comparing the results of two different pages that have just one thing different.

Even massively successful companies like Amazon and Google have to test to find out what works best. There was an Ecommerce study done where Amazon's mobile site was still suffering from things like unclear primary buttons, and product pages that were hard to find. So, Amazon went through a small redesign. The point is, even Amazon is improving things on an ongoing basis. That is the attitude you want with your crowdfunding project page, too.

One key metric that you need to check even before you launch is Page Load Time. Without exception, if your Page Load is over three to five seconds here in America, and New York specifically, that means you're too loading too slow. In China, anything over a 20 second load is too long. Australia, a 30 second load, and in Russia a 40 second load. All that it takes for a 5 second page load is 5-10 megabytes on your page. So, if you have a normal sized page with 3 GIFs that are five seconds long, you've pretty much cutout half the population in terms of how long they're willing to wait to look at your page.

To clarify page load: page load is how long it takes for that page to appear in the browser window after somebody clicks a link to go to your Kickstarter page.

To help your page load fast we recommend you limit page GIFs to three to five seconds. That's about 5 one-second GIFs, or one five-second GIF.

To test your page load, you can use Pingdom.com. Pingdom.com is a good, free speed testing website, and when we use it, we like to compare and check New York, Stockholm, Sweden, Node1, Australia, and San Jose, California.

Conclusion: It's Not About You

As human beings, we are naturally egocentric in the sense that it's difficult for us to imagine a world that's not our own. When you are designing something for potential customers, it's therefore vital you find ways to speak to them, rather than to the world just inside of your head. As the creator, you are in a position of power, and one of the quickest ways to ruin your Kickstarter campaign is to make a campaign for and about yourself.

The exception to this is when you are dealing with a tiny niche that you are familiar with. For instance, there was the guy who sold monster trucks, or racing trucks. And there was a group of around 14 people that drove racing trucks. This guy made the argument that he personally knows everyone in this category, and they were all like him. In that case, he is undoubtedly correct. So, if you're going after a niche where you can pretty much talk to everybody and meet them, then it's probably safe to assume everybody is somewhat like you.

However, for most crowdfunding projects, this is not going to be the case. If you're dealing with a market of more than 100 people, you must avoid using your biases, otherwise, you'll end up with an inefficient design.

Again, that's why it's so important to use "Triple F" (As discussed in Chapter 5). Utilizing your Friends, Family, and Fools network, for that input gives you the answers you need before you launch. They can review your page design and look at your rewards structure. They can give you feedback about aspects that you probably can't identify yourself because you live in your world. You then must use that feedback to help you get into the minds of people who are likely interested backing your product, so that your copy and page *will* resonate with them, rather than what you *think* is going to resonate with them.

Most creators do not actually have the skillset to design and develop the most efficient crowdfunding page. From what we've seen, only about 10% of computer literate people can create a page that allows people who are less computer literate to have a good experience on that page. As a small example, for a good user experience, no navigation should be required to access the information. When you are computer literate, you assume people know how to use a navigation system. That is untrue. This is kind of the same thing as the recommended reading level for most self-help books - 5th grade level.

Everything on your page has to be able to appeal and be accessed by people who know far less than you. Again, it's about their world, not yours. The job of the page is to convert anyone who visits your page. You want them to have a good experience, to get excited and want to become part of your tribe. You have to avoid the trap of wanting to show how much you know, or how smart you are. Everything needs to convey: there are no hassles, there is great information, and there are so many benefits are coming your way. If viewers don't feel all that from the moment they enter the page, they will leave.

We are going to repeat this because it's so important - don't assume knowledge. Many, many people have no idea what crowdfunding is, or what Kickstarter or Indiegogo are even about, even still today. As co-founders of Funded Today, we are always curious about what people think, and as we are out and about, we ask people if they've heard of Kickstarter.

Usually, a long pause is followed by something like, "Is that a website?" Or once - we asked a lift driver and she said "Kickstart, isn't that a soft drink named kind of like Mountain Dew?"

You are dealing with a group of people who are going to give you money with the hope that one day, perhaps in three months, six months, maybe even a year or more, they will receive the product they have given you a couple hundred bucks for. In fact, we've found most people think they're just making a purchase, they don't even realize they're backing something that may or may not ultimately be brought to life. That distinction is especially important.

What we're saying is that you have to put yourself in the mind of the customer that buys on Amazon - who in two days, or sometimes even less, receives their product. That's what you're up against, and that's the type of person you're designing this page for.

How do you resonate with them, how do you communicate nuances with that particular profile? By the way, all this information applies to company websites and such, also.

So, you're a start-up, you're trying to generate sales as effectively as possible, right? By its' nature we are assuming that because you are on Kickstarter and putting a product out there, you want to make money. But your users have different goals. They just want to get things done, so you can't let your goal of making money get in the way of the information they're trying to get. They need to be able to get their tasks done.

We're in a global market now. More and more pledges on Kickstarter and Indiegogo are coming internationally than ever before. So, if you're not resonating with that broad population, many of which do not use English as their first language, you're losing out on a lot of backers.

We know this can all begin to sound very complex, but you don't have to do it on your own. You can hire a professional copywriter who understands the world of selling online, or you can, of course, hire us.

Key Takeaways

- By imitating successful campaign presentations, you can often glean valuable insight. Just don't presume that the most-funded campaigns must also have the most effective pitches, because such campaign media may have been redesigned mid-campaign (and not always wisely), and also because total funds raised depends upon more factors than presentation alone.

- Discussing your project with real people long before you launch your campaign can help you to develop a sense of how to most effectively pitch your product to potential backers.

- Your campaign page's sales pitch should load quickly to avoid losing viewers, start powerfully to persuade viewers that it'll be worth their time to continue reading or skimming further, and then continue in a manner that's easy for viewers (including non-native English speakers) to both navigate and understand. It should avoid needless complexity or marketing hype to embrace both short sentences, and plain language.

- You should customize your pitch to likely backers through persuasive copywriting (which is more vital than good visuals) that focuses primarily upon the benefits you're offering viewers, and secondarily upon other factors, like costs, or your team.

- As a startup, focus on basics like both traffic and conversions, and on presenting your team as likable, competent, and trustworthy. Don't worry about your company's branding until it's much further developed.

- After your campaign launches, test everything about your design (as best as you can), and alter it as needed-in response to data rather than speculation.

- Your campaign marketing exists to bring traffic to your campaign page, and your campaign media exists to convert traffic into backers, but neither is as important as your product and price.

- Appeal to hearts AND minds. Make it emotionally compelling, while also providing information that will provoke thought, and appeal to the consumer's sensibilities.

- Focus on benefits, not features. Remember to highlight those benefits, not just as a laundry list of cool things, but as compelling, make-your-life-better things.

9

Setting Your Pledge Levels

A blazing fire makes flame and brightness out of everything that is thrown into it.
Marcus Aurelius

You launch your campaign and away you go, staring anxiously at your screen, watching for the pledges to come rolling in. To your dismay, your expectations are less than fulfilled as you quickly discover the major "B" of crowdfunding.

That's right, the big, the bad, the beautiful...the **BACKER**.

The backer is the key to your crowdfunding success, yet, we often overlook the path the backer must take to pledge.

How to Win the Backer

In traditional marketing, both online and in brick-and-mortar storefronts, we are told repeatedly to eliminate purchasing obstacles for the consumer. In a storefront, we eliminate purchasing deterrents by ensuring products are in stock and various payment methods and options are available.

If you are running an E-commerce site, you can eliminate purchasing deterrents by removing captchas, using auto-fill options during checkout, and offering sign-in methods, allowing consumers to store their information for quicker check-out. We use these methods because we want to eliminate obstacles for the consumer, so the purchasing process is easy.

Crowdfunding is no different. To put it simply, the key to winning your backers (after you have your 7P's in place) is to keep your funding goal and your rewards structure the same way you want to keep your potential obstacles… LOW!

Remove Obstacles

When running a crowdfunding campaign, you want to make the pledging process as easy as possible for your backers. You do this by removing the obstacles.

What obstacles, you ask?

Simply put, your funding goal and your reward structure are among the biggest obstacles your backers will face.

Obstacle 1: Your Funding Goal

Imagine walking into a store and finding a really cool gadget that you couldn't wait to get your hands on. You have watched the demos, checked out all the cool features; this product is just for you. Then a sales associate approaches you and informs you that only 20 of the 100 really cool gadgets have been reserved by customers and unless 80 more people this month reserve the product, you won't be getting that really cool gadget.

Now, if you find yourself in a fairly empty store, would you take the time to reserve the product? Probably not. You likely feel discouraged. This is the very obstacle your backers face when your funding goal is set too high. In this same scenario, had 80 of the 100 really cool gadgets been reserved, would you be more likely to reserve yours? Chances are, you would be feeling much more optimistic about getting your hands on the product at this point, and so you take the time to reserve yours.

The best scenario is to eliminate this situation entirely by reaching, and exceeding, your funding goal as quickly as possible. This way, when you are standing in the store holding that really cool gadget and the sales associate tells you, "look at this product, we have sold 150 of these really cool gadgets when we only set out to sell 100," you have not only received instant validation that this is indeed a really cool gadget, but your risk of reserving the product now and not receiving the product later is completely gone.

So, your job as the creator is to aim to quickly remove the funding obstacle. Ironically, once the funding goal is met, that leads to more backers. As we said previously, backers like winners.

Obstacle 2: Your Rewards Structure

The other common obstacle we see for backers is the project reward structure. Often, as creators, we get so excited we want to offer every reward level we can think of, so that no backer is left behind.

Trust us when we say that you won't be leaving anyone behind by limiting your reward structures. Offering more options is generally better than offering too few options, but only up to a certain point—backers might start to feel a little overwhelmed any time they're presented with too many options. Having too many rewards is counterproductive because too many rewards puts more obstacles in front of your prospective backer. For example:

- Do I want the really cool gadget with feature x, or do I need feature y, or z?
- What color do I need?
- How many should I buy?
- Wait, these rewards have add-ons?

You get the idea. The more questions your backers ask themselves, the longer it takes them to consider their pledge. This puts a greater burden on both you and the backer.

So, here is our advice based on our hard-earned experience from countless campaigns: limit your reward structures to your main product as often as possible. Doing so removes obstacles.

If you want to offer add-ons, or options to buy more than one, consider stretch goals (see below), reward and pledge fulfillment service providers like CrowdOx, and upsells. These are great tactics to turn would-be obstacles into additional revenue.

Along with your core product, it's only worthwhile to offer more-expensive packages, that feature multi-packs or additional accessories or paraphernalia (like T-shirts or mugs or stickers) or perhaps even an exclusive experience with yourself (like a fancy dinner together or a guided factory tour), for certain types of offerings.

For the most part, though, stick with your core product offering.

Remember, even if nobody buys your higher-priced options, psychological studies show that their mere existence can sometimes help your lower-priced options sell better.

Your Reward Structure

With all that information in mind, here is a sample reward structure for you to use as a guideline:

1. Thank You Pledge Level: This is your $1 level that Kickstarter now automatically includes on your campaign. This will allow backers to support your idea without having to pledge to a specific reward level. Granted, IF you cannot get more than 200 people to pledge at this level, we recommend NOT focusing on it, as it "bumps down" your main/core reward levels. But, IF you can get 200 or more backers to this reward level WITHIN the first 8 hours of your campaign launching, this will greatly increase your "Trending/Popular" rank on Kickstarter, thereby exposing your campaign to Kickstarter's organic and direct user base, which will help you to raise more pledges (If your campaign converts well).

2. Early Bird Pledge Level(s): Early Bird and Super Early Bird levels are great to have because they create a sense of urgency. If you run early bird deals, you should limit the number of backers allowed to back or claim these reward levels. While you can't change the pledge amount once your campaign is live, you CAN change the number of backers allowed to pledge on each level. Our advice is to use the same tactics here as we recommend you use on your funding goal.

3. Kickstarter Special Pledge Level: This is the level that has special pricing for your Kickstarter backers and is where the bulk of your pledges will come in, so make sure you have pricing that allows for your margins.

4. Double Down Pledge Level: It is okay to have a reward level for buying more than one, but don't get too carried away. You can also allow backers to add $xxx.xx amount to their pledge at any of your levels to double down on your product.

5. Distributor/Reseller Pledge Level: If you have a campaign that has multiple color and features to choose from, we would highly suggest using a Backer Management/ Pledge Confirmation System like CrowdOx (after your campaign) to provide your backers with these options. There's no need to include this reward/pledge level on your live Kickstarter project.

Kickstarter automatically includes a "donate without rewards" option, so in some ways, it's redundant to include this option anyway.

You can unofficially survey some of your backers mid-campaign to estimate which styles or colors they will prefer, and you can officially survey all of them post-campaign to confirm their choices.

Reward Pricing

You should set a price for each rewards package that covers not only any basic manufacturing costs, which you should already know from your prototyping phase, but also what your other crowdfunding campaign expenses are estimated to be.

These additional expenses may total 50% altogether. It's important to consider all of these costs carefully, because severely underestimating your prices can lead to severe fulfillment problems, especially for projects that prove wildly popular. These extra expenses may include:

- Platform usage (5% fee from Kickstarter or Indiegogo)
- Hiring marketing agencies (plan for 25-35% of your total gross pledges)
- Third-party payment-collection (3%-5%)
- Wire transfers
- Post-campaign pledge-management
- Packaging
- Shipping
- Lenient return policies
- Taxes (for which you should consult a tax advisor)

We recommend offering "free" shipping by the way, because it normally increases sales despite higher prices.

Not offering free shipping increases "bounce" rates (people who leave your crowdfunding page without purchasing) during checkout. However, if free shipping is not an option for your project, then you might consider charging for shipping only after your campaign has ended successfully, through a service like CrowdOx.

Along with these campaign expenses, your prices should also allow for discounts, which may include bulk discounts, surprise upsell discounts to reveal near the very end of your campaign (see below), or "early bird" discounts.

Lastly, you might also leave some profit for yourself, but many creators prefer to reinvest all of their profit margins into increasing their respective customer bases. You must factor all of these costs together to help you determine roughly how much to charge for each rewards package.

As for finalizing that rough amount into an exact amount, it helps to use "charm pricing," which involves setting prices that end in 9, such as $39 rather than $40—but not $39.99 because both Kickstarter and Indiegogo prohibit decimals.

And please remember from our 7 P of Pricing that it's better to err too high than too low in setting your crowdfunding pledge level prices, because potential backers react better to lowering prices than to raising them - so, after your campaign launches, if you suspect that your prices are set too high, then you can simply hide or close down your existing rewards while offering new, lower-priced ones in their place.

Describing Your Rewards

Package descriptions should be both clear and simple. It can help to mention the range of styles and colors that your backers will get to choose after your project ends. It can also help to include expected retail prices for comparison, so that your potential backers can see instantly how much they'd save by pledging now, rather than buying later.

As for your delivery date, please note that unexpected fulfillment delays are normal, and that it's generally better to overestimate. Please also note that, after your campaign has launched, as long as a reward remains claimed by at least one backer, you won't be allowed to change its description at all, but will be obligated to fulfill it exactly as promised—so, it's important to compose these descriptions correctly before launching. Remember that after your Kickstarter project is live, you can only edit your pledge descriptions for your pledge levels that have no backers.

It will help to strictly limit the availability of each reward from the beginning and (after your campaign launches) to gradually increase that availability for each reward as it nearly runs out, which will instill a constant sense of scarcity that, just like urgency, also has the tendency to boost your conversion rate. This will boost your sales. Indiegogo's "secret" perks pledge level option encourages sales for similar reasons.

Stretch Goals

Indiegogo defines "Stretch Goals" as promises stated on your campaign page that, if you raise enough additional funds above-and-beyond your campaign's official goal, you will then improve upon your core product with certain additional features, like new functions, accessories, styles, or colors.

You may want to peruse similar projects to help you brainstorm good "stretch goals" to include in your own project.

As a specific example of a stretch goal, let's say you are offering a wallet that is only going to be in the color black, and you have an initial funding goal of $10,000. But, if you reach $20,000 in funding, you're also going to create a red wallet option. The red option only happens if you reach the $20,000 mark.

That means If your project gets to $19,999, you're still only going to offer black wallets. But if your project makes it to $20,000 or more, your backers will be able to select a red OR a black wallet.

Be aware, though, these stretch funding goals should inspire, not daunt backers. You should never include features in your stretch goal that you could just as easily include WITHOUT any added funding, because this will upset your backers.

Most importantly, you should only include stretch goals if you are certain they won't stretch *yourself* to fulfill on your core offering. Sometimes, in an effort to raise a lot of money on Kickstarter, we've seen overzealous project creators offer the world in terms of stretch goals, only to be unable to fulfill on these extra offerings down the road. The Coolest Cooler is perhaps the most infamous example of this. Trust us, you don't want this to happen to you.

You don't necessarily need to finalize all, or any, of your stretch goals before your campaign launches. In fact, some creators like to survey their backers mid-campaign for recommendations about these additional goals before finalizing, and ultimately introducing them.

If your campaign ends successfully without achieving all of its potential stretch goals, then you might consider offering these same improvements as part of a future follow-up (2.0) campaign that improves upon your initial product or service.

Upsells

Upselling is an effective strategy used in sales that gives customers the opportunity to spend a little more in order to receive more of your products, or complementary add-ons.

For instance, you're buying a drink and the barista says, "Would you like a scone with that?" That's an upsell that results in a greater number of sales at the end of the day.

In crowdfunding, the upsell is a great way for you to utilize people who already love your product - in other words, those backers who have already pledged to your project.

Your upsell message encourages all backers to pledge for a 2nd, or 3rd product (usually at a slightly discounted price to incentivize them).

Here are two generic upsell messages to give you an idea of how this works in crowdfunding:

- Upsell 1: Now is the time to get a gift and get the best price on product xyz you will ever see! This means you can take advantage of our early bird prices one last time.
- Upsell 2 (offered when you are getting ready to ship): Our product is finally ready to ship! These prices will never be the same again. So, go ahead and purchase a few more of XYZ and add them to your order before we ship, because you're going to love them, and we don't want you to have to pay retail price.

And here are a couple of actual upsell messages our copywriting team has written for our Clients:

1. We want to personally thank you so much for supporting "INSERT YOUR PRODUCT NAME HERE." With your help, we have surpassed our goal with over "INSERT X NUMBER OF BACKERS HERE!" None of this would be possible without you. We are so excited about this product and can't wait for "INSERT YOUR PRODUCT NAME HERE" to be

your favorite "INSERT YOUR PRODUCT TYPE HERE!" As you may know, we are in our last days on Kickstarter. That means it's your last chance to take advantage of the Kickstarter pricing! Once again, we recognize that none of this would be happening without you - so THANK YOU.

2. First and foremost, I want to personally thank you so much for supporting OhSnap. With your help, we are closing in on the $500,000 mark! None of this would be possible without you. We are so excited about this product and can't wait for OhSnap to massively improve your smartphone experience.

3. As you may know, we are down to our last few hours on Kickstarter. That means it's your last chance to take advantage of the Kickstarter pricing! Based on the requests of many, we are offering you this one time, unlimited use, deal on additional OhSnaps! You can increase your CURRENT pledge level by $15 and we will include an additional OhSnap. If you want two, increase by $30, and so forth. Just $15 per each additional OhSnap that you want. Don't let this offer pass. Now is the time!

4. If you would like an additional OhSnap, just click this "link" and increase your CURRENT pledge amount by $15. Click continue and click confirm. That's it. No need to re-enter payment info.

Can a Backer Pledge More Than Once?

Be aware that you can't have your family and friends commit to more than one pledge level in an attempt to "boost" the number of backers. Kickstarter lets you know about this in their help section[29]:

> *It's only possible to pledge to a project once. Accordingly, backers can only choose one reward tier per pledge. This being said, we encourage backers to reach out to the project creator directly to inquire if it is possible to accommodate for a combination of rewards while a project is still live.*
>
> *Creators will typically accommodate multiple of rewards for backers in one of the following ways:*
>
> *Creators may create a new reward tier that includes a certain combination of rewards while the project is still live on Kickstarter.*
>
> *Creators may ask backers to adjust their pledge amount and reward selection for multiple items before the project has reached it's deadline.*
>
> *To message a creator, visit the project page and click on the creator's profile name. This will open up their bio page where you can then click the blue "Contact me" button to send them a message via Kickstarter.*
>
> *Please note: As each project on Kickstarter is unique, each project creator might also have a unique solution to address backing for multiple rewards. For this reason, we strongly encourage backers to contact the creator first to seek a personalized arrangement.*

---

[29] "Can I pledge to a single project more than once? – Kickstarter ...." 30 Oct. 2019, https://help.kickstarter.com/hc/en-us/articles/115005132333-Can-I-pledge-to-a-single-project-more-than-once- . Accessed 8 Nov. 2019.

Prepare Yourself: Backers are Going to Cancel

Cancellations are going to happen, and that's okay. It happens on every crowdfunding project.

Maybe backing your campaign was an impulse purchase and after thinking about it, a backer may decide they don't need your product, or can't afford it. So, do your best not to get overly worked up about it.

How many cancellations is normal, you ask? According to Stonemaier Games[30], around 5%:

> *Over the course of my 28-day Kickstarter campaign for Euphoria, 298 people canceled their pledges. If you added those backers to the final count of 4,765 backers, you would have 5,063 backers. Thus about 6% of the overall pool of backers canceled their pledges at some point during the project. Compare that to Viticulture, during which 41 backers canceled their pledges out of an overall backer pool of 983 (4%). This is a small sample size. But based on what I've heard from other projects, a 5% cancellation rate is pretty normal.*

Reward Yourself

Since we're talking about rewards, we want to take a moment to say, good job on getting this far on your project: many, many, people have great ideas and, as we've mentioned before, never do anything with those ideas. Hey, if this were easy everyone would do it, right?

---

[30] "Kickstarter Lesson #38: Be Mentally Prepared for Cancellations." 12 Jul. 2013, https://stonemaiergames.com/kickstarter-lesson-38-be-mentally-prepared-for-cancellations/. Accessed 8 Nov. 2019.

You are in a select crowd now. No pun intended. So, give yourself a pat on the back and realize you are closer than you think to bringing your big idea to life. It's almost time to launch!

In the next chapter we're going to talk about Preparing for Launch Day, so this is a good moment to take a short pause and acknowledge how well you're doing. You've made it this far, and that already sets you apart.

It's time to celebrate just how far you've come. So, treat YOURSELF to one of your favorite rewards. Perhaps a specialty drink from your favorite coffeehouse (and maybe even say "yes" to that upsell scone).

And remember, we are here to help you every step of the way. Should you decide you'd like help with your crowdfunding project, either one aspect, or the entire campaign, give us a shout. We are here and we always work deeply for our clients.[31]

Now, let's get ready to launch!

---

[31] "How We Work "Deeply" for Our Clients | Funded Today." https://www.funded.today/blog/how-we-work-deeply-for-our-clients. Accessed 12 Nov. 2019.

Fun fact:

Did you know Funded Today was the 2nd fastest-growing, privately-held company in Utah and the 27th fastest-growing, privately-held company in all of America according to the Inc. 500 list in 2018 having grown 8,798% since 2015?

10

Preparing for Launch Day

The supreme accomplishment is to blur the line between work and play.
Arnold J. Toynbee

There are a number of other things you need to be aware of, PRIOR to launching. Preparing properly for your launch goes beyond your video and your page's presentation.

This chapter will give you an overview of what you need to focus on so you are thoroughly ready to launch. And in subsequent chapters we will deep-dive into the areas requiring more in-depth information.

We have an entire prelaunch checklist for you (which you can find in **Chapter 21: Resources)**. Let's review some of those items now so you best complete your preparation.

Your Final Preparations

Know Your Platform

- By this time, you should have accounts on both Kickstarter and Indiegogo, and have explored those websites thoroughly. You've most likely decided which platform is best for your project: again, we recommend launching on Kickstarter if at all possible, and on Indiegogo only if necessary (you can always transition smoothly and directly to IndieGoGo InDemand after your successful Kickstarter project ends). You should also have backed some projects on Kickstarter, so you've become part of the crowdfunding community.

- You should be very familiar with the rules of your chosen platform, so you know exactly what is required for creators to run campaigns.

Plan Your Launch Schedule

- It's optimum to allow at least 2 months to prepare your project's media and marketing before launching it. This will also give you some time to do some email lead generation and list building, leading up to your launch.

- We recommend you avoid campaigning during both December or August. Beyond that, plan on launching your project either when your product's seasonal demand peaks, or as soon as you're ready.

- If possible, plan your launch day to fall between Monday and Wednesday, but not on any major American holidays. Plan to launch while it's still morning in the USA, where most crowdfunding backers live.

- Recognize you need to keep your launch dates flexible (as delays are common), and know you need to inform people accordingly.

- Plan to campaign for 30-45 days, and to extend an Indiegogo campaign up to 60 days total.

- Schedule to finish between Wednesday and Friday, and before evening in the USA.

Your Prototype

- Your product's functionality is minimally viable, with costlier enhancements deferred until later.
- Your prototype's form is maximally appealing, derived from its beneficial functions.
- The product's name is easy to pronounce and read, and lacks any negative connotations.
- You've filed to patent your product in your country, your manufacturer's country, and elsewhere as needed.
- You've hired a manufacturer via NNN agreement (to protect your IP/intellectual property in China if you go that route) to mass-produce the product later, in variable amounts.
- They've produced and you've tested and personally reviewed at least one of their product prototypes for testing, reviews, and photographs.
- Your product's form and function have been sufficiently refined via feedback from market testing, and your product's iterative development, plus reviews, have been recorded sufficiently for use in sales.

The BIG M - Marketing

Ideally, you should start marketing your project months before launching, in order to prepare as many people as possible to pledge to it during its first few days. Those first few days are when campaigns normally enjoy a spike in "organic" attention, and your prelaunch marketing will synergize with that spike, ideally helping your campaign surpass your funding goal as quickly as possible. This gives you a great advantage.

There's no "magic number" of backers and funds to arrange in advance, but more is generally better than less. Kickstarter research shows that any projects that are 20% funded within 48 hours are 78% more likely to succeed[32]. Some additional data suggests that any crowdfunding campaigns that are 30% funded within 48 hours are 90% more likely to get fully funded within 30 days. So, Indiegogo recommends arranging at least 30% of your funding before launching.

Should You Hire an Agency?

You will find that once you do launch you are going to suddenly receive dozens of messages from marketing agencies and individuals who make pitches to you about promoting your product. Often, our clients are overwhelmed by so much attention and find it's hard to make sense of it all. So, as a guideline for every creator, we'd like to make sense of those offers for you BEFORE you launch to you are prepared.

First off, there are only a handful, or so, legitimate crowdfunding marketing agencies on the market. In addition to **Funded Today**, Jellop is another agency that is reputable enough to be worth considering. You could also look at:

- Enventys Partners
- Agency 2.0
- Matix

---

[32] (n.d.). Hiring For Crowdfunding Marketing? Why Fewer is More .... Retrieved November 18, 2019, from https://www.funded.today/blog/hiring-for-crowdfunding-marketing-why-fewer-is-more

Just like us, these agencies have strengths and weaknesses, a number of successes and failures - but they have a positive reputation within the industry, and they won't just run off with your money. There are a number of black sheep in the crowdfunding marketing space, and by choosing one of the five agencies just mentioned, and passing on those not listed, you are on the safe side.

(Please note: In all fairness, this is a reference for full-service marketing agencies only. There are plenty of special service providers for crowdfunding campaigns, such as Backerland, GadgetFlow, or CrowdOx, who are also reputable in their specific space. So, if you're unsure about someone who contacted you, feel free to reach out to us).

Now back to the question at hand - do you hire one? Or multiple? Or all?

We've crunched the numbers of hundreds of our clients who have all raised at least $50,000 with us - and we've got a strong suggestion for you (beyond simply saying "hire **Funded Today"**).

As of November 19, 2019, Funded Today has raised over one million dollars with exactly 49 different clients. Of these campaigns, only 8 (or 21.6%) had hired another agency in addition to Funded Today. Of the 12 campaigns that raised over two million dollars, only 1 (our eighth-most funded campaign ever) had hired another agency. That's only 8.3%.

In the segment between $750,000 and $1,000,000, 50% of the campaigns we worked with had hired an additional agency. In this segment, we also find the highest-raising campaign that worked with at least 3 agencies, in the 40th spot of all **Funded Today** clients overall.

One segment lower, between $500,000 and $750,000 (yes, we're still in the top 0.1% of all Kickstarter campaigns!), nearly 50% had also contracted with another agency, and about 25% of clients in this segment had hired 3 or more.

The next $250,000 section is quite exhaustive already, as more than 100 of our clients have raised between $250,000 and $500,000. The trend here continues, with now more than half of campaigns bringing on an additional agency - and again, some 20% of campaigns hiring 3 or more agencies total.

In the final segment we chose to look at, between $50,000 and $250,000, we find that now nearly 60% have hired more than 1 agency, and almost 30% have hired 3 or more agencies.

Now, all of the campaigns we analyzed were strong campaigns. Only about 5% of all projects on Kickstarter raise at least $50,000, and for Indiegogo, the fraction is much smaller. But, as this data set of 567 campaigns illustrates, our empirical suggestion for you is to put all eggs into one basket, with an agency that is versatile and delivers one complete marketing package.

The numbers show that million-dollar campaigns, rare as they are, are made from the fabric of strong and dedicated partnerships, and not from hiring everybody.

If crowdfunding marketing is not one of your skill sets, then you should consider hiring a company to handle most, if not all, aspects of your project's marketing. The right marketing certainly makes a difference on how much money your project makes.

In some of the upcoming chapters we will be breaking down certain aspects of marketing. But for now, let's start with some basics.

Marketing Backend Basics

If you are going to tackle the marketing yourself, here are some of the backend basics we highly recommend you do now:

- Create a Google Analytics account with properties for both your website and project page[33]. Copy the Google Analytics' tracking code or ID to those pages and fully activate its features[34].

- If you are unfamiliar with how Google Analytics works, study it and learn it.

- Familiarize yourself with Kicktraq[35].

- Make sure you've prepared 200+ personal/business contacts ("FFF" - **Chapter 5**) who are committed to backing your project within the first 8 hours of launch.

- Create project and company social-media profiles, and began to build an active community of fans for them. For marketing crowdfunding campaigns, some entrepreneurs love to regularly share similar posts (without dumping too much content at once) across multiple company-owned social-media sites (especially Facebook), and perhaps even to run ad

---

[33] (n.d.). Google Analytics. Retrieved November 18, 2019, from https://analytics.google.com/analytics/web/

[34] (n.d.). Google Analytics. Retrieved November 18, 2019, from https://analytics.google.com/analytics/web/

[35] (n.d.). Kicktraq. Retrieved November 18, 2019, from https://www.kicktraq.com/

campaigns in order to build active communities of followers. Such fans (just like your personal contacts) can both provide useful feedback about your product as you develop it, AND help you to refine your pitching. DO NOT wait until you launch to actively engage followers on social media. It's about building relationships in advance, not just posting when you have something to sell.

- Double check that your project webpage is designed to both inspire viewers' trust, captivate their attention, AND make them want to subscribe to e-mail about your project. Whenever you have any size email list make sure you are periodically nurturing your subscribers with updates and preparing them well for your project launch.

- Continue to solicit email subscribers though your contacts, and previous networking.

- Arrange for the right social-media influencers to review your product to their large audiences.

- Identify the best newscasters (one per source) to report your project to relevant audiences. You should periodically contact those reporters to nurture a relationship that might lead to publicity. (See Public Relations section below.)

- Join a crowdfunding affiliate-marketing agency and to recruit your backers into it, and be prepared to arrange cross-promotions, especially with campaigns that attract similar backers. We offer the largest cashback and affiliate network for all things crowdfunding[36]. (https://www.funded.today/cashback#learn-more)

- If you already run a business, and if your crowdfunding project will benefit people who resemble its existing customers, then you should contact those customers to invite them to pledge.

- Design and create landing pages. These are the pages your ads will send viewers to so they will hopefully become part of your email list. See the Landing Pages section below.

Your Email Leads

As a benchmark, we normally spend about $2-$3 per lead over about 4-6 weeks generating leads for our clients.

Landing Pages to Increase Email Leads

As for designing landing pages, they should use a memorable, short and intuitive domain name, sport your company logo and name, function well on a variety of devices, both impress and inspire viewers with a professional design that looks consistent and authentic,

[36] (n.d.). Cashback - Funded Today. Retrieved November 19, 2019, from https://www.funded.today/cashback

"hook" attention with a captivating tagline, and then simply yet realistically overview your project by showing and telling an overview of key features and benefits, plus reasons to trust your product. However, this should not be done in nearly as much detail as your Kickstarter page will provide later.

You may want to incorporate a tentative launch date and countdown timer, as well as some positive quotations. Unlike your Kickstarter page, you can A/B test this landing page indefinitely toward perfection, progressing gradually from its' vital generalities to its' trivial details. Doing this may give you some insight into which images and messaging will sell your project best.

Your landing page should persuade viewers to provide their e-mailing address so that they can be among the first to know when your campaign launches, and also enjoy a pre-launch promotion or an "early bird" discount. **It should explicitly invite** viewers to do this. Pre-launch giveaways normally attract more leads than post-launch discounts, but those extra leads usually suffer from lower quality.

As you build your own e-mailing list, it's important to present opt-ins with clear expectations about content they may expect from you, while refraining from violating those expectations with irrelevant content that prompts them to lose interest in your communications.

Communicating with Your Email Leads

After you've built your e-mailing list, you should remember that your leads will grow less likely to pledge if you allow too much time to elapse before you launch your campaign. You may contact your leads regularly before your campaign to nurture them in order to help keep them warm, and possibly to solicit helpful feedback from them. This may involve not one, but a series of emails, conveyed in conversational story-like fashion (with "cliffhanger" endings) to keep your subscribers engaged.

For fundraising, you may want to contact your leads about 24 hours before your campaign launches to prepare them so make sure you get that on your schedule. (And then 24 hours after your campaign launches to report its progress, and weekly thereafter for its remainder, except daily again during its final 3 days). You can typically expect about 2%-4% of these leads to pledge to an average-priced project, and maybe 6%-10% to pledge to an unusually-cheap project.

**Although email marketing has proven well-suited for nurturing long-term customer relationships,
for the last two decades, it is now yielding to instant-messaging marketing aided by bots, which is more conversational, involves less friction,
and is better-suited to mobile-device users.**

Public Relations (PR)

This technique involves attempting to persuade reporters and influencers to publicize your project after it launches, and (except for paid editorials) it normally doesn't cost money. It just costs time—and, because it costs time, starting it sooner is better than starting it later. Although, it can still yield worthwhile results, even when started during the campaign's final days.

This kind of coverage is both popular and powerful among crowdfunding campaigners, with tremendous advantages in both objectivity and longevity; however, news lacks the urgency of ads, which means that its fruit is usually slow-growing (hence talking about it during the prelaunch phase).

This all renders PR a valuable tool for increasing long-term sales, but also reduces its effectiveness as a tool for short-term fundraising, which is why (in our experience) PR usually raises fewer pledges than most other forms of crowdfunding marketing. Even so, for the right (rare) campaigns, it can still raise tens-of-thousands of dollars by itself.

Influencers

As for influencers, one way to find them is to upload a similar crowdfunding campaign's image to Google, and then perform a Google image search to see which sites featured that campaign. It's best to target influencers with sizable audiences who best fit your product or service. Then you might try to catch their attention by following them or adding them to a Twitter list before initiating contact with them.

It's best to arrange their cooperation well before your campaign launches. Keep in mind it requires time for them to receive a product sample, examine it, and prepare a review of it to release shortly after your campaign starts.

If you want an influencer to return your review sample, then you may want to accompany it with a prepaid return label.

Reporters

As for reporters, some creators hire news release distribution platforms, but such platforms don't normally produce good results because they communicate impersonally to "mainstream" news sources. The way to do it effectively is through regular, personalized communication with niche news sources - this is far more likely to yield good results.

One way to identify good PR prospects is to search the Internet for similar campaigns (via name or image) and then see which sites reported about them. You can use sites like Alexa[37] to compare their viewership. Since your goal in crowdfunding is to raise funds quickly, it's generally best to target sources that don't necessarily enjoy the highest visibility, but that do enjoy the highest conversion rates (such as product directories).

See **Chapter 13: Marketing Your Campaign** - **Press** for intricate details on how to obtain and nurture the press and earn media for your crowdfunding project.

And, Finally...

All of the above forms of prelaunch marketing will actively attract pledging visitors to your campaign page, which will raise your project's rankings (as measured by either Indiegogo's "GoGoFactor" or Kickstarter's various algorithms), which will render your project increasingly visible to the worldwide crowdfunding community as its members actively browse projects.

---

[37] (2019, May 28). Alexa: Keyword Research, Competitive Analysis, & Website .... Retrieved November 19, 2019, from https://www.alexa.com/

This increased visibility, combined with both an enticing image-and-title and impressive statistics (like making rapid progress toward/beyond a minimal funding goal), will boost the flow of "organic" visitors to your campaign, along with their likelihood in pledging. Kickstarter's popularity rankings, especially, are closely followed by many serial backers, which means that any projects that rise into this category's top dozen will normally enjoy a substantial boost in their daily pledges for as long as they maintain that high ranking; those popularity rankings are primarily determined by backers-per-day, and to a lesser degree by both percentage funded and total funds raised.

We know this is a lot. Preparing to launch a crowdfunding project isn't simple, or easy. Marketing can be confusing and entire books (in fact, multiple books) have been written on each aspect of marketing. Don't worry. We've got you covered.

Upcoming chapters will give you more details on how to best market your project:

- Chapter 11: Launch Day
- Chapter 12: Marketing Your Campaign - Paid Media
- Chapter 13: Marketing Your Campaign - Press
- Chapter 14: Marketing Your Campaign - Other Traffic Methods

And now, the moment you've been waiting for - **Launch Day!**

11

Launch Day

***Some lack the fickleness to live as they wish and just live as they have begun.* Seneca**

Have the Right Mindset

You've done all your prelaunch tasks, such as taking full advantage of the Triple F strategy, your email list is bulging with committed followers, and your project page and elements are ready to go.

You want to make as much money as possible. Right? You don't care how many sales you get, as long as the money keeps rolling in.

You imagine that you hit your funding goal and the backers keep knocking on your door. And suddenly you start thinking about the fact that you'll actually have to fill those countless orders. Worry creeps in. And you wonder, is there such a thing as too many sales?

Wait - do people actually worry about too many sales?

But yes, this does happen. In fact, we've had people who don't want to hire **Funded Today** for that exact reason. Namely, they don't want more sales!

Why? Because more sales means more trouble and more hassle.

And, trust us, that is not the mindset you want to have as you near launch. If you launch and are crushing it on Kickstarter, keep crushing it. Your crowdfunding campaign is only live once, so make the most of it. Once the campaign is over, you WILL NOT generate sales like you did during the campaign.

Sure, you might be able to ramp up digital media campaigns, TV buys, and PR hits, and over the course of a year, or more, grow a business. But, in terms of generating sales for your product, when your crowdfunding campaign is live is when you have the opportunity to sell the most.

People are much more likely to open their wallet when your product is on Kickstarter compared to when it's on your website. More people become a customer during a live crowdfunding campaign than after (with all other factors being equal).

As a general rule, you will raise 1000% more during a Kickstarter campaign than you will the month after your campaign. Said another way, after your crowdfunding campaign, you're only going to raise about 5% to 10% of what you made then in the next month. (These are average numbers we have seen after working with hundreds of campaigns).

If you do have concerns that you could hit a threshold where fulfillment is going to be a lot of work, and you won't be able to deliver on time, here is a quick method to solve that issue:

- If you sell so many units of your product that manufacturing and shipping on time is difficult, or impossible, close all your pledge levels by limiting the number of backers for each pledge level. Then create new pledge levels for each one that you closed, but with a 2nd shipment date. People who back for the new pledge levels will know and understand that they will be receiving their product later.

Whatever you do though, don't enter into launching your campaign with an overhanging worry that might throttle your sales when your campaign is live. Generate as many sales as you possibly can. You only have this opportunity once. Make the most of it.

Launch Day Final Prep

There are a lot of things you need to be aware of in the final days leading up to, and including, launch day. You will need to be well organized with your time, familiar with all the tasks you'll need to stay on top of, and set enough time aside to accomplish everything. If you also work outside of your crowdfunding project, consider taking time off - especially on launch day itself. You will be busy. Here is a quick bullet list of items to be aware of:

- You will want to contact personal or business contacts, reporters and influencers, and any other leads you've generated in the previous months. This may include customer lists if you've already been in business.

- Your project has a private preview link. You will want to (if you haven't already), send that link out to a handful of your tech friends to double check for anything you've missed, or that reads as confusing. (See **The Private Preview Link** section below).

- If you have a social media following, post about the launch on your profiles and in some relevant groups. Don't be spammy, and don't expect much in the way of results, but it certainly doesn't hurt.

- If you haven't already enrolled in an affiliate program (such as Funded Today's cashback program[38]), do so.

- If appropriate, start arranging cross-promotions.

- Get a personal process ready that allows you to thank new backers one-by-one as they pledge. The messages, perhaps as templates, should ideally be set up before launch day and verified. Not after you launch.

- Notify any marketing partners that you're working with about the upcoming launch date.

- Be prepared to start monitoring comments, and responding to them.

- As soon as you launch you will want to monitor how quickly rewards are disappearing, and increase available quantities as appropriate.

- The FAQ's cannot be done until you have actually launched, but you should prewrite out common questions and responses. (More about this in **The FAQs** section below).

---

[38] "Cashback - Funded Today." https://www.funded.today/cashback. Accessed 23 Nov. 2019.

The Private Preview Link

No matter how many times you read through and review something, there are always items you missed, typos, and other things that need improvement.

You don't want to wait until your campaign is live to find out there are issues, or that something is very confusing. The campaign private preview link gives you the opportunity to discover issues your project page might have, so you can make those tweaks before you push that launch button.

For our clients we recommend that they send out the preview link to as many of the Triple F connections as possible, as well as interested parties on your lists, so that they can review your page. You'll want to do all this enough in advance (at least a few days) so they have time to get back to you with their input and questions. When they do follow the preview link, it will look something like this one:

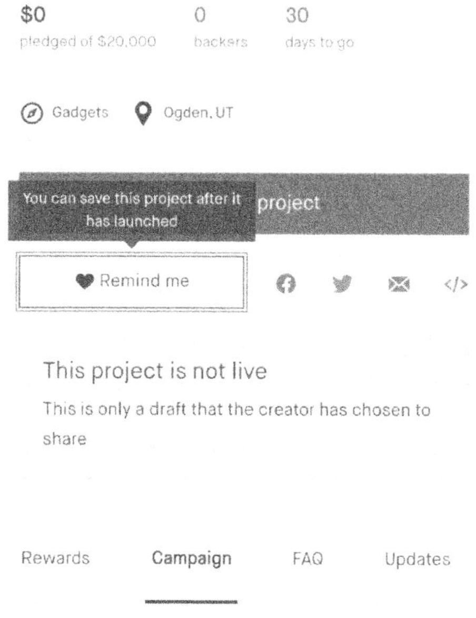

Make sure to let everyone know to click the "black heart" icon at the top of the page once they log into Kickstarter. Once they do this, they will automatically be reminded by Kickstarter when the project launches. Also, be aware that the moment your campaign goes live that preview link will redirect to your live Kickstarter link.

The FAQs

One thing to be aware of on Kickstarter is the fact that you can't fill out your FAQs until your campaign has gone live. Of course, you can't know all the questions before they are asked, but you can project likely questions and your responses, and have these prewritten and ready to go.

This is, in part, what Kickstarter says about the FAQs[39]:

> "The FAQ section of each project page is an area where the creator can address common questions they receive from backers and potential backers of their project. This section is accessible via the FAQ tab on each project page. Backers can always directly message the creator or post a comment to ask questions about the project or rewards. If a creator notices that particular question keeps being asked, or they notice a common area of confusion, they can navigate to the "FAQ" tab of their project page and click the "Edit FAQs" button. From there, a creator can add a new question and the corresponding answer. From this page, they can also rearrange or delete FAQs. This section is a great place for creators to post helpful, to-the-point information about their project and for backers to learn more about the project or rewards. For instance, a creator could use this section to share more information about their timeline, specifics about rewards, and/or a deeper dive on technical specifications."

Here is an example of what the FAQ section of your dashboard looks like. This one is from the "OhSnap" (the phone grip that doesn't suck) campaign[40]:

---

[39] "What is my responsibility for answering questions ... - Kickstarter." 25 Sep. 2019, https://help.kickstarter.com/hc/en-us/articles/115005135254-What-is-my-responsibility-for-answering-questions-from-backers-and-non-backers-. Accessed 21 Nov. 2019.

[40] "Ohsnap: The Phone Grip That Doesn't Suck by ... - Kickstarter." 4 Sep. 2019, https://www.kickstarter.com/projects/ohsnapofficial/ohsnap-the-phone-grip-that-doesnt-suck/faqs. Accessed 22 Nov. 2019.

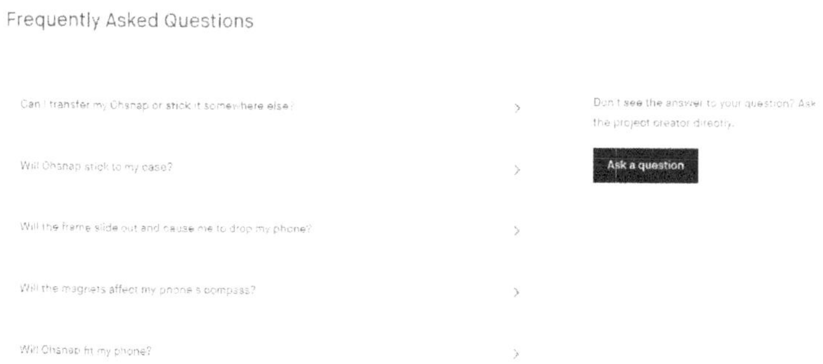

Frequently Asked Questions

Can I transfer my Ohsnap or stick it somewhere else?

Will Ohsnap stick to my case?

Will the frame slide out and cause me to drop my phone?

Will the magnets affect my phone's compass?

Will Ohsnap fit my phone?

Don't see the answer to your question? Ask the project creator directly.

Ask a question

You are certainly aware of FAQ sections on websites. They are not complicated, but it does pay to have some ready to post as soon as your campaign is live. If you're drawing a blank, just think back to what some of the questions your Tripe F connections asked when you were telling them about your project. Or, the questions you were asked when you sent out your private preview link for review.

Prepare to Launch

You'll need to send your project for final review. On Kickstarter[41] it says:

> "Once you're ready to launch your project, you'll want to click the "Send to review" button to submit the project for review. If the project is auto-approved, you will see a "Prepare to launch" button. This gives creators the flexibility to launch their projects whenever they're ready.
>
> If your project is not auto-approved, our Trust & Safety team will need to review it before being able to launch. Once the project is

---

[41] "How does "Prepare to launch" work? – Kickstarter Support." 18 Oct. 2019, https://help.kickstarter.com/hc/en-us/articles/115005134694-How-does-Prepare-to-launch-work-. Accessed 22 Nov. 2019.

reviewed and approved by our team–which can take a few days–you can go live."

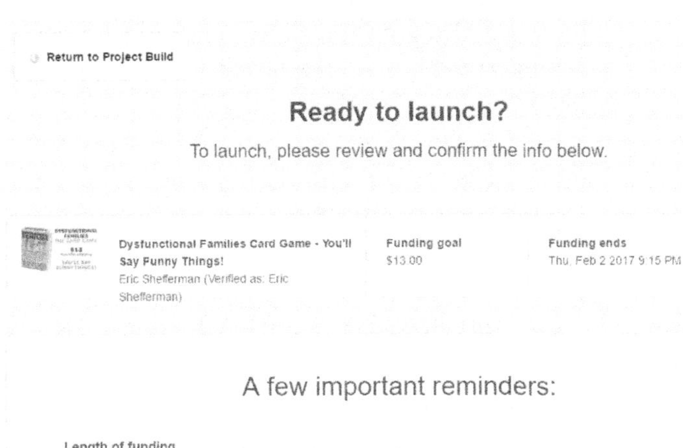

Ready to Launch?

Kickstarter

When you press that tantalizing "Launch Project Now" button, Kickstarter reminds you to review a few details one last time - things you won't be able to change once you hit the "Launch Now" button.

1. Your launch date and time determine how much time you have to reach your goal. If you launch now, you'll have until Date, Date, Time, to raise $Goal Amount.

2. Funding is all or nothing. If you reach your goal, money will be transferred to (Your Name bank account, ending in XXX) within 21 days of project completion. Kickstarter's fee (5%) and payment processing fees (3% - 5%) will be deducted from your total.

3. If you reach your funding goal, you must complete your project and fulfill each reward as outlined in our Terms of Use.

Once you click the box that shows you agree to the terms, you can click the "Launch Now" button.

I have read these important reminders, the Terms of Use, the Privacy Policy, and the Kickstarter Rules.

Indiegogo

The process for launching is similar on Indiegogo[42]:

1. Log in to your Indiegogo account and click '[Your Name],' located above the search bar

2. Select 'My Campaigns' from the drop-down menu

3. Locate the campaign you'd like to launch and click "Edit Campaign," from the 'Actions' Drop-

---

[42] "How to Launch a Campaign – Indiegogo Help Center." https://support.indiegogo.com/hc/en-us/articles/202530233-How-to-Launch-a-Campaign. Accessed 22 Nov. 2019.

Down menu. You'll be taken to your Campaign Editor.

4. From your Campaign Editor, you'll be able to launch by clicking the "Review & Launch" button. If any required fields are missing, you'll see an error message which outlines the tab that has missing info. Just go to the corresponding tab and fill out the missing fields.
5. If you've completed all the required fields, you'll be taken to a final "Ready to Go Live!" confirmation. This will allow you to confirm key areas that you will not be able to change once you are live. If everything looks good to go, click the "Launch Campaign" button.

This is what it looks like on Indiegogo:

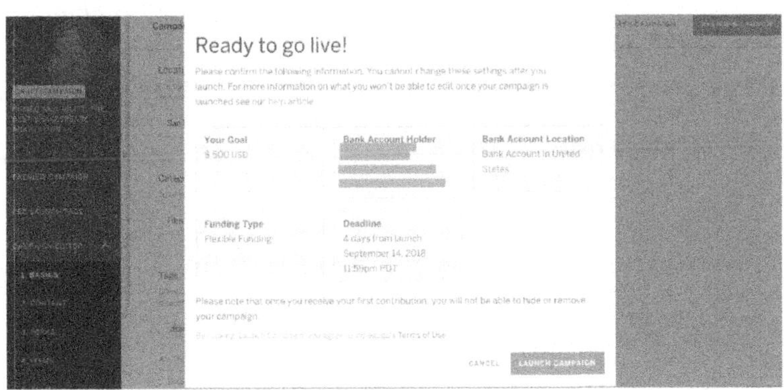

Familiarize yourself with what you can't change once you go live on Indiegogo[43]. Indiegogo does allow you to do a onetime extension on the deadline (as long as it doesn't go over their 60-day maximum).

---

[43] "What You Can & Can't Edit After Your Campaign Is Live ...." https://support.indiegogo.com/hc/en-us/articles/205154117-What-You-Can-Can-t-Edit-After-Your-Campaign-Is-Live. Accessed 22 Nov. 2019.

Launch Day

Launch day is a special day, and though you may feel as if you deserve to kick back and celebrate your hard work, be prepared to be busy and focused. Responding to comments and questions is all part of the process, and you want to establish a reputation for great service right from the first minutes.

Stonemaiergames has a good article about Launch Day[44]. Here are some of the things the article says about Launch Day:

> "Your project is going to be on Kickstarter's "recently launched" page, so as long as it's decent looking and reasonably priced, you're going to get a few backers right away and throughout the day. It will feel like magic (but don't get spoiled by this–the rest of the magic takes a lot of hard work). You're going to want to be there at your computer, thanking those backers individually and asking them if they have any questions (which could help augment your FAQ)."

As Soon as You're Live

Google Analytics

Chapter 16: Analyzing Your Campaign, goes into depth on Google Analytics and other important tracking. But once you do go live, you will immediately want to make sure that Google Analytics is tracking properly. That means study how to do this ahead of time if you're not hiring someone to help you.

---

[44] "Kickstarter Lesson #16: Launch Day – Stonemaier Games." 1 Mar. 2013, https://stonemaiergames.com/kickstarter-lesson-16-launch-day/. Accessed 21 Nov. 2019.

Emailing

As soon as your project goes live, you will want to email all your lists, and any press that you've developed a relationship with. Clearly, you want to follow through with all those on your Triple F list.

The trick to effective emails is to make them personable. Do not spam mass emails by blasting everyone you know on every list. This is about connecting with niche lists, and others that you've already established a rapport with on some level.

Writing effective emails is a bit of an art. A few tips:

- Have a tantalizing subject line
- Be personable
- Be clear about the purpose of the email
- Be precise - don't ramble
- End with a call to action

If you really have no idea what you're doing, we highly recommend you hire a professional copywriter. The point of the email is to get people to not only actually open the email, but to read it, and take some action such as going to your project page and becoming a backer. Well written emails can make all the difference in your success rate.

We talk more about emails in **Chapter 15: Prelaunch Community Building and Email Lead Generation**.

Responding to Comments and Cancelled Pledges

You will basically be glued to your computer on Launch Day. Beyond all the other tasks we've mentioned, you will need to stay on top of comments. This, of course, is important throughout the length of your campaign, but the first day is likely to be one of the busiest.

Only backers can make comments, so it behooves you to be personable and upfront in your interactions. DO NOT go long periods of time without responding to either comments, or questions.

Kickstarter has an awesome feature that allows you to connect with all backers, even those who cancel. You can, and should, reach out with a personal message to anyone who pulls out of backing your project, to see if you can answer a question or be of service.

A Note About Trolls

We would be remiss if we didn't give you the heads up that there will be trolls. These are the people who pledge, but aren't true backers. They might pledge something like $1 and then spend their time bugging you with complaints, and such. Once you recognize someone as a troll, don't engage. Don't worry, once they remove their pledge, their comment disappears like this:

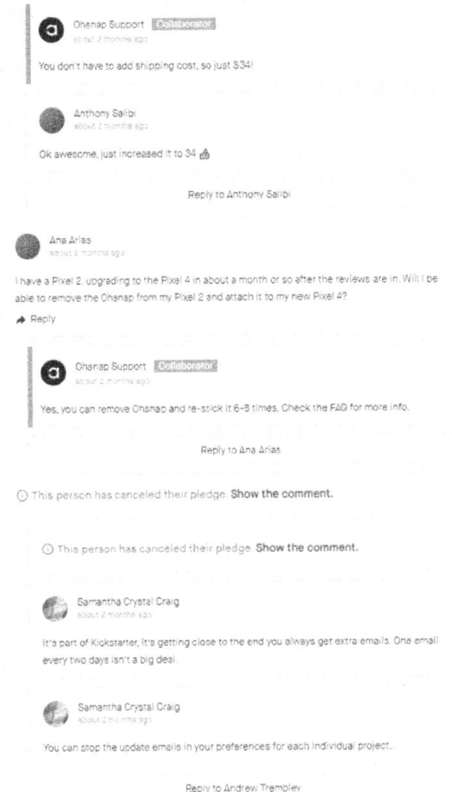

The Bigger Picture...

Even as you are focused on responding to comments and questions, and sending out those individual replies, keep in mind that there is also a bigger picture that you'll want to be aware of.

Bear with us, because we're going to talk about the Kickstarter algorithm a bit. You may be wondering, "What is this algorithm thing, and why does it even matter?" It matters because it explains why you need to keep working hard to get as many backers as possible while your campaign is live.

The algorithm is the power, the benefit, of any platform. For example, consider the Amazon Algorithm or the Google SEO Algorithm. It's the same thing with Kickstarter - it's how your project ranks on Kickstarter. This is the reason why you pay Kickstarter a 5% premium, and aren't launching your project or campaign on your own website.

Kickstarter has all this traffic, and the algorithm determines how your project is going to rank on Kickstarter.com, so people that you haven't connected with directly can discover it.

If you want to see how a project is ranking on Kickstarter - just go to kickstarter.com and click on the little button in the top left called Explore. When you click on explore, they have all kinds of different ranks you can choose from. For example:

- Recommended For You
- Projects We Love (See more below)
- Trending
- Nearly funded
- Just Launched

If you click on the Trending one, and then sort again by trending, live projects (that are trending, of course) will be seen by rank, which is determined by the Kickstarter Algorithm.

There is also "Magic": which is a special thing that Kickstarter does. Magic includes Popularity, Newest, End Date, Most Funded, Most Backed, and Near Me. (More on Magic below).

And there's an algorithm for "Projects We Love" (used to be known as "Staff Picks"), those campaigns that Kickstarter employees determine they like. These campaigns get a special badge, and are ranked algorithmically, as well.

For your own project, if you go to Google Analytics, or to the Kickstarter or Indiegogo Dashboard, it will show you the referral sources where pledges are coming from. So, for example, if somebody saw your campaign from a Facebook post, or a Facebook Ad inside of Google Analytics, it would show a visitor from Facebook, and maybe a pledge for $50. The same with the Kickstarter Dashboard. It would show a pledge from Facebook and how much in dollar value of that pledge amount.

Inside of Kickstarter and Indiegogo, as well as the Google Analytics Platform, you can see the pledges that are coming from these sources. So, for example, if you were a "Project We Love", you'll see the pledges coming from that. We've seen big campaigns where they have an extra $30,000, $40,000, $50,000, $60,000 in pledges, just because it was a "Project We Love" that Kickstarter had selected.

We believe in something called Positive Externalities. You could call it "The Trickle Effect." This means that the more money you spend on advertising, and the more time and effort you put into earning media and press attention, and the more cross collaborations and email lead generation you do, the more you are able to influence the algorithm. All of those other marketing forces come into play, and then Kickstarter kicks in with their algorithm and makes up the difference. The difference being the Positive Externalities, The Trickle Effect, that makes all of those efforts doubly, triply, or sometimes even five or six times more effective in terms of what you're paying for them.

These Positive Externalities are literally what can make or break the launch of a company. This is why Kickstarter is amazing, why the algorithm is so powerful.

One of the most influential factors that dictates how high you're ranking on the Popularity or Trending category is the number of backers that you're getting per day, or within a time frame. So, if you get 1000 backers the first day, and then the next two weeks you have 0 new backers, you will probably be ranked number one in terms of Popularity or Trending for a day, and then after that, you'll completely die off.

This can be frustrating, because you might have a campaign that has a price point of $500 and is raising $50,000 a day, but in that case, you're only getting 100 new backers per day, so, not ranking that high. Then, you might have another campaign that has a price point of $10, and they're getting 500 backers per day, so they're able to stay in the top of the Trending or the Popularity category.

A word of caution...

> *There are some random, sketchy services out there that guarantee you that they can rank you higher- and quite frankly they actually can rank you higher. But, the way they rank you higher is not going to rank you higher in the categories that actually matter. They will say "Well, you pay me this much money and I'll get your campaign to rank higher in the Technology category, and you pay me this much more, I'll get you rank this much higher." Ultimately, it doesn't work. We've seen this time and time again. Even if your*

campaign ranks higher, we've never seen it make any difference in terms of total pledges. Yes, you need backers, but your backers need to be legitimate, and real backers matter way more than money.

The Magic Category

If you can get 300 or more backers within the first 8 to 10 hours of your campaign, legitimate and real backers, from your friends and family and your folks and whoever wants to back your campaign, that's a very powerful way to rank very high in Trending, and to possibly take advantage of the Magic category on Kickstarter, as well.

It's very powerful to rank high in Magic, because Kickstarter puts a lot of clout into Magic and has a lot of exposure on their website for campaigns that are ranking high in this category.

Most of these metrics come down to how much exposure you're giving to Kickstarter, or how many backers - here's an interesting fact - 80% of all people who back a Kickstarter campaign are actually serial backers, meaning that for every person backing a campaign, there's an 80% chance that that person is backing that campaign for either the second or subsequent time. There are 15 million backers in that category.

This is why Kickstarter values you bringing in new backers so highly. Kickstarter believes in that customer lifetime value. Because they believe so much in that customer lifetime value, their algorithm, as far as it relates to Trending, is heavily weighted towards bringing new people to their platform. If you can bring new people to the platform, Kickstarter knows they're not just going to back your campaign, they're going to back future campaigns, and so they want to reward you and rank your campaign a little bit better.

Magic combines all sorts of factors, including user activity, previous pledges, etcetera - at least from everything we've gathered, and what we can see. (This is actually why we focus primarily on Facebook Ads, and not so much on Google Ads). We don't know exactly how the Magic Search Filter works.

But, here is a bit of what Kickstarter says about it:

> "The default sort of our Advanced Discover Tool Magic displays a rotating cross-section of compelling projects on Kickstarter by surfacing a mixture of projects we love and what's popular from each of our 15 categories in order to exhibit the creative spectrum of our community we've just designed the Magic sort to be dynamic. This means it refreshes often if you see your project pop in and out of this magical sort don't worry, it will still be searchable using the other finite sorts and filters".

That is interesting, and here's why. The default search on Kickstarter is Magic, and so you need to be taking advantage of that one as much as possible, because people who go to the page are first going to see campaigns that are ranked by Magic, and not by Trending or any of the other types of searches.

Kickstarter's "Projects We Love" Category

You should also be aware of the "Projects We Love" Category. Getting your campaign into this category will give your project a huge boost. Spend some time studying how that works, so you can do all that you can to heighten the chances of having your project selected.

We suggest you go onto Kickstarter[45] and study this category. Here is just a bit of it:

Our team is constantly keeping an eye on the projects that are launching on Kickstarter. When we see one that stands out, we make it a Project We Love and sometimes even feature it on the site or in a newsletter. These projects usually have a super crisp project page with a clear description, captivating images or video, a thorough plan for completion, an excited community, and of course, a lot of creativity. Interested in becoming a Project We Love? We'd recommend browsing through other Projects We Love for inspiration, checking out our newsletter to get an idea of which projects we feature, and making sure your project hits these notes[46].

You Did it!

Now we've taken you through many of the items and tasks you'll need to complete, or be aware of, immediately before, during, and right after launch. We've given you a bit of an overview on the big picture. You've launched your campaign, and everything is moving right along.

Be proud, and be happy. You deserve it! Hey, if this were easy, everyone would do it.

---

[45] "How does my project become a Project We Love? - Kickstarter." 19 Nov. 2019, https://help.kickstarter.com/hc/en-us/articles/115005135214-How-does-my-project-become-a-Project-We-Love-. Accessed 22 Nov. 2019.

[46] "How to Get Featured on Kickstarter — Kickstarter." 29 Jun. 2015, https://www.kickstarter.com/blog/how-to-get-featured-on-kickstarter. Accessed 22 Nov. 2019.

Fun fact:

When we ran the marketing for Evolution Bra, American actor, George Takei, most famous for his role as Hikaru Sulu, helmsman of the USS Enterprise in the television series Star Trek, promoted the project on his personal Facebook and in one single post, raised over $100,000 singlehandedly!

12

Marketing Your Campaign - Paid Media

***If we did the things we are capable of, we would astound ourselves.* Thomas Edison**

At Funded Today, we not only believe in marketing, but rely upon it.

We've seen it turn five-figure campaigns into six-figure ones, and help formerly failing projects far surpass their goals. Sometimes, all that a struggling project needs is to reach out to just the right audience, and effectively invite its members one-by-one to come consider it.

Marketing is marvelous in that respect. But, we also recognize that marketing has its limits.

Marketing is Not Magic

Marketing cannot supernaturally change the fundamental nature of reality, including the nature of either products or shoppers. And, objective reality always constrains subjective perception. For instance, whether you view a glass as half-full or half-empty, it won't quench your thirst any more or less. Similarly, a wise real-estate agent might call a small kitchen "cozy" rather than "cramped," but this still won't alter its size. No. matter how skillfully a store clerk may present a sow's ear to you, it will never mystically transform into a silk purse.

An Old-But-Good Marketing Joke –
The Dogs Don't Like It

Marketers may sometimes retell an old joke about a hubristic dog-food company executive who attempts to promote his product through the best marketing that money can buy – the greatest endorsements, the highest-profile news coverage, the most persuasive ads, the slickest packaging, et cetera – but then doesn't see any improvement in sales...and as he struggles to determine why, he's finally informed by one brave employee that the dogs just don't like it.

Humor often conveys truth in surprising ways and, in this case, this persistent joke conveys a rather profound truth about marketing, which is, again, that its' success is innately limited by what it's trying to sell.

So, although a skilled seller can present a given product as persuasively as possible to a potential buyer, the buyer's response will ultimately depend less upon the pitch (although the pitch definitely helps) than upon the costs-and-benefits of the product itself, which are entirely beyond the marketer's control. A superior product-and-price combination is, and will always be, the single most vital factor in sales. No matter how skillfully it may be presented and promoted, even the best salesman on Earth can only do so much to talk people into a bad deal.

In short, the pitch can never exceed the product.

This principle is both timeless and universal, applying not only to old-fashioned retail sales, but equally to new-fangled e-commerce, including crowdfunding.

Pitching Online Products

Creators normally believe wholeheartedly that their products and services are highly desirable, or else they wouldn't devote so much time to developing them. They may spend countless hours slowly perfecting their creations, until those creations are finally ready to be released to the world.

At that point, if they're selling via the Internet (or raising funds on a crowdfunding website), then they may create a well-designed attractive webpage that will effectively showcase their creations while skillfully persuading viewers to become buyers—and they may also adeptly invite their most-likely buyers to come view it.

As those potential buyers respond to such invitations by visiting the webpage and considering its sales "pitch," they may agree that they're being shown a highly desirable product at a highly-affordable price - but not always. Marketing can't coerce people's feelings and thoughts - it can only persuade.

A persuasive presentation can potentially influence their perceptions for the better by presenting reality in the very best light possible—but, ultimately, it can never change that reality, which innately constrains it. Or, in other words, marketing can always focus on the sunny side, but it can never change the weather.

In some cases, marketers might attempt to defy reality by overstepping its limits to engage in outright fraud, but that's both wrong and (ultimately) counterproductive. Although some marketers might temporarily delude people into believing that black is actually white, reality (and justice), will ultimately prevail.

The truth is, your product is going to be good for some people, and not for others. Again: in sales, how something is presented is ALWAYS less important than *what* is being presented!

The best products and services innately tend to sell themselves, in which case a skilled presentation and/or promotion will merely enhance their success, whereas the worst ones will never catch on, and even the best marketing on Earth can never ultimately save them.

When it comes to paid media, a lot of creators will feel pulled toward publications that everyone knows: Huffington Post, Buzzfeed, and the New York Times, to name a few. Often, those are not worth utilizing as a platform for marketing because they have horrible conversion rates. That's because the people who read these publications don't necessarily have a strong affinity to crowdfunding.

In fact, we would argue that the most important demographic for determining a good crowdfunding publication is how likely its' readers are to be active on Kickstarter.

The Single Most Effective Type of Marketing

Paid media has raised more money than all of our other methods combined.

Paid media is what it sounds like - getting exposure on media, but you're paying for it. So, it's predictable. For example, you go to Facebook and pay $10 to do $10 in Facebook Ads. That's Paid Media. If you buy a commercial on TV, that is also Paid Media.

It's important to understand that becoming good at paid media takes time. As an example, we'd like to share with you how our expertise in paid media began - and how Thomas got started in crowdfunding.

Well, way back in the day (well before **Funded Today**) Thomas was learning Google AdWords. He bought some courses and started going through the content. It was probably 6 to 12 months until he got some traction. He had a few different business ventures but there just wasn't quite a product to market fit. For example, he had created an Online Immigration Self-Help where you have step-by-step information on how to file a government immigration form, and if you needed help, you'd have access to an attorney. He turned Google AdWords on, and began getting five to ten leads a day, for $1 or $2 per lead. That probably would have worked out tremendously, except there's a lot of fraud in immigration, and people wanted to meet in person. So, that stopped. Then, he got involved in the political arena and was working with some Governor and Senate races. He was doing political Email Lead Generation, and it was going well. He was making $10,000 to $20,000 a month. It was around that time that Zach reached out and asked him about some Paid Media.

Thomas would have a new campaign here, a new campaign there, and he was optimizing Google Ads for his family's business as well as reading some content on copywriting. The entire thing was a process. In other words, it took a while. The success we have with Funded Today now was not some kind of overnight success story, even though it kind of feels that way with what

Funded Today has become. But we didn't follow a road map. Through Thomas' experimentation, he essentially created an entire world - nobody was doing this strategy.

He got a political client and they wanted him to generate leads with about $2.50 per lead. Now, in the political arena the typical way that you generate leads is through petition. You have an ad – "Hey, sign this petition!", and when people sign it, they opt into the email list.

He had set up a few campaigns with the cost per lead around $5, $6. That was not going to work this time. This is what he says:

"I remember I got up early one day, I think 5:00 in the morning or so, maybe at 6:00. I got up, I went to the office, and I had an idea for one more campaign. During all this time I had learned a little bit of coding, and so I put together a web page, I sent some traffic, I was trying a new approach. I turned on the ads, went home, had breakfast with my wife and then an hour or two later I went back. I turned things on and I thought holy smokes are you kidding me? I was blown away, I kid you not, I was getting leads for $0.10, $0.15. And not only that, on some of my ads, my click through rates were 60%, 70% and that ended up being about a $100,000 contract."

(Meaning that for every 100 people that saw it, $600 (or 60 to 70 people) would actually click through on the ad. The option rate was approximately 20%).

Many entrepreneurs are afraid to spend any money on marketing. However, with the right "formula" you can, with reasonable accuracy, figure out what your return on marketing investment is.

For Crowdfunding, you need to spend enough to test stuff out on your most targeted audience. If it's not working, why would you spend $500? And if it works really well why would you not spend more than $1,000? When it works you expand outward and increase your budget. But, if that most targeted audience doesn't convert, then you can test some other audiences. But, if your most targeted audience doesn't convert well, then most likely you're not going to have a winner.

When Thomas applied what he had learned previously to crowdfunding for the first time, it was for the "RooSport."[47]

Tracking was not as sophisticated as it is now - no Google Analytics and such. So, we turned on ads and we looked at the campaign overall. Before we did this, it was making about 2k per day, and then it began to raise around 5k per day.

Now to test and see if was actually the ads that were doing this, we turned them off. Yes, things died down. So, we turned them back on, and raised another $50,000 to $60,000.

And that was it for crowdfunding. Or, so Thomas thought. Then the "FreeWavz Campaign," who was a friend of the "RooSport Campaign" that we just finished, saw what we did. They needed to raise another $100,000 in less than 100 hours, and basically came and begged us to run the marketing. We did, they hit their goal, and that's essentially how Thomas got started in Crowdfunding Marketing. Now, here we are.

---

[47] "RooSport 2.0 Wallet: World's First Magnetic Wallet ... - Kickstarter." 11 Oct. 2016, https://www.kickstarter.com/projects/theroosport/roosport-20-wallet-worlds-first-magnetic-wallet-po. Accessed 3 Dec. 2019.

Our Best Practices for Crowdfunding Paid Media

What we're sharing here is based on our experiences, and what we know works for crowdfunding specifically.

Custom Links

If you are running a Crowdfunding Campaign, if you are not working with **Funded Today**, or another marketing agency, you should go to your dashboard in Kickstarter or Indiegogo and create a custom link. This is the link that, when clicked on leads to your Crowdfunding Page. If they make a pledge, it will track back to that custom referral.

For example, you have a dashboard that shows all the pledges and where the pledges have come from. Some might come from Facebook, Google, TechCrunch, or Huffington Post, etcetera. When you use a custom link, it allows you to track where different pledges are coming from. You can create multiple custom links.

We actually have a Link Shortener called FND.to, and it's kind of like Bitly - if you are familiar with Bitly. The redirect tracks on the dashboard, and so, when we run a campaign, we have tons of different unique links tracked, that track back to all of our different divisions and their marketing efforts. But even if you have no marketing department, you have to track what you're doing. You don't want to spend blindly so you need to know what your ROI is for all your marketing efforts.

Facebook

Facebook is always going to be the best platform to start with.

That's because Facebook has almost 2.5 billion users[48], so if you want to have the ability to target anybody, Facebook is currently the best way to get there. Your crowdfunding project is only going to run for, say, 30 days. Facebook gives you the most traffic, the cheapest clicks, and the most *targeted* targeting.

Yes, we've tested different channels and Facebook, so far, is always the best. Whenever we've had a campaign that converts really well on Facebook, we've tested Twitter, we've tested Pinterest, we've done things on Google AdWords, do they give you a return? Can you generate pledges? Yes. Can you generate pledges at as good of an ROI as at Facebook? No, never.

So, you have your custom short link, you create an ad using that link. The ad set level within Facebook is structured with three levels:

1. Campaign
2. Ad set
3. Ad

A campaign would be your Kickstarter or Indiegogo campaign.

Your Ad Set

Then within that, you breakout your marketing based off of your ad set. At the ad set level, you're specifying your demographics - where your ads are going to display and things like that. So, for example, you might have one ad set where you're targeting males in the US who are between the ages of 18 and 35, who like Kickstarter, and you target through their Facebook News Feed. We

---

[48] "Top 20 Facebook Statistics - Updated ...." 12 Nov. 2019, https://zephoria.com/top-15-valuable-facebook-statistics/. Accessed 3 Dec. 2019.

actually start with the News Feed on desktop as we've found that will give you the best return for your money.

You can usually optimize, for instance, for clicks. If you're optimizing for conversions, Facebook will run all of their algorithms and analytics to try to generate conversions for you, or in this case, purchase for the cheapest price possible.

Your Ads

And then within the ad set, you can have different ads. Let's say you are selling a watch. You have one ad that has a certain title with a picture of a female wearing the watch. Then you have that same text, but it's a male wearing that same watch. Then maybe you take both of those same images and you change the title to something different. You then have four different ads, and each of those ads can have a unique URL that people go to.

When we run ads at Funded Today, we don't break things down at the ad level in terms of link tracking and seeing what's giving us an ROI. But we do, in fact, do it at the ad set level. For example, if we were targeting males between the age of 18 to 35 on the Facebook News Feed on desktop, we would have four ads. All four of those ads will have specific nomenclature, so if a pledge happens, you know what demographic that was.

The most important element of any ad is the image, not the title, and not the little blurb up above. All those obviously influence it, but it's actually the image that has the most importance. Why? Because when somebody is scrolling through Facebook, you're trying to take their attention away from other things, and make them stop so you need an image that invokes curiosity. Curiosity is what we always go for. Now to be clear, curiosity is not clickbait. The difference between the two is that in clickbait, you hang out a carrot and people click, and then when they land on a landing page it's not what the carrot leads one to believe. Curiosity is where you pique their interest, and it's intriguing that they want to know more, so they click through, and it ends up being related.

Here's a more specific example. We worked with a company that decided to take over from their grandfather a watchmaking business. The picture that we used to great effect was the two grandchildren - you couldn't see them too well, but they were in the frame. And then, there was the grandfather. On one of the grandkids' wrists was a watch that you couldn't even make out. And then, there was an arrow pointing to it and the text read "72-year-old grandfather passes on legacy of watchmaking to grandchildren."

Do you see how that image, and that text, and the idea of the story all combine together to form the perfect ad leveraging? It didn't even show the watch - you couldn't even see the watch until you clicked. The ad is not meant to sell - the ad is simply to drive curiosity to your sales page, to your Kickstarter page, to your video. The job of your Kickstarter video, and your page, and your reward structure, is to sell.

What if you don't want to use your own image? You think your too old, or too young, or too… something?

Here's the thing - your image may hit a different demographic, but that can work to your advantage. You want things that look different, that stand out. Never try to create an ad that looks polished and glossy and beautiful, because people have their sensors on, and when they see an ad like that, they naturally just ignore it. You want to look organic and authentic. (Ironically enough, on your Kickstarter video you actually need to convey professionalism that you're going to be able to bring this new product or idea to life that you can bring it to fruition - but not in your ad).

Facebook, and most ad networks, are social networks, and so you want to connect socially- that's often why we think a founders' image performs the best.

The Custom Audience

One of the other factors that is going to influence your conversion, that you'll see at the ad set level, is the different demographics that you're driving traffic to or from. They're all going to convert differently - an 18 to 35 year old male will convert differently than an 18 to 35 year old female, for different products. So, depending on the audience, your ad will convert differently.

We have thousands of audiences at **Funded Today** that allow us to hone in our marketing, so if you have a widget that is like X, we probably have a few past campaigns that were similar to your widget and that had a similar audience. So, we're able to market or create lookalike audiences, and market to those people.

To create a custom audience, you upload a list of emails, or other information, into Facebook. Facebook matches that to people that they have in their system, and that's called a custom audience. Then once you have a custom audience, and you have to have at least a minimum number, you can then tell Facebook to create an audience that looks like the custom audience you just uploaded. Then, they'll analyze the age, the demographic, the psychographic, the interest, the behaviors, everything they have. They will say: "here's 10% of the population that looks like the people that you uploaded." (This, by the way, is another reason to hire an agency rather than to go it alone, because they're going to have access to these custom audiences that it will take you time to build.)

Typically, the audience size is such that within a two to three-week time frame you can reach all of the people in a demographic that you're ever going to be reaching. You don't need to be advertising for 60 days. So, in two to three weeks, you're going to have enough time to reach all of those people without having to increase your budget so much that your costs become too high.

A note on hiring multiple paid media agencies: when you have multiple agencies, all targeting the same audience they're all going to have pretty similar audiences. So in a sense they will be competing against each other – with your money.

Metrics

You have to know what's working and what isn't. If you're really focused on ROI, and you don't have other objectives outside your crowdfunding campaign, such as raising funds from investors, or getting to retail, then you usually want to focus on having a better margin so you can take that and go fulfill.

Click-Through Rate

What conversion rate should you be looking for? At Funded Today, typically we'll see between a 2% to 4% click through rate. If we're below 2% we keep working on finding an ad that will work better. If we're at about 5%, that's phenomenal, and we're really happy about it.

The dynamic of how you pay your Cost Per Click (your CPC) is a combination of both your click through rate and your CPM (cost per mill), which is kind of confusing if you're not familiar with the terms. When you pay for an ad on Facebook, the billing terminology that Facebook uses is CPM, which stands for Cost Per Mill. This basically says for every 1,000 impressions, or for every 1,000 times that your ad is shown, how much do you pay? For example, you might pay $16 for every 1,000 impressions. Now you might only have 100 impressions, in which case your CPM would be $16, but you would only spend about $1.60.

So, you look at your CPM. Let's say you have a click through rate that's 2%, and you double your click through rate to 4%. Then, whatever you're paying in your cost per click, you will literally have just cut that in half. If you were previously paying $0.40 per click, now you're paying $0.20 per click.

You have control over your cost per click by creating a better ad that has a better click through rate. If you double your click through rate, you're going to decrease your cost per click by 50%. You don't really have control over the CPM because you're bidding against other people and it's what the market sets, what in the marketplace, what the equilibrium is. So, the one way you can affect CPM though up or down is by your budget, and your audience size. If you have an audience size of, say 1 million people, and you spend $1 per day, your CPM is going to be pretty low because Facebook basically has a million people that it can show your ad to. You're only going to spend a dollar a day, so Facebook can be very picky about who it shows to, and if there's an advertiser or other advertisers who are bidding more, Facebook can "say" that they're just going to wait until there's not a lot of other advertisers bidding and they're able to get a bid in for really low. On the flip side, let's say you have an audience of 50,000 people, and you go and you spend $10,000 a day on that audience, you might be spending $50 to $500 per 1,000 impressions - a lot of money. That's why scaling slowly is effective.

Earnings Per Visitor (EPV)

The conversion rate tells you for every 100 visitors, how many become a customer. In other words, how many make a purchase. So, if you have 100 visitors and you have three people for every 100 visitors that make a purchase, then your conversion rate is 3%. 3 divided by 100, pretty straightforward.

Now, hypothetically, what if we said there were two campaigns. One campaign has a conversion rate of 5% and the other campaign has a conversion rate of 10%. Which campaign do you wish were yours? You'd probably say the 10% one.

Well you may be right, or you may be wrong. We actually have no clue which one is better. What if the product that has a 10% conversion rate sells their product for $8? That means for every 100 visitors there are 10 people who are purchasing, because it's a 10% conversion rate, and those 10 people are making a purchase for $8.

So, every visitor, in that case, is generating on average $1 per visit because, again, you have 10 visitors who each make a $8 purchase. That's a $80 in revenue, and you had 100 visitors.

If you were to look at that and say, "What is the average amount raised per every visitor in this example?" It would be $0.80, because if you take 100 visitors multiplied by $0.80, you get $80 in revenue that was generated.

Now, let's go back to the other campaign that had a 5% conversion rate. What if that product actually cost a $1,000? That means there were five customers, or purchases, for every 100 visitors and they each spent $1,000. That would be $5,000 in revenue for every 100 visitors. Well, would you rather have $80 in revenue, or $5,000 in revenue for every 100 visitors? Well, obviously, you want the $5,000. The earnings per visitor would be $50, so on the one campaign that has a 5% conversion rate, on average, the earnings per visitor is $50. Now, on the other campaign you have an 8% conversion rate, but you only have an $0.80 earnings per visitor.

Those are some basic metrics to look at the cost per click for your ads, and specifically, the earnings per visitor for your ads. Different traffic sources will have a different conversion rate. So, if you have your Friends, Family, and Fools backing, your conversion rate and earnings per visitor will be way higher than, say, paid media. And if you land Press it's going to be different, and with Cross Collaboration it's going to be different. Basically, now you can see that for your ads you're spending *this* much per click, and your earnings per visitor is *this* much.

If your initial sales are all from your FFF, because your conversion rate is so much higher than a "normal" audience, you can't calculate your EPV accurately until you have other sources of traffic come through.

You'll go to Google Analytics to see your metrics. That's why it's important to have your tracking enabled from day one, so you have those metrics. Out of the gate, you're going to see those metrics, and that's also why it's important to have unique links for each of your different traffic sources so you can see what's happening. Otherwise you might go spend $5,000 or $10,000 on Facebook, and you're like "Hey, look, I raised $50,000 on my campaign in the first week!" But, maybe you spent $10,000 on those Facebook ads, and you actually only generated $2,000 in pledges- and it was actually press or something else that was generating that money.

You have to be willing to break it all down granularly (if you're doing this yourself, so you can see what's working and what's not). You need to look at each source, and then based upon each source - Facebook, Instagram, Pinterest, Press, Cross Collaborations, Cashback, Affiliate Marketing, and Influencer Marketing. Then determine from there what you are willing to spend based upon that key number: your EPV.

And, Finally...

Don't get discouraged if you have a low budget, or you can't keep scaling up. One of the most successful Crowdfunding companies of all time is "PopSocket." We've mentioned this before - how much did they raise Crowdfunding? It was something like $18,000, four or five years ago. Last year, they had 160 million in revenue.

Don't compare your raise to other campaigns. You don't know the backstory. A few years ago, there was a campaign they had raised $600,000 to $700,000. Basically, this campaign had prototypes, but they actually didn't *have* prototypes. Their whole goal was to raise this money, and then go find some investors to be able to create the product. So, even though it looked like they were flying high, they hadn't even created it. By the way, doing this is against Kickstarter rules.

We know, especially if you have never done anything like this before, that this can seem a bit confusing. This is certainly not a comprehensive list of all aspects of paid media, but it gets you started and, essentially, gives you a Facebook formula so that you can run ads.

Key Takeaways

- Crowdfunding advertising, compared with other forms of marketing, is unusually steady in raising pledges, and typically raises higher pledge totals than any other method.
- Start advertising on Facebook through desktop news-feed ads (optimized for clicks, but billed for impressions) and then possibly expand to other social-media platforms.
- In choosing audiences to test, consider lookalike audiences of people who have backed similar crowdfunding campaigns. These tend to perform best.
- For each audience targeted, try to maximize click-through rates by testing a variety of different image-and-text combinations.
- Exclude images that look too obviously like professional ads.
- Include creator images when possible.
- Aim to attract viewers' attention and arouse their curiosity, not to sell your project, but to draw traffic to your campaign page.

- Start advertising by testing your most highly-targeted audiences to determine their profitability, then expand your ads targeting, as long as it remains profitable. Then, continue running ads (while slowly scaling-up spending on them) as long as they remain profitable, realizing that their ROI will diminish over time on Facebook.

- Use custom links, plus analytics like CTRs and EPVs, to calculate profitability accurately, rather than speculating, while considering the fact that ads typically yield more pledges than those that are directly trackable to them.

- It can help to outsource your campaign marketing to a crowdfunding agency, since agencies typically enjoy skilled labor plus a variety of backer lookalike audiences—but you should verify their claims to have worked on various campaigns, and hire only one agency at a time to avoid them hurting each other's success.

Fun Fact:

Did you know that Funded Today has worked on 54 projects that were million/multi-million dollar projects?

13

Marketing Your Campaign - Press

***A pessimist sees the difficulty in every opportunity. An optimist finds the opportunity in every difficulty.* Sir Winston Churchill**

In sociology, there is a phenomenon called the "Matthew Effect."[49]

It's the idea of "accumulated advantage." The idea that the rich get richer, and the poor get poorer. The Matthew Effect basically says that if you are the top dog, you will stay the top dog, because you are the top dog.

As an example, if Sarah gets her book on the New York Times best sellers list, Sarah may likely stay on the New York Times best sellers list, because being on the New York Times best sellers list helps her sell more books!

The power of the press, right?

The Odd Kid on the Block

PR, within the world of crowdfunding marketing, enjoys a reputation of being the odd kid on the block. Often forgotten among the much more prominent ingredients

---

[49] "Matthew effect - Wikipedia." https://en.wikipedia.org/wiki/Matthew_effect. Accessed 3 Dec. 2019.

of the marketing mix (such as paid advertising, email marketing, and affiliate marketing), PR can be forgotten. While only about four percent of all crowdfunding pledges track back directly to media mentions, a strong PR showing can add significant credibility to your campaign and make a financial impact across the board. This can apply even after your campaign ends, and you move on to the next stage of selling your product.

Things You Should Know

No, PR will (most likely) not save the day for your campaign.

Too many creators have the impression that if things don't go well with their other forms of marketing, that then it's time to do media outreach... if we could just get on Mashable, then things would go through the roof!

We would like to shatter this illusion immediately, before we take you through how to best use PR.

Almost always, the groundwork for a successful PR campaign is laid by some other type of marketing - usually by either word-of-mouth and leveraging your FFFs, or by paid advertising. Think about it this way: If you can't get the people who know and love you to back your campaign, why would a journalist find it relevant enough to write about it? Or, if you know you can't make money by showing your campaign to strangers, why should it magically start working better when you show your campaign to even more strangers?

Here's the truth of it:
journalists and bloggers embrace campaigns and ideas that have already proven their market value, but they are usually timid about projects that struggle.

If you find that you do not receive much responsiveness from your associates and you can't generate a positive ROI on advertisements (and there is absolutely no shame in this), your next best destination is probably the drawing board, to make your product more attractive to the market - and not the office of a PR specialist.

Uniqueness Counts

If you're active in the crowdfunding world, you may be aware of some of the product categories that just won't go away: such as wallets, watches, or phone cases, as examples. It seems like there are dozens of them on Kickstarter at any time, and this is no surprise, as crowdfunding has a pretty solid track record of financing wallets, watches and phone cases.

While having a product that is relevant to a large number of people (and often relatively easy to manufacture) can be excellent for your campaign, media outreach can be a struggle. Here's why: journalists - even those at publications that don't report on breaking news - are generally obsessed with newsworthiness. They may receive 50, 100 or even 500 pitches every day, and they are always looking for the two or three leads that are most likely to be relevant to their audience. Even if your wallet has a completely novel feature or amazing design, the "check out this revolutionary wallet" pitch gets old in the journalist's mind very quickly, because it also gets old in their readers' minds. They can only publish the same story so many times.

So, is selling a watch or a wallet or a phone case detrimental to your PR efforts? No, but it is essential that you have something compellingly unique about your product - and it probably shouldn't just be some abstract feature, but something that can lead a journalist to tell a great story with your product.

Take Swiss watch manufacturer Werenbach[50], for example. They were one of many companies selling upscale watches on Kickstarter, but they had something unique about them: they built their watches from pieces of Russian Soyuz rockets. This allowed their backers to literally own a piece of history, as one journalist wrote in his review. This one piece of coverage tracked with nearly $12,000 in sales and likely contributed even more to the significant spike Werenbach experienced during the last week of their campaign. Werenbach's story went above that of a "standard luxury watch," and this is why we were able to generate good coverage for it.

In most cases, however, products that are unique and that solve common problems have the greatest chances of PR success.

PR Leads to Validation - not direct pledges

The most likely outcome of PR is validation of your product, not necessarily pledges. As mentioned earlier, only $1 in every $25 raised on Kickstarter tracks, on average, to a media placement. Of course, there are some campaigns that raise much more from media

---

[50] "Watches built from spaceborne rockets. by ... - Kickstarter." 6 Dec. 2017, https://www.kickstarter.com/projects/rocketwatch/watches-built-from-spaceborne-rockets. Accessed 5 Dec. 2019.

coverage than 4% - but these are usually the types of projects that could also do very well with other kinds of marketing - like paid advertisements or cross collaborations. You may be reluctant to dedicate many resources to PR during your actual crowdfunding campaign, but we think it's very worthwhile anyway.

Here's why.

Let me start with perhaps the biggest advantage PR has over all other types of marketing we use at **Funded Today**: the glory of media coverage is (usually) eternal. Your obvious short-term goal is to raise as much money as possible on Kickstarter or Indiegogo, but the underlying reason why you are on Kickstarter is probably a different one. As the name conveniently implies, you most likely want to "kickstart" your business. This means that you want to continue selling your product and growing your business after your crowdfunding campaign clock hits zero.

While most of the hundreds of creators we've met do not want to surrender their business after their Kickstarter ends, a good percentage of them believe that their marketing and PR efforts only work while they crowdfund. However, media coverage has, at least occasionally, brought some of the following to our clients after the end of their campaigns:

- interested investors
- retailers who want to sell the product
- prospective clients who are eager to learn where to buy the product post-crowdfunding.

In varying degrees, all of these benefits from media coverage can help businesses make a successful transition to the big dance of long-term retail.

The other indirect, hard-to-track, benefit is third-party validation during the campaign. Imagine, for example, that you sell a product for $500 - so, rather pricey for a Kickstarter product. For simplicity, you drive traffic to your campaign page in two different ways: paid advertisements, and media outreach. You will find that even the many people who see your ads and really like your campaign will be reluctant to spend $500 on your product, so they engage in a completely natural step of the buyer decision-making process - research. In modern times, this means asking Google for wisdom.

If you are mentioned in multiple credible publications and have received positive reviews, the prospective backer is much more inclined to buy than before. Depending on their exact action, the transaction will be recorded as either a sale from ads or from media coverage, but in the much more complex real world, both helped facilitate the sale equally.

How to Get Started

Everybody wants to get press. That's the dream, right? Yet, many entrepreneurs are afraid of the press. For each source, it's good PR practice to identify one, and only one, reporter to target at any given time. It's generally best to contact your targeted reporters between Tuesday and Friday mornings through email. Use an attention-grabbing, accurate title that entices them to read, and brief, snappy, entertaining, informative content that is customized to both their style and their audience. DON'T forget to add your preview link to your campaign page as soon as it's available.

After your initial contact, you should follow-up with them regularly to try and nurture a relationship that may lead to news coverage. Such coverage is generally easier to obtain for campaigns that enjoy naturally newsworthy elements - such as clothing that never stinks nor stains - or campaigns that have already surpassed their respective funding goals.

Unlike paid media, you can never guarantee any news coverage, unless perhaps you buy an editorial. Anytime you successfully persuade one press source, large or small, to feature your project, it's usually easier to persuade other sources to do likewise, which can lead to a "snowball effect."

For newscasters who choose to report about your project, you should prepare a press kit which they can download from Google Drive or Dropbox. The kit should include minimal, but helpful content, such as:

- a polished news release that presents both your project and your company, including links to learn more
- personnel backgrounds
- basic organizational facts
- any relevant branding guidelines
- company logos in vector format
- a product fact sheet
- high-resolution product photographs
- a copy of your finished campaign video
- awards lists
- positive customer reviews

All of this should be organized as conveniently as possible.

Crowdfunding PR

With a crowdfunding project everything is on a faster timeline because your project is only going to last a month or a bit more. Not a lot of people understand the crowdfunding arm of public relations. It's a really unique animal.

One of the aspects that makes it so unique is that the goal here is to help bring in more pledges. In traditional PR, the goal is to get the brand name out there and to build those long-term relationships and rapport with other agencies and companies. In crowdfunding, we really just want to bring brand awareness quickly, in a way that converts well, to bring in pledges RIGHT NOW, while the campaign is live.

In other words, your spin has to appeal to readers to buy rather than the more traditional, "oh yeah, I heard about this company one time." Crowdfunding requires a different kind of pitch, not so much about the brand, more about the product, and driving traffic to get people to click on a link and go check out the product.

To be clear, general exposure is still good, because as we mentioned above, some exposure can lead to more exposure. What you're aiming for in crowdfunding is that focus on making the product interesting in this moment. So what we do for our clients, and recommend you do, is target a lot of websites that cycle through content really frequently, rather than something like Forbes, which has a big audience, but they don't necessarily buy a lot of products. Forbes is more of a scroll and read website. What you want are those websites that will convert better because they are product-based websites.

Go for Conversions, Not Greatness

You've no doubt gathered by now that we would not recommend you go right to Forbes to pitch. For some reason, everyone wants to be featured on Forbes, but here's the thing - even when **Funded Today** gets written about in Forbes, sometimes it gets exposure… and sometimes it doesn't. So, let go of the myth that Forbes is *the place* to be featured. Yes, it can be good for long term brand awareness, but that's not your goal right now.

Any press that is going to raise you money is the most important press you can have at this time in your entrepreneurial endeavor – and for your Crowdfunding campaign. Always keep in mind why you're doing Kickstarter in the first place - to help raise money for your product.

Timing

Press is an interesting animal. It can be hit or miss, and could have nothing to do with your product, or anything related to your project. It might just have to do with the journalists, and what they ate that day. On a good day they might be excited about your project, and on another day… not so much.

Press can be more confusing and complex than most people realize. A poorly worded email can turn a journalist off to your product, so make sure whoever writes your emails knows what they are doing.

In our experience, Fridays seem to be the best days to pitch. A lot of people think first thing Monday morning is the best time, but we completely disagree - in part because everybody is pitching either Friday night, or first thing Monday morning. Many journalists can have 1,000 emails in their inbox. By Friday, they've probably cleared out their inbox and then you can be the first in line if you pitch Friday, sometime before lunch.

Now, what about the holidays?

Most journalists are out of the office on the actual holiday, so pitching them then wouldn't make any sense. However, a lot of journalists will keep content that they already have completed to post during those off times. So, let's say you have a campaign that's going to deliver to its' backers right before Christmas. You can message a journalist at Digital Trends and say, "Hey, I have this really cool product, it would be a great post for something you can buy your husband for Christmas, and it will be delivered before the holidays, what do you think?"

Aim to pitch at least a week before the holidays, preferably two, depending on the product.

Where to Pitch

The first thing you need to figure out is what kind of market you want to engage: are you a tech-based product? Fashion? Something else? You want to stick with your niche, and maybe branch out into related areas.

Once you've determined your niche, then make a media list - basically just a big spreadsheet full of outlets, like websites and YouTube Influencer channel names, Instagram handles, everything that fits within the niche you've chosen.

The best place to start is with the places where you tend to read content the most. So, for instance, if you look at cool products on, let's say, thisiswhyimbroke.com, start there. Find a good contact for them and talk to them first. The more the merrier, so don't stop at just a few on your media list. Talk to all of the places you want to be featured.

Okay, now you have your media list, you've got your 500 people that you want to contact. Remember, they get pitched a lot. So, you have to make your pitch stand out - you have to be consistent, and you have to be unique. Most journalists get hundreds, if not thousands, of pitches a day. You have to send an email they want to look at, with that super interesting title. Once you have them looking at it, they need to be able to spend as little time on it as possible - so here's that snappy, and maybe funny, part.

Then you have to be informative. Journalists want good information, and they want it quickly. So, you need to spend the time to figure out how to craft your pitch in a way that they can say, "Okay, this is a really cool product. I have the information; I want to go look for more." Then, there is your link, so they can go straight to your page and pull the assets they need right from your Crowdfunding page.

Even though you'll spend time crafting your pitch, you want it to feel as natural and personable as possible. You don't want journalists feeling like you're sending 1,000 emails to the same person. So, try and include their name, and something like:

"Hey, I saw this piece of press that you wrote a couple of months ago about this product, and I have something very similar. Here are some cool points about it (list 2 or 3), and here's a link to my campaign. I would love for you to check it out and let me know your thoughts."

That way, they have a call to action to go look at something, but they also have a few cool facts that get them hooked right when they start reading.

The great thing about PR is, as long as you're consistent and you follow-up with multiple different outlets, chances of getting someone's attention are exponentially higher - and that could make a huge shift in your campaign.

Be Persistent

Many journalists won't respond right away. Is there such a thing as sending too many emails? What's the strategy behind consistency and persistence, and following up in your outreach to journalists?

The goal, of course, is to get a response. If that means you send 5 or 10 emails throughout the campaign, then that's what you do. Sometimes journalists will get back to us after the first pitch. They might say they are not interested, or they have a question, or they are green-lit to write an article. In PR, persistence is key and really, too many emails is not a thing when it comes to PR (unless they've already told you they're not interested).

Our Secret Strategy

Product Directories. Product Directories are basically online malls, where people can look and digitally window-shop. These shoppers want to see an item, be convinced of why they need it, and then buy it and move on. It's all about fast purchasing and instant gratification these days.

So, you can almost always submit your campaign for an organic placement to any product directory. They always have a contact page, and they always have a suggested page - which you 100% should take advantage of, because if you get placed, your product almost always earns a listing on the website for the life of the website. So, that will forever bring in continuous coverage for your projects - even after the campaign ends - then it will redirect wherever you redirect your Kickstarter or Indiegogo page.

A few directories to get you started:

- Bouncy.news[51]
- Thisiswhyimbroke.com[52]
- Dudeiwantthat.com[53]
- Thegadgetflow[54]

This is a question we get asked a lot: Do I have to have a sample, first?

Do you need them? No.

Is it good to have them? Yes. Samples always help, and it lets the influencers and journalists have a hands-on experience with the product. However, 95% of our clients who don't have samples still landed thousands of dollars and pledges in organic pieces.

The only time we would ever suggest to have a product is if you can send it to a big outlet before you actually launch your campaign. We've learned that it just eats up too much time to send a sample to an outlet while your campaign is live, because then they have to receive the product, test out the product, see if they actually like it, and then write the piece and get it live, which can eat up 50% of your campaign in the blink of an eye. So, it's just

---

[51] "bouncy / バウンシー | 未来のライフスタイルが見える動画メディア." https://bouncy.news/. Accessed 4 Dec. 2019.

[52] "ThisIsWhyImBroke." https://www.thisiswhyimbroke.com/. Accessed 4 Dec. 2019.

[53] "DudeIWantThat.com." http://www.dudeiwantthat.com/. Accessed 4 Dec. 2019.

[54] "Gadget Flow." https://thegadgetflow.com/. Accessed 4 Dec. 2019.

as effective and more efficient, to continue pitching your product, and telling the writers why they need to write about it. Of course, if you only have one single prototype, don't send it out to anyone.

When you continue to follow up with a journalist to ask if they're interested, here are some tips.

The first 2 or 3 follow-ups should say something to the effect of, "Hey, I haven't heard from you yet. Do you have any additional questions? Is there anything I can help you with?"

Then, the emails would start highlighting some new milestones that the campaign has reached - maybe the campaign was successfully funded, or 200% funded at the time of the email. Perhaps you have a cool new version of the product that was just released for the final week. Like all the other emails, keep them short, snappy, and informative.

We want to reemphasize at this point to be very cautious about reaching out to more than one journalist at any outlet, or you might end up stepping on toes. The exception to this might be if you've contacted one and haven't heard anything back. Maybe they just wrote something like it- you never know the reasons. A new writer might have a fresh take and be eager for the piece.

Pitch to one journalist at a time at an outlet but don't be afraid to reach out to another if you never hear back from the first.

If you have multiple contacts from the same outlet and are unsure which one to pitch, you can ask if someone could get you in touch with the Director of that department, or a Manager, and coordinate with them.

You want to start by reaching out to the strongest possibility and if that person responds, great, otherwise go down the line one at a time.

The Snowball Effect

When you begin, start by pitching the smaller outlets first. Once you get a few pieces of press, this tends to create more awareness. Once this gets rolling, you get more and more. Then, the big hitter outlets like BuzzFeed, Gizmodo, and The Verge will look at these smaller websites to see what the breaking news is, and then usually cover something very similar. If you can already have coverage in those smaller outlets, the chance of getting more coverage in those bigger guys is much, much higher. The smaller outlets give that product the validation that those big outlets require before they're willing to write about a product.

Of course, though from smaller to bigger outlets is the usual pattern for the snowball effect to take hold, if the product is cool enough, innovative enough, and makes a big enough splash, it can happen where the big outlets write about the product right off the bat.

The biggest piece of advice we can give you to grab the attention of those big converting outlets is to make your product interesting to the audience that you're pitching. BuzzFeed has a different rhetoric than, let's say, Oculus or a Digital Trends does. So, what we do at **Funded Today** is craft our pitches and present the products to different outlets in a way that fits their writing style already. This means they don't have to do any extra work to write about it - the idea being that you present them with this really cool product, and basically write an article for them so it's very easy and fast for them to use it.

This means, of course, that you need to spend some time studying the outlets you want to pitch to so that you understand their style and focus. Here's an example of the snowball effect.

The Sunrise Smart Pillow[55] is a memory foam pillow that had smart features that can help wake you up with natural lights, that change colors. When we first connected with them, they had no Press so we wanted to see what we could do. We sent out a pitch and heard back from askmen.com, and that led to an article. The very next morning we had five new pieces from Digital Trends. It seemed like all these different places had seemingly written about it overnight. The whole thing continued to funnel for the rest of the campaign. Every single day there was some new coverage for them. Really, that all started because we were able to find one good contact at one outlet.

Part of this process was instantly getting back to that first journalist - time is of the essence in PR. Once you get a contact from an outlet, stay in touch with them, because if you have more products or more projects, they're going to be your go-to person to get more coverage and get more branding for your project.

Seize the moment.

---

[55] "Sunrise Smart Pillow: The Future of Sleep ...." 12 Jan. 2019, https://www.kickstarter.com/projects/modem/the-sunrise-smart-pillow-sleep-smart-wake-naturall. Accessed 5 Dec. 2019.

Tracking Press Impact

The impact of Press is much harder to pin down. As an example of what we mean, let's look at the Cubiio[56] (a small cube laser engraver tool) campaign. When we first started on that campaign, they already had a couple pieces of press but there was no more coming in. So, our PR department used the same contact at AskMen that we mentioned earlier for the smart pillow in the snowball effect section. This landed another piece with them, and then after a couple of days more people started to read it and look at the product. At the same time, we were using the product directories for placement, and we ended up raising over $50,000 in press for Cubiio. Now when we say $50,000 in press, generally speaking that's $150,000 that didn't track, because press syndicates might not use a specific link, so it's hard to keep track of where everybody is coming from. The $50,000 directly tracked from press is three to four times what actually shows up in the dashboard.

People will read an article and think, cool gadget, and then when they have some time, they'll just Google the product and go pledge directly to the Kickstarter Campaign. That you can't track at all.

One of the great things about Press is that when you get multiple coverages, more people are going to see it and have the feeling that they are seeing it everywhere, so they need to go check it out. So, even if it doesn't track directly to PR, you're still getting that brand awareness which is where traditional PR comes into the Crowdfunding space.

---

[56] "Cubiio: The Most Compact Laser Engraver by ... - Kickstarter." 15 Aug. 2017, https://www.kickstarter.com/projects/880456201/cubiio-the-most-compact-laser-engraver. Accessed 5 Dec. 2019.

The biggest key here is building those relationships with contacts AND also knowing what outlets are going to work best for your campaign.

Is it Too Late for Press?

Certainly, **Funded Today** has been hired numerous times for a campaign that didn't have any press, and there were only a few weeks left.

Clearly, the more time the better. The more time you have to talk with journalists, the more likely you are to land Press. But - no amount of time is too short. We know from working with campaigns that are already live all the time that it's possible.

If you are going to launch, or have already launched, and are having trouble landing Press, you can hire Funded Today so we can use our contacts and well-oiled process to help your project.

A note of caution - it's considered bad practice in the PR world to have two people pitching the same journalists, it's called double pitching. So, if you do bring in someone to help with Press and you've already started the process, make sure you have that shared Media Outreach Google Doc so no one gets their paths crossed.

Parting Words of Advice

Don't lose your passion! Journalists will see through that so quickly. If you're not passionate about what you're doing, those you are trying to connect with won't be excited by what you have to say. Just like in daily living, do everything you can with passion, and life will reward you back.

PR may always remain the odd kid on the block, but your long-term vision may justify that you give it some love.

Key Takeaways

- PR is best started as soon as possible, in order to allow as much time as possible to cultivate vital relationships, but it's never too late for PR to accomplish some good.

- It's helpful (but not essential) to send prototypes or samples to reviewers, especially when such product reviews are arranged in advance during a campaign's pre-launch phase.

- Crowdfunding PR, unlike traditional PR, should focus more on short-term fundraising than on long-term positive exposure, which may mean targeting sources that enjoy less prominence but better conversion rates, such as product directories.

- Crowdfunding PR should involve compiling a list of hundreds of news outlets that serve one's target market, identifying only one reporter (at a time) to contact at each outlet.

- Pitch to those reporters via email (ideally on Friday mornings, but whatever you do, not on Mondays or holidays).

- Follow up consistently with any reporters who haven't yet responded.

- Each pitch to a newscaster should include a title that will easily stand out among hundreds of others. Content should be brief, snappy, entertaining, informative, and highly customized toward the writing style of each news source, along with the interests of its audience. Also, include a link to whichever campaign page is being promoted.

- It's easier for popular, well-funded campaigns to get featured, especially those with newsworthy elements—and getting featured in one news source (whether big or small) renders it easier to get featured in additional news sources.

- Public relations is both hectic and "hit-or-miss," and sometimes rather slow to yield results, but it can potentially raise tens-of-thousands of dollars for the right campaigns, and can create good exposure for your project.

14

Marketing Your Campaign - Other Traffic Methods

Whatever your present environment is, you will fall, remain, or rise with your thoughts, your vision, your ideal. You will become as small as your controlling desire, as great as your dominant aspiration. James Allen

The Single Best Marketing Strategy We Use

We're talking about Cross Promotions, or CCs. Here at **Funded Today** we call them Cross Collaborations. When you are running a live campaign, and even after the campaign ends, you will want to keep your backers updated through emails. These are also posted to your campaign. At the bottom of those updates, you can share other campaigns that you like, or that have reached out to you. Maybe they are similar products. You share those in your update with a link that promotes those campaigns. In return, those campaigns will also promote yours in the bottom of their updates.

This is a great system, because Kickstarter is a community, so a lot of the same backers will back similar products in similar categories. This means your backers get those Cross Collaborations and look at them, because they're looking for new ideas to back. It's highly effective.

As an example of how a CC works: suppose you're selling a new type of water bottle. You spot a campaign that is selling a backpack that has a slot for a water bottle. You would approach the creator of the backpack and say something like, "Hey, you've got a really cool backpack. I have this awesome water bottle that looks like it fits perfectly in that little slot. How about you tell your backers about my water bottle, and I'll tell my backers about your backpack, and together we'll make some money?"

Now, do the Cross Collaborations need to have a synergy like that of a backpack with a water bottle holder and then the water bottle campaign? Do the products have to be that closely aligned to work?

If the products do fit that closely you may have a slightly higher conversion rate. But, you could do a CC with a set of earbuds and a backpack, or a set of earbuds and a water bottle and you will still see great conversion - in fact, sometimes you may not even see a difference in the conversion rate. That's what makes Kickstarter Cross Collaborations so neat and unique. It's a community. Most Kickstarter Backers aren't just on Kickstarter shopping for a specific item, or only in one category. They're looking to back a new, cool, different invention that comes across the Kickstarter platform.

Why Even Do Cross Collaborations?

What is the point of doing Cross Collaborations? Why are they so important?

Even though you're running Facebook Ads and other things will drive more traffic and therefore more pledges, Cross Collaborations, 95% of the time, are going to be your highest converting source of traffic.

We are saying 95% of the time rather than 100% of the time, because on occasion we've seen ads convert higher. Once in a while there is that rare campaign where press converts very highly. Even so, most of the time, it's going to be Cross Collaborations that are converting to the highest rates.

The flip side of this - if your CCs are not converting, that tells you chances are there's something wrong with one of your 7-P's. (See Chapter 4: The 7 Ps).

A pretty good mantra in the crowdfunding world is if Cross Collaborations don't convert, nothing's going to convert.

Best Strategy for Cross Collaborations

CCs are somewhat newer to Crowdfunding, and have really only taken off in the last few years. So, on the chance that not all your backers know what it is, you may want to put in some sort of introduction there, such as, "Hey check out some of these other great campaigns we think you might like." Or, "Here are some campaigns that are helping us reach our goal. Let's return that favor, and help them reach their goals, as well."

On average, we see our Cross Collaborations convert anywhere from 4%, all the way up to 20%. That means that if we send 100 visitors, they click on that link of Cross Collaborations, and it takes them to your page. Out of those 100 people, anywhere from 4 to 20 of those will convert (back your product).

Let's suppose you see a shoe campaign that you want to do a Cross Collaboration with. You go to that shoe campaign and they have 1,000 backers. If the Cross Collaboration is going to have an average conversion rate of 4% you can I expect to get 40 new backers by doing a CC with the shoe campaign.

When we do Cross Collaborations when we first start out, we are just testing things - and suggest you do the same. If you are finding that your Cross-Collaboration conversions are very, very low, you may have to dive a little deeper into your own campaign to look for issues.

Understanding Conversions

Of course, it's not quite that straightforward. There are many factors that influence the conversion rate on any Cross Collaboration, such as:

1. The Split - you will want to look at the Community Tab to see what a campaign's "split" is - the number of returning backers (people who have backed Kickstarter campaigns in the past) and new backers. The higher the percentage of returning backers, the higher the conversion rate is likely to be, because you have an audience of

people who are already predisposed to backing an additional campaign.

2. Product Price - the price of the product impacts conversion. If your product is on the expensive side, say $150, your conversion rate will be lower. However, you're also driving your pledge dollars up more with each conversion.

3. Actual Click Throughs - you might have a Cross Collaboration with another campaign that has 1,000 backers - but not all 1,000 of those backers are going to click on the link of the update email from that campaign that has your product at the bottom. So, maybe out of the 1,000 backers you would get 70% who open and read that email update. Then, of those people who read it, you might get 20% - 30% of the people who click through. Even though you have a Cross Collaboration with a campaign that has 1,000 backers, you might only get 200 people to actually click through to your page. Out of those 200 people who end up on your project page, you will get your 4% - 20%.

   As an example, let's take the shoe campaign again. They have 1,000 backers and have agreed to cross collaborate with you. They message all 1000 of their backers and of those 1,000 backers, 200 end up clicking through and seeing your page. If you're converting on the low end, you'll have 8 conversions, but on the high end, you might have 40 conversions.

Now, if you're not used to dealing with the world of conversions, 4%, or even 20%, may not sound all that great. But, if you were to take all of your traffic sources across the board, across every campaign, you might be between 1% to 3% on your conversion rate. Again, that number varies so much depending on the conversion rate of your page, the traffic source, your price point, etcetera. Generally speaking, 1% to 3% is what you're looking at on average.

To do your updates with Cross Collaborations, pick any weekday other than Wednesday. Do your updates twice a week, but never on Wednesday. Monday-Thursday or Tuesday-Friday schedules work fine.

For the best time, you should be aware of where the majority of your backers are living – obviously, if most of your backers are in Europe you don't want to be sending out updates according to a U.S. clock.

We've seen CCs work well when sent out at 9:00 AM, 3:00 PM, or 4:00 PM. Especially going into the weekend, when you post them on Thursday or Friday in the afternoons, people have time over the weekend to look at your updates.

If you notice that your backers simply love getting updates, you could send out 3 per week. It all depends on how engaged your backers are. Begin with 2 per week, and experiment a bit with the days of the week.

Dealing with Naysayers

Yes, there will always be a few people who complain about the Cross Collaborations, but the gain far outweighs that. In other words, your net positive is good. Consider that if you weren't doing Cross Collaborations, they would probably complain about something else.

There are always those who want to complain about something. As a creator you need to be prepared for this – never take it personally.

Let's pause for a moment to talk about this. A lot of people who are launching a business, or putting themselves out there, find the negative people who say critical things. As a creator you can't start thinking, "Oh no, they can't be saying this, I shouldn't be doing this."

Realize that in any marketing medium where you're able to get feedback, you're always going to have negative comments. Sometimes we will have a campaign that is absolutely crushing it, and literally every single comment is negative. Maybe the negative people just want a place to vent. Just think about all the negativism you see on social media channels, and you'll be reminded how much negativity does go on.

As far as your campaign goes, the people who like it are not even spending their time in the comment section. They've voted with their wallet, so to speak.

To keep the negative impacts from feeling personal, think about it this way. Not everybody loves iPhones. But there are millions and millions of people who have iPhones. Let's say there are about one million or so who absolutely despise iPhones. What if Apple was trying to cater to that one million who hate them, versus the multiple millions who love them?

The Kickstarter Community

Many backers feel like they are mini investors. There are some companies that come on Kickstarter that are full-fledged and already well-known. But, the majority of crowdfunding creators are getting their start on Kickstarter, as the name suggests.

The Kickstarter community gets invested in seeing how creators bring companies to life, rather than just shopping for a product. This is, in part, why the conversion rates for Cross Collaborations are so high. This is one of those intangibles that makes Crowd Funding so exciting. Many backers love the feeling that you want them to come take a look at your product so they can help with your campaign.

Yes, of course there are those people who don't even realize it's Crowdfunding, and actually think it's an e-Commerce Store. They don't realize that they're helping put money in now for something that is coming out later. So, they don't realize this is Kickstarter and they're not going to get a product right away, or that a lot of these companies are building brands.

Occasionally we get a creator who has heard that doing CC is going to hurt their brand. Building a brand on Kickstarter is definitely not going to hurt your product. Here's why.

These backers (the ones who are into crowdfunding) are on Kickstarter to look for what's fun, what's cool, what's new, what's different. So, if they've backed your campaign, a very high percentage of the time, like 80% or 90%, they backed somebody else's campaign, as well. These people have received Cross Collaborations from other campaigns, so they're already getting them. When you do it, it's not going to make them mad.

You might as well be doing Cross Collaborations on your campaign and gaining the fruits from doing them. Cross Collaboration can lead to thousands more for your campaign, for essentially 10 minutes of your time a couple of times per week.

Getting Other Campaigns to Collaborate with You

One of the things to keep in mind when approaching other campaigns to Cross Collaborate with your campaign is that you need to use your best sales tactics. If you're a campaign with a lower number of backers and you are reaching out to a hyper campaign - like one that has 10,000 backers, suggest something that benefits them. Maybe you'll do more Cross Collaboration posts about them than they will for you. The worst thing they can say is no, right?

If you have a previous campaign that's got 300 to 400 backers on it, use it. Reach out to the campaigns you want to collaborate with and say, "I know my campaign is a little bit older, but I'll post about your product on this 300 or 400 backers campaign, if you'll post about my product on launch day one or two."

If you don't have a previous campaign, which a majority of you probably won't, reach out to the campaigns that are live, or will be live when your campaign launches, and say, "I know I don't have any backers right now, but here is my product, and since it's a quality product I imagine I'll have 300 to 500 backers, or more. So, if you post about mine from the launch day, I'll post about your products when I have 200+ backers.

If you set up enough of these before launch day, it can help drive you up in the Kickstarter Algorithm, which moves you up on pages. That's one of the advantages of Cross Collaborations - there is not going to be a trickle effect in pledges, but more like waves of pledges that come once those updates go out.

How to Do Great Updates

With all this talk about putting your Cross Collaborations at the bottom of your email updates, we thought we should spend a bit of time on just how to do the most effective updates.

As a creator, let's say you're running your campaign for 30 days, and roughly twice a week you are sending out updates. There are many, many things you can focus on in your updates such as stretch goals, milestones, and press announcements.

6 Tips for Effective Updates:

1. The first thing to keep in mind is that you do not need to write a novel. There is no reason to send out a two page update. Think more in terms of short and sweet.

2. Images that serve the update well can enhance the message. You can even shoot a video for your updates.

3. Think personality and building trust. People can be nervous about backing a campaign because there is the chance that things can go wrong. So, if you can show your face, demonstrate your capabilities and credibility by showing your face and doing a video, that can greatly enhance the trust element.

4. Pay attention so you know what your backers are responding to. Then try and give them those elements that they seem to love. Unless you are absolutely certain your backers will love just getting information on Cross Collaborations, don't make that the main message. Focus on your campaign and your product, and offer those other campaigns for a little spice. You never want to drag away attention from your own product. It's probably not a great idea to collaborate with a campaign that has the "same" product. In other words, if you're producing a wallet, don't collaborate with another wallet campaign.

5. One of the worst things you can do is not keep your backers updated. If your campaign runs for 45 days and you only send out two updates, that's NOT enough.

6. In general, 3-5 Cross Collaborations at the bottom of an email is about right. Make sure to test this out with your backers, and adjust accordingly.

Kickstarter put out an article *(50 Ideas for Sending Great Project Updates*[57]*)* which had some awesome update ideas. Here are just 12 of their suggestions for updates while your campaign is live:

1. Highlight campaign milestones, like when you reach your goal mid-point.
2. Share community milestones as your backer count grows to 50, 100, or 500 backers, and beyond.

---

[57] "50 Ideas for Sending Great Project Updates — Kickstarter." 12 Aug. 2016, https://www.kickstarter.com/blog/50-updates-to-keep-up-with-your-backers. Accessed 10 Dec. 2019.

3. Announce any changes you make to your campaign, such as new rewards or stretch goals.
4. Celebrate when you've been featured as a Project We Love or in one of our newsletters.
5. Spotlight your backer's comments, drawings, videos, and other contributions.
6. Introduce members of your team.
7. Invite collaborators to write posts that introduce themselves and share how they contribute to your project.
8. Running a Food project? Share your favorite recipe.
9. Running a Publishing or Journalism project? Write a little feature on a writer that has inspired you.
10. Countdown the final days of your campaign with a new update each day.
11. Share personal news/events, like the adoption of a new kitten, children's graduations, etc.
12. Be transparent about any challenges that come up, like a bug in your code or changes to the cost of supplies.

Conclusion: Cross Collaborations DO NOT Hurt Your Campaign

There are even marketing companies that recommend you don't do Cross Collaborations. Clearly, as you can see from this chapter, we wholeheartedly disagree. Think of your backers like investors. They have spent money, but don't have a product yet. In our experience, they absolutely want to hear from creators through updates, because they have invested in the journey that is crowdfunding - that is, your campaign.

Key Takeaways

- It's important to update backers regularly—usually about twice weekly, depending upon exactly how communicative they want you to be, which they'll generally tell you—at the time of day that's best for wherever the majority of them live.

- It's helpful to end each backer update by introducing no more than five cross-promotions (which may also be called "cross-collaborations" or "CCs") arranged with other campaigns, even if a few backers complain about it.

- Cross-promotions should never feature competitors' projects, and they fare best when featuring *complementary* projects. They still do well featuring unrelated campaigns, especially campaigns that have attracted high percentages of repeat backers.

- Not all backers will read cross-promotions, nor click on them, but those who respond to them will normally convert at unusually-high rates of up to 20% or so, which is far more than the average rate of about 1% - 3% (depending upon average pledge size). Conversely, if cross-promotion traffic doesn't convert, then it's almost guaranteed that no other traffic will convert, either.

- Some popular campaigns have raised over $50,000 directly from cross-promotions alone—and, just like with other forms of crowdfunding marketing, increased pledges from cross-promotions generally encourage increased pledges from all other sources.

Fun fact:

Did you know that on April 16th, 2020 Funded Today surpassed the $329,000,000 in total pledges raised milestone?

15

Prelaunch Community Building and Email Lead Generation

Always remember Goliath was a 40-point favorite over David. **Shug Jordan / Auburn Head Football Coach**

If you are running your first crowdfunding project, chances are good that you are a single proprietor. This means you must fill every role, from CEO to janitor, in your business. That makes it especially important to understand that not all work is of equal value.

This is where the Pareto Principle comes in.

The Pareto Principle

The Pareto Principle guarantees that 20% of your efforts will yield 80% of your results. That means if you want to focus more time on what's most important, as you should, then you'll need to start recruiting additional personnel who specialize in various tasks, which they do even better than you do, while building those specialists into a team to help bring your vision to reality.

This introduces both leadership and management into your business - management is more about keeping operations running well (or the "how" that engages people's minds), whereas leadership is more about providing common direction for all of those operations (the "why" that engages people's hearts).

Attracting others to rally around you is important, because your business cannot succeed in isolation. Your business can only succeed through developing a mutually beneficial relationship with the rest of the vast, ever-changing marketplace.

It's only by benefiting customers well, that they will bring prosperity to you in return - and help draw additional customers to you, as well. Their unsolicited praise through news reports, expert recommendations, celebrity endorsements, and customer reviews is generally more powerful than your self-promotional efforts alone, although your paid marketing (see Promotion below) can both amplify and hasten their word-of-mouth marketing.

Although their words are potent, their actions through sales are even more so. Citing such "social proof" (see Presentation below) is exceptionally powerful in persuading additional people to transact business with you. It's through these, and other person-to-person interactions, that the market will collectively determine your success in business from moment to moment.

Although you can help persuade these choices, you can't control them. You can only control your own choices. So, focus on doing your best at serving other people's needs, while constantly improving your performance, and this will render it easy for other people to freely favor you to serve them. Ultimately, business is centered around people- it's about how well your personnel serve other people in mutually beneficial ways by selling them products or services.

The Crowdfunding Success Matrix

What are your chances of success with your crowdfunding project? Of course, there is no way to know for sure until you go through it, but there are ways of understanding and increasing your odds for success. The paradigm we like to use here at **Funded Today** is the Crowdfunding Success Matrix. Here's what it looks like:

Understanding which quadrant you fall in will give you insights into where you might need to adjust what you're spending your time on. Even though it's super simple, it actually has a lot of implications that matter substantially, because if you have a campaign, or a business, or an E-commerce website, and things aren't going the way you wish they were, it's important to form an understanding of why it's not working. Do you have a product problem? Or a marketing problem? As you can see in the image, the "Crowdfunding Success Matrix" is just like those Business Matrixes you've seen if you've ever been to business school.

How the Success Matrix Works

On the Y-Axis you have your product, and your product is either bad or good. The X-axis is your marketing, and your marketing is either good or bad. So, if you have bad marketing and a bad product, you're in "Quadrant 4"; the bottom right. If you have good marketing and a bad product, bad marketing and a good product, or both good marketing and a good product, you're in "Quadrant 3"; "Quadrant 2"; and "Quadrant 1" respectively.

Products: Good vs. Bad

> We consider a product "good," if it converts. That is, when people see the product, do they buy? If visitors go to the crowdfunding product page, a high percentage of these visitors should pledge or contribute. On the other hand, we consider a product "bad" when it does not convert well, or not at all. In this scenario, even after many visitors go to the crowdfunding product page, there are few to no buyers. There's little to no demand for the product, so few people put in their money.

Marketing: Good vs. Bad

> The marketing is deemed "good" if it meets two elements: First, the marketing must drive A LOT of traffic to the crowdfunding product page. Second, the marketing must drive TARGETED traffic to the product page - people who then convert.

These are the four quadrants your crowdfunding campaign will fall under:

- Outer Darkness
- Black Hole
- Shooting Star
- Supernova

Outer Darkness - Quadrant 4: "Bad" Product "Bad" Marketing

Clearly the least desirable quadrant to be in. We'll wax religious here for a moment. Outer Darkness is a place you simply do not want to be. In Christianity, it's a place that sounds extremely painful and unpleasant and includes, "weeping and wailing and gnashing of teeth!"

When your Kickstarter or IndieGoGo Campaign combines a bad product with bad marketing, outer darkness is what you get. These are the sorts of ideas, inventions, or crowdfunding campaigns that are not even backed by your friends, family, or fools. You want to avoid this quadrant at all costs.

For crowdfunding campaigns that are Outer Darkness, no amount of marketing or ad spend will matter. If you find yourself in such a position, it's best to cancel your crowdfunding campaign; or better yet, learn how to NOT create an Outer Darkness campaign in the first place.

Black Hole - Quadrant 3: "Bad" Product Good Marketing

In reality, although we classify this as the second worst quadrant to fall under, a Black Hole might very well be the worst of all quadrants. A Black Hole crowdfunding campaign indicates good marketing but a bad product. When you combine good marketing with a bad product, your ROI is going to suffer. You're essentially throwing your money away, as if into a black hole.

No amount of marketing will ever produce the sorts of returns necessary to justify turning your crowdfunding campaign into an actual business. Generally, your crowdfunding campaign will not get funded, either.

Black hole products are sometimes difficult to target. At Funded Today, we have worked with a few. One example that comes to mind is Orka[58]. While this product might not necessarily be a completely "bad" product, there were elements of the project that were most definitely a "black hole."

For instance, while the idea was originally created because the Creator was getting headaches while working at a desk job, in the video and the story for the campaign, Orka was pitched as a way for athletes and active people to remember to be hydrated. Now, I don't know about you, but when I'm running or playing a sport, when I'm thirsty, I simply drink! I do not have to be reminded through an app on my phone to do so.

---

[58] "Meet ORKA, the Smart Water Bottle by Zach Thurston :: Kicktraq." 7 Aug. 2019, https://www.kicktraq.com/projects/999956853/meet-orka-the-smart-water-bottle/. Accessed 17 Dec. 2019.

Had the story remained true to why the product was originally hatched, perhaps the marketing would not have been for nothing. On this product, timing was also a problem. Orka launched following in the footsteps of the most successful crowdfunded "Smart Water Bottle" of all-time, HidrateMe[59]. By not allowing enough time to pass between the end of HidrateMe's Kickstarter campaign and Orka's launch, backers likely were not quite ready to back another product so similar. They already had what they needed. This made Orka a bad product, and no amount of good marketing could lead to good conversions. Ultimately, this campaign was cancelled by the creator.

Shooting Star - Quadrant 2: Good Product Bad Marketing

Of all the four quadrants at Funded Today, this one is actually our favorite. A shooting star crowdfunding campaign starts off with a good product, but the marketing simply does not last. It is fleeting, just like a shooting star. Therefore, we classify this type of case as having bad marketing but a good product. We like these sorts of crowdfunding campaigns because when it comes to marketing, we are the best in the world. If you have a good product, there's an extremely good chance that with great marketing your project will succeed.

Supernova - Quadrant 1: Good Product Good Marketing.

This is exactly where you want to be if you hope to raise millions on Kickstarter. Some of Funded Today's past

---

[59] "HidrateMe Smart Water Bottle by Hidrate, Inc. — Kickstarter." 18 Jun. 2016, https://www.kickstarter.com/projects/582920317/hidrateme-smart-water-bottle. Accessed 17 Dec. 2019.

clients who fit into this criterion are: BauBax Travel Jacket[60] (we helped them raise over $4.4 Million USD), and Pugz[61] ($1.43 Million USD raised).
In short, a supernova is an explosion of a star that briefly outshines an entire galaxy, radiating as much energy as the sun or any ordinary star is expected to emit over its entire life span. Normally, this "shining" and energy radiation lasts several weeks, or maybe even many months! That's exactly what you want to do during your 30-60 day crowdfunding campaign.

The Importance of Recognizing Your Quadrant

So, after reading about the quadrants, can you picture where your project might sit? It's important to have a good idea about which quadrant you're likely in because it can guide you when it comes time to decide where to put your time (see The Pareto Principle above). If your product isn't good, you should be putting your time into creating a product that is great - not in throwing money into something that has little chance of succeeding.

Yes, it's hard to admit when your product just isn't very good, but if your friends and family aren't responding well, we encourage you to seriously reevaluate. If people you talk to are enthusiastic and are excited about backing your product, then your probably aren't going to end up in the dreaded outer darkness.

---

[60] "The World's Best TRAVEL JACKET with 15 Features || BAUBAX." 15 Jun. 2016, https://www.kickstarter.com/projects/baubax/the-worlds-best-travel-jacket-with-15-features-bau. Accessed 17 Dec. 2019.

[61] "PUGZ-World's smallest wireless earbuds charged ... - Kickstarter." 23 Nov. 2016, https://www.kickstarter.com/projects/pugz/pugz-worlds-smallest-wireless-earbuds-you-charge-w. Accessed 17 Dec. 2019.

Imagine you've created this great highly cost-effective computer because your dream is to get it into the hands of people who live in remote areas so they can join the computerized world. But, you've neglected the fact that in many of your target areas they don't have electricity, much less the Internet. Well, your computer will do them no good, and no amount of marketing will make this a good product for them.

We are talking about this now because before you do any Pre-Launch marketing, you need to be certain that your product is useful and desirable to enough people. Remember **Chapter 4: the 7 P's**? Even the 7 P's start with product.

As you move further into your campaign and marketing, keep the quadrants in mind. If you know your product is being well received, but you're not getting enough people looking at your campaign page, or the conversion rate is too low, then reexamine your marketing.

Who knows, with constant tweaking and fine tuning, perhaps you can even shift your project into that Supernova quadrant.

Pre-Launch Marketing

So, you've just reestablished that your product is a good product, so you're not hanging in the outer darkness. Ideally, you should start marketing a campaign weeks before it launches in order to prepare as many people as possible to pledge to it during its first few days. These first few days are when campaigns normally enjoy a spike in "organic" attention, and your pre-launch marketing will synergize with that spike, ideally helping your campaign to surpass its funding goal as quickly as possible, which is a great advantage.

There's no "magic number" of backers or funds to arrange in advance, but more is generally better than less. Kickstarter research shows that any projects that are 20% funded within 48 hours are 78% more likely to succeed. Some additional data by Planting Justice suggests that any crowdfunding campaigns that are 30% funded within 48 hours are 90% more likely to get fully funded within 30 days. So, Indiegogo recommends arranging at least 30% of your funding before launching.

Warning!
Kickstarter doesn't' like creators donating to their own projects, and it uses sophisticated techniques to detect self-funding, so please don't do this!

Target Groups for Pre-launch Marketing

Personal Contacts

You should generally discuss your project with people whom you know as you develop it, so you can solicit their honest feedback, and also practice your sales pitch on them to zero-in on the best way to market your product. As your launch date approaches, you should prepare to mobilize as many personal contacts (family, friends, acquaintances, co-workers, old college roommates, etc.) as possible to support you, persuading them to commit to pledging to your campaign (whether to obtain a reward or not) as it launches, and then obtaining their permission to contact them at that time.

Even if each personal contact pledges only $1 each, this affects Kickstarter's popularity algorithm about the same as if they'd pledged $100 each, and a higher popularly ranking raises visibility, which increases "organic" pledges in turn. This is one task that you can't delegate very well to an agency. (For more details on this go to **Chapter 5: Triple F - The Single Most Important Prelaunch Strategy**).

Business Contacts

If you already run a business, and if your crowdfunding project will benefit people who resemble its existing customers, then you should contact those customers to invite them to pledge. You can also use their contact information to identify lookalikes to target with social-media ads.

Social-Media Fans

Social media, despite its name, is less used for socializing than for identity-construction, which renders it a useful tool for branding. However, branding, as we've mentioned in earlier chapters, shouldn't become a high priority during the startup phase.

For marketing crowdfunding campaigns, some entrepreneurs love to regularly share similar posts, without dumping too much content at once, across various company-owned social-media sites (especially Facebook), and perhaps even to run ad campaigns, in order to build active communities of followers. Such fans, just like your personal contacts, can both provide useful feedback about your product as you develop it AND help you to refine your pitching. However, they may prove relatively hard to mobilize to pledge after your project launches—in fact, your social-media followers are only a fraction as likely to read your posts as your e-mail subscribers are to read your emails. This is why, unless you plan to use Facebook Messenger marketing, you may want to focus your social-media time less on accumulating followers while sharing posts, than on running ads to build an e-mailing list.

Influencers

As for influencers, one way to find them is to upload a similar crowdfunding campaign's image to Google, and then perform a Google image search to see which sites featured that campaign. It's best to target influencers with sizable audiences who best fit your product or service. You might try to catch their attention by following them or adding them to a Twitter list before initiating contact with them.

It's best to arrange their cooperation well before your campaign launches - it requires time for them to receive a product sample, examine it, and prepare a review of it to release shortly after your campaign starts. If you want an influencer to return your review sample, then you will want to accompany it with a prepaid return label.

Reporters

We talked about press in Chapter 13, but we'd like to discuss it here as well. Some creators hire news release distribution platforms, but in our experience, such platforms don't normally produce good results because they communicate impersonally to "mainstream" news sources. Regular, personalized communication with niche news sources is far more likely to yield good results.

One way to identify good PR prospects is to search the Internet for similar campaigns (via name or image) and then see which sites reported about them. You can use sites like Alexa[62] to compare their viewership, but since your goal in crowdfunding is to raise funds quickly, it's generally best to target sources that don't necessarily enjoy the highest visibility, but that do enjoy the highest conversion rates (such as product directories).

Utilizing Email

Email Leads

Email leads have proven to be our single most effective form of pre-launch marketing. Such leads may be generated through showing social-media ads, especially on Facebook, to well-targeted audiences that arouse their curiosity enough to draw clickers to a landing page that will persuade them to provide their e-mailing address.

What to Look for With Your Email Responses

You will want to consider tracking:

- The Open Rate (OR)
- The Click Through Rate (CTR)
- Click to Open Rate (CTOR)
- The Conversion Rate (CR)

Open Rate

A great open rate (OR) is anything above 15%. 20% open rates and above are really great. So, if you have

[62] "Alexa." 28 May. 2019, https://www.alexa.com/. Accessed 16 Dec. 2019.

an email list of 10,000 people, expecting 1,500 people to open each of your emails is the industry standard.

Click-through Rate

Click-through rate (CTR) for email is the percentage of your subscribers who clicked on at least one link in your email message. To calculate CTR, simply divide the number of total people who clicked by the number of delivered emails, and multiply that ratio by 100 to arrive at your email CTR percentage. A good CTR is anything above 5%. Industry standards are roughly 2.5%. So, if you have 1,500 people open your email (at 15% OR), expect 500 people (At 5% CTR) to click through to your offer, or whatever your CTA (Call to Action) is.

Click to Open Rate

The best way to think about CTOR (Click to Open Rate) is to imagine, of those who opened your email, what percent found the content inside valuable and relevant enough to click on? CTOR can be calculated as: (unique clicks/unique opens) x 100. In the example above, if your email receives 500 clicks, and 1500 opens, your CTOR is 33.33%. Generally speaking, a good CTOR can range between 20% and 30%.

Conversion Rate

This is simple to calculate. If 100 people visit your website, and 10 people purchase, that would be a 10% conversion rate.

Email Leads: Landing Pages

Landing pages should use a memorable, short, and intuitive domain name, sport your company logo and name, function well on a variety of devices, and impress and inspire viewers with a professional design that looks consistent and authentic. You have to "hook" attention with a captivating tagline, and then simply and realistically overview your project by persuasively showing-and-telling about key features-and-benefits. You must also provide reasons to trust your campaign, although none of this should be done in nearly as much detail as your Kickstarter page.

You might want to incorporate a tentative launch date and countdown timer, and some positive quotations. Unlike your Kickstarter page, you can A/B test this landing page indefinitely toward perfection, progressing gradually from its vital generalities to its trivial details, which may give you some insight into which images and messaging will sell your project best later on.

Your landing page should persuade viewers to provide their e-mailing address so that they can be among the first to know when your campaign launches, and also enjoy a pre-launch promotion or an "early bird" discount - and it should *explicitly* invite viewers to do this.

Pre-launch giveaways normally attract more leads than post-launch discounts, but those extra leads usually suffer from lower quality. As you build your own e-mailing list, it's important to present its opt-ins with clear expectations about content they may expect from you, while refraining from violating those expectations with irrelevant content that influences them to lose interest in your communications.

Email Leads: Communication

After you've built your emailing list, you should remember that your leads will grow less likely to pledge if you allow too much time to elapse before you launch your campaign. You may contact your leads regularly before your campaign to nurture them, in order to help keep them warm, and possibly to solicit helpful feedback from them. This may involve a series of emails conveyed in conversational, story-like fashion (with "cliffhanger" endings), to keep your subscribers engaged.

For fundraising, you may want to contact your leads about 24 hours before your campaign launches to prepare them, during launch to mobilize them to pledge, 24 hours after your campaign launches to report its progress, weekly thereafter for its remainder, and daily again during its final 3 days.

You can typically expect about 2%-4% of these leads to pledge to an average-priced project, and maybe 6%-10% to pledge to an unusually-cheap project. After your campaign ends, you may want to continue to email your remaining leads either weekly or monthly, for as long as such communication proves worthwhile. Although email marketing has proven well-suited for nurturing long-term customer relationships for the last two decades, it is now yielding to instant-message marketing aided by bots, which is more conversational, involves less friction, and is better-suited to mobile-device users.

"Organic" Enticements

All of these other forms of pre-launch marketing will actively attract pledging visitors to your campaign page, which will raise your project's rankings (as measured by either Indiegogo's "GoGoFactor" or Kickstarter's various algorithms), which will render it increasingly visible to the worldwide crowdfunding community as its members actively browse projects. This increased visibility, combined with both an enticing image and title, as well as impressive statistics (like making rapid progress toward and beyond a minimal funding goal), will boost the flow of "organic" visitors to your campaign, along with their likelihood to pledge.

Kickstarter's popularity rankings, especially, are closely followed by many serial backers, which means that any projects that rise into this category's top dozen will normally enjoy a substantial boost in their daily pledges for as long as they maintain that high ranking; those popularity rankings are primarily determined by backers-per-day, and to a lesser degree, by both percentage funded and total funds raised.

Key Takeaways

- You should NOT focus on what you can't (or shouldn't) control, but on your own stewardship, as nobody is more responsible for your success than yourself!

- Success in business depends upon how well you serve both the market generally and the customer specifically, which should guide every business decision.

- Plan to regularly evaluate your own performance for that purpose.

- Follow the Pareto Principle - focus on the 20% of your efforts that will yield 80% of your results, and delegate your work as needed to competent specialists who share your vision.

- Customers are more likely to transact business with people (or companies) whom they know, like, and trust - so develop good inner character, and then convey it accurately to develop a good outer reputation.

- Always start improvement with your heart, and then work outward to your actions. Begin also with yourself, and then work outward to others.

- Marketing is most potent when others do it on their own, including via reviews or "social proof," but word-of-mouth is always both hastened and enhanced through your own marketing, especially while your business remains too new to have earned a clear reputation.

- Marketing can potentially multiply funds raised by your crowdfunding campaign, but it effectiveness is innately limited by even-more fundamental factors like your products or services, prices, personnel, presentation, and platform, which is why you should always prioritize these other factors.

- Crowdfunding marketing is both synergistic and recursive, so it's best to engage in all forms of it, while prioritizing your focus on its most effective forms.

- Pre-launch marketing synergizes with your campaign's natural spike in "organic" attention during its first few days, and it's helpful to get fully funded as quickly as possible, so it's good to engage in as much pre-launch marketing as your budget will allow.
-
- Post-launch marketing maintains your campaign's fundraising momentum after its initial surge in "organic" attention would otherwise dwindle, and it may include running skillfully-targeted, intriguing, segmented social-media ads (especially on Facebook), arranging cross-promotions with other projects, engaging in affiliate marketing, conducting public relations, appearing in newsletters, offering upsells to current backers, and posting content on social-media.

16

Analyzing Your Campaign

Be hard on yourself but indulge others.
Ryan Holiday

If you're not tracking and analyzing your campaign and the traffic coming to it, you're just guessing. You're guessing at what you think is working. You're missing the opportunity to test different aspects of your marketing. Sometimes, small changes make all the difference between failure and success.

Tracking your campaign traffic is not as hard as you might think. Kickstarter has made it simple to add your Google Analytics tracking code right from your dashboard[63]:

You'll want to get this set up and running BEFORE your campaign goes live.

---

[63] "How do I enable Google Analytics for my project? – Kickstarter ...." 13 Nov. 2019, https://help.kickstarter.com/hc/en-us/articles/115005135134-How-do-I-enable-Google-Analytics-for-my-project-. Accessed 18 Dec. 2019.

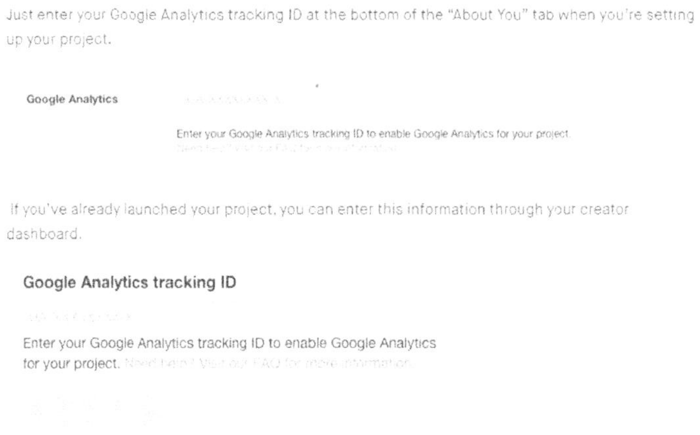

Just enter your Google Analytics tracking ID at the bottom of the "About You" tab when you're setting up your project.

Google Analytics

Enter your Google Analytics tracking ID to enable Google Analytics for your project.

If you've already launched your project, you can enter this information through your creator dashboard.

Google Analytics tracking ID

Enter your Google Analytics tracking ID to enable Google Analytics for your project.

Once you have it set up, that Google Analytics tracking ID will help you gather lots of useful data that you can use to improve your campaign and to understand what marketing is working… or what's not.

Your Google Analytics Primer

Let's start with some basic information about how Google Analytics works, especially with respect to your crowdfunding campaign. If you are going to continue in E-commerce, you will want to be well-versed in this, but we are going to cover some of the basics below so you can better understand how your campaign is doing through Google Analytics.

Google Analytics tracks website activity (according to Wikipedia[64]):

---

[64] "Google Analytics - Wikipedia." https://en.wikipedia.org/wiki/Google_Analytics. Accessed 17 Dec. 2019.

> Google analytics is used to track the website activity of the users such as session duration, pages per session, bounce rate etc. along with the information on the source of the traffic.

Go to your Google Analytics account at analytics.google.com. If you don't have one, set it up now[65]. To start collecting basic data from a website[66]:

1. Create or sign in to your Analytics account:
   Go to google.com/analytics
   Do one of the following:
   - To create an account, click Start for Free.
   - To sign in to your account, Click Sign in to Analytics.

Set up a property in your Analytics account. A property represents your website or app, and is the collection point in Analytics for the data from your site or app.
Set up a reporting view in your property. Views let you create filtered perspectives of your data; for example, all data except from your company's internal IP addresses, or all data associated with a specific sales region.
Follow the instructions to add the tracking code to your website, so you can collect data in your Analytics property.

Your crowdfunding page is your website.

---

[65] "Google Analytics." https://analytics.google.com/analytics/web/. Accessed 18 Dec. 2019.

[66] "Get started with Analytics - Analytics Help - Google Support." https://support.google.com/analytics/answer/1008015?hl=en. Accessed 17 Dec. 2019.

The Google Analytics Menu

If you go to your Analytics account and examine the menu in the top left corner, you'll see that your GA (Google Analytics) data is organized into a hierarchy of folders. Its topmost folders represent accounts, and each user normally has only one- although, in our case, we have a growing list of accounts (either that we've created or that our clients have shared with us in part) for monitoring our various clients' webpages.

Within each account folder, you can create subfolders for each one of your "properties" (for example, one for their Kickstarter webpage, another for the Indiegogo InDemand webpage, and yet another for your product website, et cetera), each with its own individual GA tracking ID number. Within each of these property subfolders, there will be at least one (default) "view" of the data that Google Analytics is collecting about that site, from which you can create other customized views as desired.

If you select this menu's property for your crowdfunding webpage, and its' default view of data about that property, then you can start exploring it. You'll be welcomed by an "Audience Overview" page that presents some basic information, and it includes a menu in its leftmost column that allows you to explore this data further. This menu's Real-Time submenu allows you to watch visitors come and go from your page in real time, and its Audience submenu can also show you some helpful demographic data (such as genders, ages, locations, and interests) about the sort of people who visit your webpage and/or pledge to your project, not only generally, but also specifically from your ads.

We've observed that interest data isn't often very useful, since it remains fairly steady from one campaign to another; however, there are rare exceptions, such as when it helped us to see that Breton's business-style backpack was finding unexpected popularity among college students who preferred something more classy than average to carry their textbooks. (And, by the way, you will normally observe an unusually high pledge rate from Virginia's Ashburn area, where Kickstarter's Internet servers are located.)

Traffic Sources

What normally interests us most, and what may also interest you most, is found in this view's Acquisition submenu. If you click on "Acquisition," then on "All Traffic," and then on "Source/Medium," you'll see a webpage that features a list of sources (along with their respective source-types) for your webpage's visitors. If you don't see this entire list, then you may use a pull-down menu in the lower-right corner to display additional rows of data for additional sources of visitors.

You may also adjust the timeframe shown through another more-complex pull-down menu in the upper-right corner, although you can't examine your data for time-periods smaller than a single day. By default, this list of sources is sorted by Sessions (total number of webpage visitors from/through that source), but it may also be sorted in other ways, including by either Ecommerce Conversion Rate (pledgers/visitors) or Revenue (total dollars pledged). Or even Bounce Rates, which are normally very high for crowdfunding pages, since their visitors normally "bounce" elsewhere without visiting any sub-pages unless they're interested in pledging. Due to these high "bounce" rates, all GA data about time spent viewing your page may be inaccurate.

In this list, you'll see "direct / none," which is a broad category that includes not only people who visit your webpage by typing in its address character-by-character (or by copying-and-pasting it) into their Internet browser, but also those who select that address either from their browser's bookmarks or from its list of previously-visited webpages, as well as those who visit your webpage from any other source that GA can't easily identify, which includes referrals from certain secure webpages, as well as from some (not all) search engines, some (not all) e-mail providers, and various mobile applications. Along with "direct / none," you'll also see "google / organic," and perhaps some other "organic" entries, which represent those visitors who find their way to your webpage through various Internet search engines.

If/when any of these referrals return to your webpage on another occasion, then they'll most likely be categorized as either "direct" or "organic" visitors rather than "referrals." GA's Model Comparison Tool submenu can provide an approximate estimate of the percentage of ad referrals who pledge on their first visit versus the percentage that return on another occasion to do so; we've noticed that, for every 100 ad referrals who pledge on their first visit, another 15-50 (or more) ad referrals may return later as either "direct" or "organic" traffic to pledge, which means that GA will normally under-report the full effects of ads. Plus, GA doesn't account for synergistic effects between ad pledges and pledges from other sources.

We've noticed from extensive experience that, for past campaigns with which we've successfully partnered, our ad referrals will normally pledge at a rate of at least 1-2% (depending upon average pledge size), while "direct" traffic will normally pledge at a rate of at least 6%, although there are other factors that must be considered also. Along with these E-commerce Conversion Rates, we believe that an even more important quantity is Per Session Value (which is also known as Earnings Per

Visitor or EPV), and we've noticed that successful partnerships normally involve EPVs of at least $1 for our ad referrals and about $4-5 for "direct" traffic.

Note: We are giving values that we've experienced over time to give you something to compare to.

If these values are relatively low for our ad referrals but not for "direct" traffic, then it could indicate that our ad targeting needs improvement; if these values are relatively low for both our ad referrals and direct traffic, then it could indicate that your product is relatively niche, or that either your product or your presentation is not as good as it could be.

If you suspect that your page-design could use some improvement, then you're welcome to visit our **Ultimate Crowdfunding Page-Design Analyzer** (please see Resources), and you're also welcome to consider hiring our creative team anytime, either to revise your existing media, or to provide professional consultation at an hourly rate.

Toward the top of this page, the blue line chart normally shows only webpage-visitors per day, but you can use the second pull-down menu—the one that reads "Select a metric"—toward the upper-left corner to select E-commerce > Revenue so that this chart will display dollars-pledged per day, as well. You can have this chart display various other sorts of data over time, as well, but both Sessions and Revenue will likely interest you most.

Learn More

If you want to learn more about how Google Analytics works, then we'd highly recommend visiting the official Google Analytics Academy[67] webpage to watch some of its free training courses.

Kickstarter also has some articles to help you utilize Google Analytics for your campaign.

This primer is enough to get you started. The good thing about collecting traffic data is even if you don't understand it all, you have it. When it comes to data, having it is always better than not having it.

We highly recommend that you keep an eye on your analytics multiple times per day, so you can get a feel of trends and ways that you can improve your marketing to boost your conversions.

With data collection, 'the sooner the better' is always the best answer. **Marissa Mayer**

---

[67] "Google Analytics Academy." https://analytics.google.com/analytics/academy/. Accessed 18 Dec. 2019.

17

Creating a Campaign that Won't Get Banned

80% of the results come from 20% of the causes. A few things are important; most are not. **Richard Koch**

Remember earlier in this book when we spoke about being invested in success itself, rather than in one idea? It's important to keep that in mind, especially when your campaign hits a snag, or you end up having to relaunch or begin again with a new idea.

Most people don't realize this could happen. Many creators come into their campaign and think, "Of course this is going to succeed, everyone is going to love it. They're all going to bow down to the product and give me all my money because my product is absolutely amazing."

That's the dream, of course, otherwise we wouldn't be putting in sleepless nights, capital, and many sacrifices, all to bring an idea to fruition. The reality is: campaigns fail about twice as often as they succeed. When we say fail and succeed, we're just talking about hitting the funding goal. Some people might hit a goal at $50,000, but really in their mind, they wanted to raise $200,000.

You have to realize going into this process that failure is normal, so don't set yourself up. Realize that people might buy and people might not buy - you really don't know. One of the great ironies we see in crowdfunding is that the people who go on to raise a million dollars very often are the people who are like, "Holy smokes, I thought I was going to raise $75,000, maybe $100,000. This is blowing my mind!" Then there are the people who are like, "Ah! my campaign is the best, I'm going to raise a million, I'm going to raise five million!" and they get $3,000. All this to say… failure is normal.

Your job is to ask enough questions and get all the feedback you can. We find that Crowdfunding backers are generally very willing to provide you with feedback about your product, the problems with your product, your price, your platform, your funding goals, your reward structure, your timing, your media, your marketing, or something else. The only way you can really fail is to not be honest, and to not gather enough information so you can go forth with an improved product (or a new idea altogether).

Remember, bad feedback is still good feedback, because it's letting you see where to improve.

Voluntarily Relaunch

Now, in some cases you can easily solve any problems without ever needing to relaunch. Sometimes it's confusion about what people are getting, or sometimes it's a too-high price point and you can lower the price while your campaign is still live. However, in other cases, your problems may be serious enough that is actually best to just completely start over.

Believe it or not, this can be an amazingly effective strategy. When you launch a new campaign, most often you're going to see a spike in organic attention during the first few days of your campaign, and it's nice to get a second chance if you didn't have everything right the first time. This is especially true when your products, your prices, your goals, your timing, or your presentation all need serious revision.

Part of being a good creator is to recognize one's tendency to become so entrenched in your own product that they can't see things honestly. That's why fresh perspectives are vital. Listen to the feedback you get. Use it, and change aspects of your campaign accordingly. There is no shame in a relaunch, and it may end up being the best thing for your project.

On Kickstarter when you cancel your project, you lose your campaign information. So, before you cancel, get all your backers names, phone numbers, and any other information you can, even if you only have 50 to 100 backers. Those 50 or 100 backers are going to be your first, earliest supporters for a successful relaunch. It's important to gather that info as best you can. Connect with them and say something such as, "Hey, it didn't work out this time and my plan is to relaunch a month from now," or "I'm cleaning up the following things based upon the feedback that all 50 of you gave me, and I want you to be my early supporters. I'm going to give you the early bird discount when we relaunch. Can you please give me your name, email, phone number, so that I can let you know the moment we launch?"

You can cancel your campaign, and still do updates through the platform, but you're limited to that.

Campaign Suspension

Sometimes you don't have that luxury to voluntarily cancel your campaign. Occasionally, out of the middle of nowhere, you get a dreaded email alerting you that your campaign is going to be suspended. In general, this is a 48-hour warning. So, even though your project is doing really well, your campaign may be cancelled, and you'll have to relaunch after addressing whatever issues there are. "Involuntary Cancellations" arise because platform staff on Kickstarter or Indiegogo believe that you violated their rules.

Here is what it says on the Kickstarter site[68]:

> A project may be suspended if our Trust & Safety team uncovers evidence that it is in violation of Kickstarter's rules, including:
>
> Misrepresentation of support, through self-pledging.
>
> - Misrepresentation or failure to disclose relevant facts about the project or its creator.
> - The creator provides inaccurate or incomplete user information to Kickstarter or one of our partners.
> - The characteristics of the creator account overlap with the characteristics of backer accounts that pledged to their project.
> - A party related to the creator is posing as an independent, supportive party in project comments or elsewhere.
> - The creator is presenting someone else's work as their own.
> - The creator is offering purchased items, claiming to have made them.
> - The creator or an affiliated service is spamming potential backers with promotional materials.

---

[68] "Why would a project be suspended? – Kickstarter Support." 20 Dec. 2019, https://help.kickstarter.com/hc/en-us/articles/115005139813-Why-would-a-project-be-suspended-. Accessed 26 Dec. 2019.

- The creator is repackaging a previously created product, without adding anything new or aiming to iterate on the idea in any way.
- The creator has outstanding fulfillment issues related to a previously successful crowdfunding campaign

- Projects may also be suspended if they were approved through 'Launch Now' but, on closer inspection, do not fall within our rules.

Kickstarter does warn against making exaggerated claims, such as saying "the world's best," or "the world's fastest xyz" because in reality, that is likely not a true claim.

Once a project has been suspended, it can not be unsuspended.

When a project is suspended, funding stops, and all pledges are canceled. Everyone is notified via email[69].

So, obviously, you want to do everything you can to avoid having your campaign suspended. That's why it's key to know their rules[70] and keep them in mind.

Here is a quick example of one of our clients who did a follow-up campaign on Kickstarter after Indiegogo. They put in a larger battery in their product as well as a few

---

[69] "What happens when a project is suspended? – Kickstarter ...." 24 Oct. 2019, https://help.kickstarter.com/hc/en-us/articles/115005136354-What-happens-when-a-project-is-suspended-. Accessed 26 Dec. 2019.

[70] "Our Rules — Kickstarter." https://www.kickstarter.com/rules. Accessed 26 Dec. 2019.

other changes, but they didn't make those changes very obvious. So, Kickstarter sent a notice of cancelation. In this case, the client was able to explicitly point out all the changes to Kickstarter staff in order to avoid being cancelled.

Also, DO NOT run multiple campaigns at the same time. If you try and do a bunch of campaigns on a platform all at once, Kickstarter won't like it. They want you to fulfill one product, and then another, and another. Trust us, it's smart that Kickstarter does that. They don't want you launching 10 different projects at once, because it's hard enough to get one off the ground, and if you're trying to spin three or four different projects at the same time, you're going to have even more difficulty. More difficulty is bad for the platform, because then people think you scammed them, when in reality you probably just had a difficult time bringing new business to life. So, this is a case of "it's for your own good."

Kickstarter understands that's some campaigns will fail, and they want to mitigate the chances of that as much as possible. Some creators in certain categories will create a new campaign, say, every six months. This means they have to deliver on a lot of campaigns. Even though the prior one is still in production, Kickstarter is fine with them launching again.

These are serial creators, and if you can deliver and do what you say you're going to do, you don't have to worry about how many campaigns you launch as long as it's one active one at a time.

Just know upfront that you can't foresee all the issues that could put your campaign at risk of suspension. We have had the opportunity to prevent many campaigns from being suspended, even on short deadlines. We've dealt with more suspensions than anyone else, just because we work with more campaigns than anybody else in the world. We speak from experience when we say that, sometimes, you can pull the campaign out of the proverbial ditch.

Remember the Kuroi Hana knives we talked about earlier in the book? We ended up raising a million or two by marketing them to every country in the entire world. Then, out of the blue, we got a letter that Kickstarter has frozen the campaign and they're about to suspend it. Basically, Kickstarter gives you a 48-hour notice saying they're going to suspend your campaign - here is what you need to do. With the knives it was "Hey, you're violating German Law!" It was a little nuisance, and because of the German law, Kickstarter was going to suspend the campaign.

During the next 48 hours, with many international calls and such, we were able to solve the problem by having the client reword their campaign a bit. Sometimes it is that simple.

Just know that cancellations happen, and you often won't see it coming.

Of course, the more successful your campaign is, the more people are seeing it, the greater the chances that someone, somewhere, might see an issue. That's okay. You fix it if you can, and if you can't, you do a relaunch when everything is resolved.

We have never caused a campaign to be suspended from something we have done, in part because we always market honestly and ethically. You should absolutely do the same. People don't expect your product to be perfect, but they do expect it to be what you say it is.

Indiegogo seems to be a lot more lenient when it comes to suspensions. That being said, we still recommend Kickstarter over Indiegogo, because the Kickstarter Suspension Policy, as much as we wish there was a little more transparency, does create a lot more trust. That trust leads to long term retention of backers, and long-term retention of backers means that you're going to have more people who back more projects, just like yours.

We hope involuntary cancellation or suspension doesn't happen to you, but if it does, here is our Involuntary Relaunch Checklist.

Involuntary Relaunch Checklist

1. Determine the reason for the cancellation.

If you can't, because the email doesn't make a lot of sense, then you are going to need to follow up insistently to get more details.

Here are some of the common reasons we've found for campaigns being suspended:

If the cancellation is due to the fact that you are running multiple campaigns (which as we've said is a no-no), then you need to cancel the other campaign and send an email such as: "Hey, sorry Kickstarter. I didn't know this was a rule. I had a campaign on Kickstarter/Indiegogo, and I have just cancelled the one on X platform, are we good now?"

If the cancellation is due to inadequate prototype section: "Hey, I'm sorry about that. I just updated my prototype section; here is a thirty second unedited, untouched, unfiltered video that shows exactly how my product works. Are we good now?"

If the cancellation is due to you using renderings, rather than actual photographs (again, don't do this!): "Hey, sorry, I've replaced all the renderings with actual photographs, are we good now?"

Copyright infringement allegations - we'd say, "Why are you trying to copy Disney or Marvel?" Don't do that! We don't want to get preachy, but it's simply not a good idea. It will get your project suspended. Here's the truth - there are no secrets. So, anything shady or dishonest is going to be exposed. Please don't go buy a product and tell us it's new from Alibaba. That's never going to work long-term, and somebody else is going to do the same thing and kill your margins, so you're not going to make any money long term anyway.

Also, don't sell your product on your website, or anywhere else before you go to Kickstarter or Indiegogo. They don't allow that, and they're going to catch on. They have entire teams of trust in safety that look into things if your project becomes successful. Now, if you want to launch your project, you don't raise any money, nobody is going to know anything because it doesn't matter.

Kickstarter is not always very forthcoming about the reasons for cancellation. You have to email them a bunch, and usually they want you to figure it out.
They don't want to tell you why because they think you should know.

Yes, sometimes campaigns get cancelled by mistake. This happened to our client "Lobster Bag" - they did nothing wrong. They got suspended and were aggressively emailing Kickstarter. Fortunately, Kickstarter realized their mistake, admitted their mistake, and let them relaunch.

But most of the time a cancellation is because you did something wrong and you weren't honest with Kickstarter. But if you truly don't think you violated any of the reasons you can't think of, the best way is to email Kickstarter. You can contact them at support@kickstarter.com or legal@kickstarter.com and start asking them, "Hey, I need to know what happened here." If you are nice and they haven't suspended your campaign immediately, they will send an email and say, "Hey we're going to suspend your campaign, you have five days to correct XYZ." Sometimes they'll do that for you, if your violation is not an egregious violation of their rules.

2. Appeal the decision.

If you believe or you know that they've made wrong determination, then you need to present Kickstarter with the evidence, including you messages from their own team showing that your project complies with its policies. We've even had campaign where somebody had a product on Indiegogo that didn't work, and then they relaunched on Kickstarter and they said, "Hey, is it okay if I relaunch on Kickstarter? Here's why I'm doing it." Somebody from Kickstarter said, "Yes, you could do that!" and then a week or so into the campaign, Kickstarter said "Hey, we're going to suspend your campaign."

So, you have to show Kickstarter your evidence so they can look at it objectively and say, "Okay, they are in compliance, it was a mistake on our end."

Look the reality is we're all human. Businesses are human in the sense that they make mistakes because it's people who are running them, or if it's algorithms, it's people who wrote the algorithms, and they make mistakes. So, if it's their mistake, you need to present evidence to help them see that it was their mistake. Now, if Kickstarter has already suspended your campaign, you need to understand they will not reinstate your campaign under any circumstances. We hope that might change in the future, because sometimes they have made mistakes, and they're like, "Oh, oops sorry, that was our bad. Tough luck…?"

But, if your campaign has not already been suspended, then you might be able to avert that action. So, please note that although Kickstarter may be callous, they are honest. If it says that they'll cancel in 48 hours, then you'll use the 48-hours to figure out what to do, or how to pursue an appeal.

3. Contact your Backers.

This is especially important we talked about this earlier. If suspension is certain, you need to inform your backers, because usually when you're suspended Kickstarter doesn't let you talk to them anymore. You want to maintain their trust as much as possible. So, you should be the first one explaining what is happening, honestly, and with transparency. This is going to come across a lot better than if their first notice is the Kickstarter automated email that's sent when your project is suspended or canceled, that basically says "this person has violated xyz", and they immediately think you've done something terrible. If you haven't done something terrible, it's good to let them know that you haven't.

So, to reiterate, if you do get a notice of forthcoming cancellation, contact your backers immediately and explain. Do your best to get their contact information so you can reach out to them again, after you've cleared up any red tape.

The backers can still message on the board, and have a discussion, but you can't participate in that, and you can't send any of them a message. So, if you haven't contacted them, the backers are left in the dark and you end up with a bunch of people on the Internet who have no concrete information, only suspicions. You know how that goes, right? It's not going to turn out favorably for you.

4. Preempt the Cancellation

If suspension is certain but hasn't already been implemented, then preemptively cancel your own campaign after you collect your backers contact information. Doing this before Kickstarter/Indiegogo suspends you looks a lot better. It's a painful thing to do, but sometimes it's the right action to take.

5. Reconsider the platform you're launching on.

If you could negotiate a way to satisfy Kickstarter's requirements in order to relaunch on its platform, it's actually worth your effort to do so. So, maybe they're saying, "We're going to suspend it, and you can't get out of it, but we'll still let you relaunch on our platform."

Or maybe it happened, and you didn't have time to notify your backers, but you can still relaunch if you can talk with Kickstarter and settle things to their satisfaction. Otherwise, you can usually transition to Indiegogo instead. Over the past few years, Indiegogo has become a little stricter, but there are a lot more open and understanding, and their customer support is usually more willing to lend an open ear.

One thing we love about Indiegogo is their ability to distinguish what level your project is at. As in, this is still just a dream, an idea in your head, or whether you've got a prototype and much further along in the process. So, Indiegogo will literally put their money where their mouth and say "This product is so good, we've reviewed everything, we've looked at their prototypes, we know they're going to ship, and we're going to ensure that if you back this project, you will get your product."

6. Remobilize your Backers.

This is the point of why you contact your backers in step 3. After you relaunch your campaign, contact your original backers, persuade them with discounts, and let them know that because they stuck with you through thick and thin, you're going to hook them up on your next project.

This is your tribe of people who decided to stay with you even after a cancellation or suspension and they help you get that initial upon launch momentum that propels you to Kickstarter trending magic and all those good categories you want to rank in. By doing that you have a much better chance of ranking higher in the platform and getting organic and direct pledges from the platform Kickstarter/Indiegogo themselves.

7. Resume your Marketing.

Proceed as before. You don't have to do anything different on the marketing side of things. Do what you need to for a strong relaunch.

Conclusion

You're always going to run into hiccups when you launch a business. This is something to have on your radar, and make sure you keep everything above board. Even if you're doing everything above-board and you still run into these issues, follow the steps above.

As an entrepreneur, you need to have both passion and faith. You should also remain humble enough to accept correction. Excessive and misplaced confidence can impede your ability to persistently learn and improve toward success. Remember, don't commit yourself to a single idea as much as to the idea of success itself. That's how you can best serve in this everchanging marketplace.

Key Takeaways

- Creators should remember that failure is normal, avoid any irrational expectations, stay humble enough to progress, work hard, and resist discouragement.
- Creators should solicit feedback from backers (and perhaps others) anytime campaigns are not performing ideally, and use it to determine how to improve.
- Creators shouldn't fear to re-launch campaigns whenever they need serious revisions in their product, timing, goal, or presentation – and, in doing so, creators should keep their backers fully informed and treat them similarly to pre-launch leads.

- It's important for crowdfunding campaigners to both know and follow the rules for their respective platforms, and to render it sufficiently obvious to reviewers that they're doing so.

- A campaign's relative popularity statistically increases the likelihood that people will notice any rules violations that merit suspension.

- Kickstarter is notorious for sometimes suspending suspicious campaigns without either warning or explanation, and it will never reinstate suspended ones for any reason whatsoever—but it does make mistakes, and creators can sometimes negotiate with it to re-launch.

- When faced with suspension, determine the reason, appeal this decision, inform your backers, preempt the cancellation if possible, re-launch on Kickstarter if possible, remobilize your backers upon re-launch, and then proceed as before.

Need help? Reach out and hire us at Funded Today.

18

Delivering on Your Campaign

***To attain knowledge, add something every day. To attain wisdom, subtract something every day.* Lao Zi**

When you're starting a crowdfunding project, the first step is to ensure you'll be able to scale - that your manufacturers who can meet the demand of your crowdfunding campaign. If your manufacturers can't meet the demand, you are guaranteed to run into problems.

This is why nearly 65% of all crowdfunding campaigns have delivery delays, and why some never end up fulfilling their promised reward. Crowdfunding creators need to be able to have manufacturing partners that can handle a wide range of order sizes, as your order will depend on the result of your campaign.

If you knock your funding goal out of the park, you'll obviously be ordering a lot more units than anticipated. This is what causes most manufacturing problems for creators. If you're really looking to crush a funding goal, take these steps to understand how you can ensure your manufacturing is scalable, while knowing ways to cut manufacturing costs and lead times.

Manufacturing Overview

"I've Got a Prototype!"

This is one of the most exciting steps in your project's progression. If you're planning to launch a crowdfunding campaign, and your prototype was made in-house, you're in for a rude awakening: you need to find a real manufacturer.

We know creators who think they want to keep manufacturing in-house or think launching with their homemade prototype is a good idea. Unfortunately, it isn't, and will cause failure in the long run. What you want to do if you've developed a homemade prototype is find a manufacturer who can produce it on a larger scale. What you learned from your homemade prototype are the basic production functions and materials needed to produce your product.

The prototyping, making sure that you have something viable and manufacturable, is critical. This is a step that some people skip over but in order to have a successful project this cannot be overlooked. In other words, having a cool concept is not enough.

Yes, this can be a bit of a chicken-egg issue. Sometimes you have to raise money to make a prototype, or even see if there's a market demand for it before you even go build it. This is where Indiegogo has different categories for what stage you're in. Are you just at the idea stage? Or are you manufacturing? Currently, Kickstarter doesn't really have that, and it can be a difficult dilemma. You might spend $20,000 to build some prototyping, and then you launch a campaign, and then you realize, "Oh, there's no demand for it." Then on the flipside, you could launch a campaign, raise half a million, and then realize, "I can't even create this thing!" It's tough.

Finding a Good Manufacturer

One of the hardest parts of starting a crowdfunding campaign is the process of finding the right manufacturer. With so many possibilities out there, sorting through them all can be a nightmare. This is why it's important to have a systemized approach to understanding who your manufacturer should be.

To start your search on the right foot, you should understand the following characteristics of your manufacturers:

Scalability

With the uncertainty of scale on a crowdfunding campaign, you're going to need manufacturers who can act fast and be prepared for bigger production runs than expected. If you really knock your crowdfunding goal out of the park, the right manufacturer will be happy to face the challenge of meeting this new demand.

Most manufacturers nowadays are familiar with or have at least heard of crowdfunding and Kickstarter. Some will even track the progression of your campaign so they can be prepared for the order of what's to come. There are some manufacturers who don't, so you're going to have to keep them updated along the way.

Use of Existing Molds

Try to find a manufacturer who has produced near identical products to the one you're looking to produce. This will help to cut lead times dramatically and save thousands of dollars. In some cases, this will enable you to use their existing mold, so you don't have to spend more money or time opening your own.

Finding a manufacturer who has an existing mold you can use is the way to go when possible. Opening a mold can cost thousands of dollars and take weeks to complete. You need to be specific about the product you're looking to produce, and conduct a thorough search to find this manufacturer. If your product is truly one of a kind, then it is not likely that you will be able to find a manufacturer with an existing mold you can use.

Location Analysis

While most of the world's manufacturing happens throughout Asia, there is some scalable manufacturing to be done in America. The difference between Asian and American manufacturers is stark. Not only will your experience differ drastically, but so will your cost.

Most of the time I recommend manufacturing in Asia, unless your company to going for the "Made in America" marketing approach. This has been big on Kickstarter and many fashion oriented campaigns have struck attention by trying to bring manufacturing back to America.

For most products though, economically speaking, manufacturing in Asia will make more sense. The value of our currency and the cost of labor dictates the reason why producing products abroad is so cost effective. The American Dollar is currently equal to 6.88 Chinese Yuan and 64.47 Indian Rupee.[71]

You can understand why the labor costs are cheap when you know the Chinese factory worker is getting paid an average of $2 USD an hour, compared to over

[71] "USD - X-Rates." https://www.x-rates.com/table/?from=USD&amount=1. Accessed 2 Jan. 2020.

$23 USD in America. The cost of living is also much cheaper in China.

When you're looking to produce products like watches, or backpacks, labor is your main cost outside of the raw material. The cost of labor in countries throughout Asia is always going to be cheaper than in America.

Your Next Steps

Once you've found a good manufacturing partner, it's time to move forward through the manufacturing process. The first step for any product is getting an actual prototype made.

To get your prototype made, you're going to need to have all the specifications set. Specifications will vary per product. For example, when creating sunglasses, you need to know the following: the material of lenses, the material of arms, colors, size and shape, logo, logo placement.

The more complex your product, the more detailed specifications you'll need.

Once you have the specifications for your product set, it's time to start producing a prototype with your manufacturer. For clothes, this could take less than two weeks, but for more technical devices, this can take months.

The key to a smooth prototyping process stems from communication. You need to be on the same page as your manufacturer. This means you should be speaking with them a few times per week, to ensure your product stays top of mind for them.

Once you have a prototype, make sure you've sampled and tested it thoroughly.

Most manufacturing production runs work on a payment basis of 30% due upfront, and 70% due once production is complete. If your campaign has already reached that production run, it could be smart to put that 30% production deposit down to get production started.

This all depends on the cash you have on hand. If you don't have enough money to put 30% down, you're going to have to wait until you get your money from Kickstarter. This can take up to two weeks after your campaign is finished so make sure you build this into the delivery timeline.

Preparing production for your crowdfunding campaign is essential to success. If you don't know how you're going to produce your products at scale before launch, you're going to end up shipping those products late, if you even ship them at all.

When launching a campaign, you should be trying to knock your funding goal out of the park, which means your manufacturing is vital because the last thing you want is to face backend manufacturing troubles when everything else is going your way.

Production: FAQs

1. At what point in a crowdfunding campaign should a product creator start seeking a manufacturer?
Prior to even finding the right manufacturer, you should have a working prototype which you've either made in your own garage or made by someone else. Already having a prototype can eliminate a lot of miscommunication with a potential manufacturer. Once you have something in hand, you can really illustrate your product points and what it does.

2. What should you, as a creator, already know, or have before you approach a manufacturer? You need to have your idea narrowed down. "I want to make this gizmo. It should do this, this, and that, and solve this problem. I would like it to be made of this material." Knowing these things is a good starting point.

3. How can you best identify your options and choose the right ones? Sort of like knowing when you have the right mechanic for your car - you just know it. Communication and trust are the founding pillars of any type of manufacturing. It doesn't matter if it's in China, USA, Germany, France, or wherever. If you can't get on the same page, or speak the same technical language, and don't understand each other's requirements, it doesn't matter who your manufacturer is- you'll never get something you want.

You can't be working with a manufacturer that makes you worried they're going to steal your idea, or wonder if they are actually going to fulfill your item. Finding the right manufacturer is really tricky, and it's really product-specific now. It is doable to do this online. You can go to www.madeinchina.com, or Google it, or go on a site like

Alibaba, and hopefully you get connected with the right person.

Of course, everything you see is online. Getting recommendations from others who have used a manufacturer at least gives you some firsthand knowledge.

Then there are companies, like “The LGG Corp”[72] whom we work with. They help product creators to transform their concepts into prototypes, to put their prototypes into mass-production, to warehouse their manufactured products, and to ship those products worldwide.

Beware of going through middlemen who won’t reveal where the factories or manufacturers are that they work. If you do this, you’ll always be held hostage to their information.

4. Why is Asia so popular for manufacturers? People are attracted to working with China and Asia, because it’s cheaper and often faster than most U.S. factories. And just to clarify, the tariff is only applied on your cost of goods and your cost of shipping - and this must be built into your profit margin.

5. What are the biggest concerns about manufacturing overseas and how do you resolve those? it's not taxes, or anything like that - it's the unknown. Most of us don't know anything about China, or how to work with a company there. We don’t know who to contact or how to speak their language. And then there is the idea of sending thousands to someone you don’t know, and wondering if you’re actually going to hear back from them. These fears are resolved by what we mentioned above - trust and communication.

---

[72] "The LGG Corp." https://www.thelggcorp.com/. Accessed 2 Jan. 2020.

6. Do you need to patent ideas before seeking a manufacturer? We strongly recommend that you do, though it's not a must. For the content creator too, it does provide some basic essential protection, so that if anything happens then you can take it to court. Something we recommend even more is to seek a patent in China. With a Chinese patent, the Chinese factory can actually read it, and they wouldn't attempt to steal the idea because they won't want it to be a legal problem later. It's more enforceable than a U.S. patent. Also, you can take that to Border Control in China, and then restrict exportation of the product, and that's more powerful than anything else.

Another important document you should look into is an NNN. This is a particularly good governing document that a lot of factories respect. An NNN is A Non-Use Non-Disclosure and Non-Supervision document. Basically, they cannot take your IP and can't make a product that is like yours.

7. How long does it take to develop an idea into a working prototype and what are you looking at, in terms of a range for costs? Every project is different, of course. In general, if you are further along in your idea, then processes are quicker and cost less. If you just have a general concept on the back of a napkin, it might cost more and take a little bit more time,
To give you a generic idea, here is a timeframe from our friends at the LGG Corp[73]:

From "here's the idea," we need a prototype. Can you make it? If this is your starting point, then you start with creating a professional technical drawing or sketch – this keeps everybody aware of what it looks like, what material

[73] "Crowdfunding Prototypes & Mass-Production - Funded Today." https://www.funded.today/podcast/crowdfunding-prototypes-massproduction. Accessed 2 Jan. 2020.

will be used, what the specs are, etc. This step takes around 5 days.

The next step is to take the 2D Sketch, or CAD, and make a 3D rendering - a 3D model that is photo-realistic. This typically takes 7 - 10 days. From that 3D model, the prototyping process begins. At LGG, they use SLA, which is state-of-the-art. This gives you an exact one-to-one model, no rough edges. This gives you a physical product that you can actually evaluate right. Typically, the printing process with SLA it's about 5 days.

So that's roughly 3-4 weeks, if there's no major showstopper.

Remember, your prototype needs to meet the minimum viability requirement for Crowdfunding.

And, again, just as a reference, the typical cost behind a functional prototype is anywhere from $5,000 to $8,000 for typical project.

Once you get your 3D model into a real prototype you can use that for an opinion group, or social media feedback. This is the magic of a good prototype - you actually get the item exactly the way you want it, and you can field test it. This is where you want to catch all the mistakes so you can improve your product from the get go. Essentially, you need at least one working prototype- that's just to prove it to yourself. You really need three to five prototypes, for market study and certifications. Some of your product might need certification, especially in the electronic world. You will need to send a physical working prototype for them to get a jump on it. If you wait until you can send the complete manufactured version, that's going to add some time, 2, 3, maybe 4 months to your clock, and that's how people get in trouble. You can't start your package design until you have a prototype.

Like all other aspects of crowdfunding, OUTSOURCE any aspect of this process that is not up your alley. All these steps are too important to not do well.

8. How much does it cost upfront to get a product ready for mass production? There's the cost of the mold. We've heard creators say something like, "Hey, we got quoted like $30,000 for the mold - is this right?"

No, absolutely not. When you first approach manufacturer, they don't know if you're actually going to take this product to fruition, so instead of wasting their time and working for free, they'll bite you on the mold so it costs three or four times more than what it should cost. Be aware of this possibility.

You will also need to put a down payment for your production, depending on the complexity and the cost of manufacturing, it can vary from 30% to 50% down from what you want to make.

9. How can you minimize delays, or even avoid failures in fulfillment? We know that around 65% of successful Crowdfunding campaigns suffer delays in fulfillment.

Why? Inexperience. You have to meet with somebody that knows what they're talking about, as far as manufacturing. You have to build in a timeline that includes contingencies, and then you have to develop a realistic timeline based on expert advice that includes, give or take, one to two months.

Knowing the contingencies is important. For instance, if your manufacturer can produce x number of units per month, what happens when your demand goes well beyond that? Is the plan to have a second mold made? Will that be cost effective in the long run? There's a fine balance between production time and long term business.

What's the best way to keep a certain level of quality control? Ideally, you should have a go-to person that you connect with at the manufacturing end who is the project manager. Whatever title that person has, and no matter how many units are being produced, the goal is to have the quality remain at a certain level.

We also strongly encourage you to do third-party verification. At the early stages of working with a manufacturer, or whomever, get a third-party verification done. As you build trust, as the project goes further and further, then you can lean off a little bit. There are firms out there that will do a QA or QC check for you, or they'll go inspect your products. They'll just make sure that everything is running. You pay them on the side as a third-party, and they'll inspect whatever you need inspected.

10. What about certifications? During the engineering prototyping phase and the manufacturing phase, someone who knows what they are doing should be looking at your product and trying to anticipate what the certification needs are going to be. For example, a specialty toy might need some Child Certification and Safety Certification before it could be exported.

Or, an electronic product with wireless capability might need the FCC Certification. So, long story short, you make sure that whoever you are dealing with has the right information so you can get ahead of the game, before the product is finished, or even before the manufacturing. Double check that these things are actually being done, don't just assume.

11. What are some tips for logistics and shipping? If you are shipping into the U.S. you will need a broker's agent to clear customs. You should have a bond. Yes, it is an option to ship your product somewhere and do fulfillment yourself, though it might not be the best usage of your time because once you start labeling, packaging and sending thousands and thousands of products, it can get old real quick. You might think you're saving money but remember, time is money. There are a lot of other options these days. Experts in these areas can often save you a lot of money in the long run, so make sure you've done all your research.

Key Takeaways

- Crowdfunding campaigners should develop their concepts into working prototypes before starting to raise funds to mass-produce them.

- Creators should ideally patent their ideas, both in their own country and in their manufacturer's country, before approaching a manufacturer — and should hire manufacturers through an NNN agreement to minimize their risk of their ideas being stolen.

- Creators should consider manufacturing in Asia due to lower costs, may use tools like Alibaba or Jungle Scout, or conduct in-person visits to explore manufacturing options for their type of product. They should avoid profiteering middlemen like sourcing agents, and should consider both communication and trust when choosing among viable options, plus the ability to accommodate unpredictable order sizes during mass-production phase.

- Some manufacturers (like The LGG Corp) can help creators through all phases of production by providing cost-effective professional services, like vetting concepts for viability, sketching them, rendering them, engineering or designing them into beautiful working prototypes, creating molds to mass-produce finished products, designing manuals and packaging to accompany these products, mass-producing and then assembling all of these items properly, warehousing them, shipping them worldwide, and handling legal requirements throughout this process — and it's advantageous to hire a single agent for all of these tasks, so they can become intimately familiar with the product.

- An average product may require several thousand dollars over 3-4 weeks to be transformed from concept to prototype, which creators may then market-test and perhaps iteratively refine—and it's ideal to make all errors during prototype phase, while it's cheapest to correct them.

- Creators should ideally produce at least 3-5 final prototypes for various purposes, which may include durability testing, product certifications, media production, user feedback, reporter reviews, and packaging design.

- Crowdfunding campaigners should avoid being overcharged for molds for mass-production, and should expect to pay 30%-50% upfront for mass-production.

- Creators can encourage high-quality mass-production through both effective project management and hired third-party inspections.

- Although manufacturers may ship finished products temporarily to creators to store and then mail to consumers, creators may hire professional fulfillment agencies like ShipMonk to perform these tasks, instead. It's generally both cheapest and fastest for creators to hire a manufacturer (like The LGG Corp) that performs these tasks.

19

Building a Company Post Campaign

By then I knew that everything good and bad left an emptiness when it stopped. But if it was bad, the emptiness filled up by itself. If it was good you could only fill it by finding something better.
Ernest Hemingway, A Moveable Feast

When you launch your product on Kickstarter or Indiegogo, the hope is always to raise a lot of money. The more the better. Of course.

However, your crowdfunding campaign might not do as well as you'd hope. Consumers may not buy your product in droves, and you might not hit your crowdfunding goal. Here are three critical lessons to understand if your crowdfunding campaign doesn't go as well as you had hoped.

3 Lessons from Kickstarter

1. View Kickstarter as a place for validation, not just as a platform for fundraising.

When we think of crowdfunding, we readily think of raising funds for a new product idea. The word "funding" is in the very name of "crowdfunding." Yet, if you view crowdfunding as simply a platform for raising funds, you miss half the picture.

Crowdfunding is like a two-sided coin. One side of the coin is money. On the other side of the coin is a product validation.

When you run a crowdfunding campaign, if your flip doesn't land on the side of money, that's okay. It can even be advantageous. How, you ask?

Entrepreneurs can spend year after year working on a new product idea and trying to make it work. Because they are slow, or delayed in getting to market, they can waste hundreds and thousands of dollars in both time and actual out-of-pocket cash. They can waste even more in opportunity costs.

Crowdfunding allows you to quickly and cost-effectively validate whether there is a market for your product. This is invaluable in both time and money. As MasterCard might say: "One failed Kickstarter – $4,565. Business validation in less than 6 months – priceless."

Truthfully, quick business validation on a product that has no future, is priceless!

So, if your crowdfunding campaign is a flop, learn from it. Take what lessons you can, pivot, and move on to the next thing.

2. Be Committed to Success, Not Your Product.

Yes, we've mentioned this *a lot* before - the most successful entrepreneurs are committed not to their product idea, but to success itself. For an entrepreneur, especially a first-time entrepreneur, being committed to success, and not the product, is a critically important distinction. (And very hard to do, which is why we are repeating this truth).

Beginner entrepreneurs are affected, even plagued by what we call entreumyopia. Entreumyopia is when an entrepreneur believes his or her new product idea 'IS' the most amazing product ever, and 'WILL' revolutionize their industry. They don't just think that this new product idea 'may' or 'can' or 'could be' amazing and make lots of money, but that it 'IS' and 'WILL.' Any suggestion to the contrary is dismissed as ludicrous and ignorant.

Truth: most business ventures fail. Yes, your new product may turn out to be incredible, and become the best ever, but there is, yes, there is a chance it won't turn out that way. That's okay.

Successful entrepreneurs don't only know success. They fail, get up and go at it again in a new way. Learning quickly that your idea isn't as great as you imagine is a blessing because the faster you learn that the faster you can move onto an even better idea.

When we're committed to a particular idea or product rather than to the idea of success, we tend to chase that singular thing much longer than we should - which usually translates into lost time and money. When you are focused on success and the idea that it may take more than one idea to help you generate this success, then you can leave a failing venture, pivot and move upward.

An untested idea is just a potential business, not an actual business. So, don't get too attached to anything. Keep at it until the market responds en-masse with a resounding "yes", by opening its wallet and giving you money for your product.

3. You Get Better with Practice, So Be Patient. Your Next Campaign Will Likely Be Better.

If your crowdfunding campaign fails, don't worry. That's perfectly fine. During the first go-round you will always learn the most, and when you come back with your next campaign, you'll most likely do better. Here are some pretty powerful examples, both outside and inside of crowdfunding:

- Barack Obama ran for the U.S. House of Representatives in 2000 and lost 60% to 30%. Yet, he later ran for and won the U.S. Senate in 2004, and the U.S. Presidency in both 2008 and 2012.

- Similarly, Bill Clinton ran for the U.S. House in 1974 and lost. He later became the U.S. President.

- George W. Bush ran for the U.S. House in 1978 and lost. He later became the U.S. President, as well.

- As one last example, Ryan Grepper of Coolest Cooler launched his first Kickstarter in December

> 2013. He only raised $102,000 and didn't reach his funding goal. He then relaunched in the Summer of 2014 and raised over $13 million.

The campaigns in which they "lost" weren't lost causes. They all learned how to better run things the next go-round. It's cliché, but it's true: "If at first you don't succeed, try again."

There is more to Kickstarter than raising money. You're also launching a crowdfunding campaign to validate your product idea. If it's a home run, run with it. On the other hand, if it's not even a first base hit, pivot to a new idea, and keep going until you hit success.

Post Crowdfunding - Getting Started

If you have the idea that you'll run your crowdfunding campaign, then have your website ready to go to continue selling your product and everything will be awesome, you may want to rethink that strategy.

The first bit of advice we'd like to share is to not get bogged down in the details. Yes, you are going to need to set your professional website and hosting, along with your Google Analytics, Facebook Pixel and Google AdWords pixel. BUT - it doesn't really matter if you're on WordPress or Shopify or whatnot. It's easy to get stuck on questions such as which hosting is best, or do you need such and such a WordPress plugin. Or maybe you need to be on Shopify.

In short you can end up with analysis paralysis. To avoid this, it's better to focus on "getting the things done that need to be done." If you don't do this you are in danger of what we call playing at business rather than actually doing business. Playing at business looks something like this:

> *You spend all your time wanting to be an entrepreneur, faking it like you're an entrepreneur, but you're never actually doing things entrepreneurs do. You just build and tinker away, and never really create anything of value. You just build, build, build, build, build, and never sell, sell, sell, sell, sell, and never do anything related to actually turning their idea into something you could be truly proud of.*

Yes, it's more comfortable to just build rather than take action. We get it, we've done it. Both of us (Zach and Thomas) have been in exactly that spot.

The first thing is to think things through and have a realistic expectation. Everyone thinks their babies are the cutest darn things in the world and it can't possibly be ugly and the market can't possibly not want it. But, even when your product does sell well, you still have to be able to see outside of that- because running a business is a lot more than just having a great product.

Not everything you touch will turn to gold. Look at the great companies of today such as Amazon and Google. Look at how many new ventures they've rolled out that have completely failed right, flat on their face even with their resources and branding. Take a look at Tesla. Their quarterly earnings statements sometimes have a huge loss of millions and millions of dollars. The next quarter might show some profit. The point is, even when they're successful, suddenly they're not.

When you're on Kickstarter or Indiegogo, you're tapping into the community of that platform, the support of the platform. It creates this idea that you're always going to have that return, when the reality is that you're always going to have your best returns, in terms of ad spend, when you're on a platform. The platform itself is giving you additional traffic, organic traffic, that's why you launch on those platforms, and place your products on platforms like Amazon.

If you ever work with Funded Today, you'll hear us talk about "Positive Externalities" all the time. You might spend a dollar to track for a dollar, but overall, you might track for $3 or $5 or even $6 or $10 if you have something that is converting really well. That extra $2, $3, $9 or whatever it is, in addition to your ad spend, is that positive externality that comes from being on a bigger platform like Amazon, Kickstarter, Indiegogo, or that sort of thing.

Once your crowdfunding campaign is over, it's important to recognize that your cost per acquisition on your website is almost always going to be lower than it was on the crowdfunding platform.

Your USP - Unique Selling Proposition

We always talk with our clients about a "USP" - "Unique Selling Proposition." When you set up your website, you need to be able to look at that page, specifically the top fold, and know in just a few seconds what it's about.

Back in the day, in newspapers it was called the "top fold" because the big headline was right there on the fold, before you opened it up. That determined whether you want to read the newspaper at all, or perhaps open it up or continue reading, or just throw in the trash. Anyway, the top fold of your website is the part you see before you even scroll. You have to have it set and optimized for mobile devices, iPads, desktops, as many devices as you can.

You USP has to be readily visible, available, and clear. What are you selling? Why does it matter? The viewer needs to know this in the first three seconds.

This is especially useful for a startup, for a new business that doesn't have a brand reputation. If you went to McDonald's website, you don't need to know what McDonald's is because everybody already knows. If you go to Apple's website, it doesn't need to say "Hey, we create cellphone gadgets and earbuds!" Right? So, where you're at, and how much the industry knows about you and who you are, is going to influence how specific your messaging needs to be.

So, if you go to apple.com they will have the unique selling proposition targeted to their latest product, not about the company in general.

We look at a lot of websites. Too often we go to one that sells, say, watches, and we want to know what's unique about their watch. But we can't really tell. That's not good. Now if you're a B2B (business selling to business) and your audience knows who you are, then maybe it doesn't matter as much.

We still see websites where we don't even know what they do, or what they are about. Then, if someone is willing to spend the time (and most are not) they can go to the about page to find out more. Bottom line, you don't want to make people have to work to know who you are, what you do, and most importantly, how to buy from you. You need to build a good website that makes all this easy.

Price Point & Cost Per Acquisition

To recap, a conversion rate means if you had 1,000 visitors come to your page, and you had a 10% conversion rate, 100 of them will purchase your $1 product.

A typical E-commerce conversion rate is very roughly from 1% - 4% depending on your price point. Imagine you have a product that sells for $1. You have to be able to run pay traffic for less than a dollar, and then, even if you had a 10% conversion rate, that's an incredible conversion rate.

When you have a lower price point, it's harder to be able to generate traffic profitably. On the flipside, as an example, if you have a product that you're selling for $3,000, and you're able to get clicks, or traffic, for $0.30 per click. You could spend $1,000 in marketing and generate 3,000 clicks and you can have less than a 1% conversion rate. If you just get one sale, you generate so much money and revenue.

So, the lower the price point, the harder the business. Typically, a price point under $20 makes it a little bit harder, though still feasible. But, if your price point is low, you might want to think about how you can have bundles, or up-sells, or cross-sales. If you have a price point that's $50, $100, or $200, it's going to be easier.

Of course, you can't just randomly set a price point. You need to know your market, to realize what similar products are currently selling for. It's also good to know the typical CPA for your product and industry. As a reminder, the CPA is your cost per acquisition. That's a metric that's not always going to be readily out there, but it's something you need to look at and evaluate.

For example, if you're selling Uber as a service, not as product but as a service, you need to know what the spend needs to be to acquire a new customer. You need to know the cost per acquisition.

Customer Lifetime Value Point

A service like Uber is interesting when you talk about CPA. They spend, spend, spend, spend, spend, have negative net revenue, negative net profit forever, but then they reach the tipping point where they've acquired enough customers now to handle their ad spend, to handle their Cost per acquisition, because of their residual income.

In this case, Uber falls under a "SaaS" because even though people aren't necessarily paying a monthly fee, they're using the service several times per day, so it acts the same as a "software-as-a-service," or a residual income model. Eventually they reach a break even, and then even a tipping point where they start to become profitable from a revenue standpoint.

Even though you may not be selling a service like Uber, it's important to consider, because we are talking about your customer lifetime value. It might cost you $100 to get that customer, but how many SKUs do you have, how many different products do you have that they might buy?

So, you're spending all this money to bring potential customers to your website. If you can think in terms of "multiples," multiple SKUs, multiple channels, multiple products, customer lifetime value. Think, "Where else can I create value for my customers so that they'll open up their pocketbooks and give my business more money?" This is always better than just selling them one thing.

As a business owner, think this through, and decide what CPA you are aiming for. What's your industry going to look like, what is your product going to look like? If you can generate a new customer at cost, that's not necessarily bad when you think in terms of lifetime value. Depending on your strategy and your growth goals, of course.

Go back to the Uber example. Your strategy can be all about growth right now, because you have capital and don't need immediate profit. Maybe you just want to dominate a market, and growth is the way to do that. But, if you're just bootstrapping it, and it's all about profit, you really need to be cognizant about what you're doing.

You don't want to be in a spot where you can't spend money to make money, otherwise you don't have a business.

You do not have a business if that's the case, because you can't spend money on Facebook Ads or Google AdWords, drive traffic to your website, and get new customers and make it profitable. You are at a stalemate with yourself.

This is worth repeating. If you can't spend money to make money, you don't have a business.

Very often, the Kickstarter creator has an idea to start a business, but only has one product idea in mind. One of the key takeaways here is that entrepreneurs, business owners, need to think in terms of multiples.

When we worked with "The Basics Wallet" campaign, it was just "The Basics Wallet." For all we knew, that was all they were ever going to create. Then, they rebranded, probably a little bit late, and became Nomadic, now a lifestyle brand and with a wallet, a watch, backpacks, travel gear of all kinds, and other things. They realized you can't necessarily make a living selling one product. Honestly, a wallet is pretty ubiquitous. Everybody could potentially use one. You need those multiple SKUs.

If you did one product on your crowdfunding campaign, and that's all you want to do, that's fine. Just beware, trying to turn that single thing into a business (unless you're one of those anomaly products - keep reading) is not the best path.

If you get nothing else out of this chapter, we hope you get the mental strategy of thinking, "What else can I sell? Where else can I bring value to this idea that I've created?"

Yes, of course. There are exceptions. There are products you can run an entire business on. For instance, the "LastSwab[74]." It's basically a reusable "Q-Tip". Something like this may be an anomaly to what we're talking about here. This is one product where it might be all you need to sell, because every person on the planet has probably used a Q-Tip, or a cotton swab before, right? Go back to our formula for success - ubiquity, plus innovation or tech, plus a cool compelling story, gives you a huge chance for success. Well, the LastSwab has all this. They've got the ubiquity covered, everybody and their dog could use a cotton swab. They've got the innovation covered, because now you literally can use the same cotton swab forever, instead of buying that pack of 1,000 that everybody usually

---

[74] "LastSwab - The Reusable Cotton Swab by ... - Kickstarter." 29 Nov. 2019, https://www.kickstarter.com/projects/193289139/lastswab-the-reusable-cotton-swab. Accessed 3 Jan. 2020.

buys. The story is pretty amazing, too, because they've created a product where they are trying to improve the environment by helping to keep the landfills from filling up with used cotton swabs.

However, even they probably have some ideas for a future product, or something that can go along the lines of great ideas, innovative products that protect the environment, but are also solving huge problems, and then creating multiple SKUs, multiple products based upon whatever that brand or company represents.

The reason behind all this talk of multiples is that if you have one product that you're selling, if you can acquire and generate a sale at cost, meaning you spend $50 on marketing and you're able to generate a sale for $70, but then you have maybe $20, and COGS (Cost of Goods Sold), your manufacturing, shipping, etcetera, you're at a break-even point - not making any money but generating a sale. That is a valuable, valuable thing - to have that contact, to have that email, to then be able to sell them additional products if that customer likes your brand and likes your product.

If they like you, if they resonate with your brand, if they like your original product, you now have the customer lifetime value. You have a customer who is free to you to sell whatever else you want to sell in the future, who is probably going to trust you because they had a great first experience with your brand or company.

Cross Sells & Upsells

Right away when you gain a customer, you can offer an upsell or a cross-sell. An upsell would be the same product but just a higher quality- it would be like going and buying a new car, but they upsell you to the next model up. Still the same car, but now you have automated windows and a better engine. A cross-sell would be, sticking with the car example, when they sell you "car washes for life for an extra $200", or leather protection for your seats.

So, a cross-sell isn't the same product, it's something that's complementary. It's good to have those in your business. You might not know what they are right away, but you'll discover what those are over time.

For instance, the iPad did not exist when Apple came out with the iPhone. iPhones didn't even exist before smartphones, which didn't exist when Apple first came out with the Personal Computer. These are complementary products, and will continue to evolve. You don't have to have it all at once, but it's good to be thinking about that.

Your Strategy & Multiple Channels

Another thing you need to be thinking about is multiple channels. You never want to have just one of anything, just one credit card processor, or just using PayPal, because what if they freeze your account and all of your sales dry up because you can accept payments, or your funds are frozen?

Really, this is all about how to make your website a cash machine. You don't want just one avenue for sales, either.

You might think selling from more places than your website can detract from your web sales because people can purchase this elsewhere. This will make your web sales suffer. Yes, you can look at it this way.

But, let's look at one of our clients, which is the BauBax Brand we've mentioned before. The travel jacket raised over $9 million on Kickstarter. They got picked up and were placed in airports all around the U.S. This is only when they had one product, now they have multiple SKUs, multiple products. They were spending money, driving traffic to their website even though it was at a break even, even at a little bit of a loss, because they knew we were running so much marketing, they're getting their brand in front of many, many people. Ys, directly tracked on the website did not generate a lot of money. But if they looked at what's happening in the retail stores, it was actually increasing the sales.

Again, there is not a one-size-fits-all solution. That's why we are giving you different examples and ideas - so you can find the best fit for your business. In contrast to BauBax, if we're not mistaken on this, Nike actually had an opposite strategy. Their brand is so prevalent, and so strong, that instead of running marketing to try to drive people to retail locations, they made a push to really focus in terms of increasing the profit to their own website, because they have a much bigger profit margin when selling direct-to-consumer.

In Nike's case, they already have the brand, everybody knows who Nike is, so that growth and branding is not as critical for them. Rather, they are saying, "Hey, how do we increase our profit in this day and age, where brick-and-mortar stores are going out of business? Where malls are going out of business? What's our new strategy? What's our new game plan? Let's take the stuff and drive more of the traffic back directly to us."

Now we're back to, what's your strategy? Is it growth or is it profit?

Having multiple channels will allow you to be able to have your website be a cash machine. If you only have your website with one product it's going to be incredibly hard - if you're selling just one wallet on your website, it's going to be super hard to scale up your marketing for your website.

In fact, if a potential client comes to us and they only have one product, and all they have is a website, most of the time we say it's not going to work. Unless, again, it's an exception, that unique niche that has high demand and low competition. This at least means that it's possible.

If your product is a "me too", and you're competing on Google AdWords with a lot of other advertisers, and it's only a one-time purchase like a wallet, the odds are really stacked against you.

If it's something people like, and can buy again, and again, and again, for 50 years, or more, including their kids, then you have something. The point is that if you have that, you have a lifetime value. Whereas if you have a one-time product that once people buy, they're not going to buy it again, and you're only selling on your website, it's going to be super hard to get that.

That doesn't mean you can't still make it a profitable business. Perhaps on Amazon you'd be able to rank higher and get that traffic and those sales, because of organic traffic and SEO.

So, again, every strategy is different, but the key takeaway is to think in terms of multiples.

Here's another type of strategy. Our very first client at **Funded Today,** the "RooSport", owned by Brenda and Earl Brundage has, essentially, leveraged the power of

Expos, Expositions, and Tradeshows, to sell their product. By doing so, their website, their Shopify Store, their Infusionsoft setup, all of that actually generates a spike at the end of every single expo.

It might only be a couple thousand dollars, but we've seen it as high as $10,000 before. This is because they give a little coupon code, something like 10% off, or 5% off something, depending. It's just a little insert, "Hey, did you like this RooSport? Do you know somebody else would like one? Here is our website." So, they get a pretty good return.

They might spend $10,000 on an expo, and then make $20,000 over the weekend. But then, they get that huge spike at all these expos, and after you've been to 500+ Expos (which might be an understatement for them), it's serious money.

Their website is constantly getting sales from all over the country, even internationally now in Canada and some other places where they've been, because of all these little coupon codes that they've distributed around the world.

Just because there's foot traffic from all these expos and tradeshows, it works. So, don't discount some of these old-school strategies of expo, to website, to long-term customer value, because they can be exceedingly beneficial and profitable.

Compare that to if they only sold on their website. No doubt, it would be an entirely different picture.

So, back to you. Think about it - your strategy and the multi-channels, multiple SKUs, multiple sales, customer lifetime value. That's the power of creating a website that is a cash machine.

Embrace Your Email List

How can you leverage your list properly, and what does that even mean… "Embrace Your Email List"?

There are maybe a handful of ways that you can get traffic to your website, or perhaps to your app. The first would be if you have a brand like Facebook, or Uber, or Amazon. It's a service and, even though on Amazon you're buying things, it's a service to help you with shopping. So, people just naturally come back because of what you're providing.

If you're an E-commerce store selling a product or service, there may not be a reason for them to come back after they've made a purchase.

Then there is SEO, depending on how you rank for certain keywords. For a new startup, for a small medium size business, usually an SEO Strategy is going to take longer to build out.

Now, you're left with paid traffic, as well as your email list. We've already talked about "paid traffic," where your spending for clicks, whether it's on Facebook, Google, Pinterest, Twitter, or anywhere else. But you're paying for the clicks to get to your website that cost money, and yes, it's "Guaranteed Traffic," but it's also guaranteed to cost you money.

So, one of the most guaranteed ways to drive traffic back to your website at virtually no cost is your email list. Once you have that email list, yes, you'll have attrition, yes, people might not be interested or opt out, but generally speaking, you will be able to send out an email and you will have between a 10% to 20% open rate. Of course, that varies by industry. You can Google to find Average Open Rate, Average Click Through Rate, and include Mailchimp in the search - Mailchimp has pages that show results of millions of emails sent for different industries which will show you benchmarks, what you can expect.

With that information, you can see if you have an email list of 10,000 people, and you know you have a 2% click-through rate, you can guestimate that if you send out an email, you'll get 200 visitors to your website. Over time you'll know, on average, that 5% of your past customers will buy. Then you can say, "Okay, I know I can send out an email and generate 10 sales on average, and maybe my average price point is $200 bucks. So, I'm going to generate $2,000 from every email that I send out."

Now, this is where you also need to have multiple products, multiple SKUs, because if you just have one product, and all you do is send out an email saying, "Hey, check out this product!" you won't have repeat buyers. Maybe if you already have a wallet, you now have a different design, "Hey, we just came out with this new design!", or "Hey, it's Christmas, we have this promo! Buy one for a friend."

You can run so many different campaigns with email marketing. The power of that email list is that once you've captured a customer email, you can continue to market to that individual, to that potential customer, again, and again, and again - at virtually zero cost to you.

A Note on Ownership

We'd also like to give you a little master takeaway on this point. We want to talk about "Ownership."

It's really easy nowadays to spend money on Facebook, and generate lots of clicks. Before it was really easy to do that on Google, and not necessarily spend a ton of money through Google AdWords, (PPC) Pay-per-Click, that kind of thing. Facebook's kind of the newer avenue. Then there's Snapchat, Twitter, Pinterest, and Reddit. There are lots of other places, too, where you can spend money to generate clicks. The list will grow, the list will change.

But here's the thing - you don't own those assets.

Facebook could go away (remember Myspace?). But, with your email list, no matter what happens, no matter what becomes the next Facebook, or the next Snapchat, or the next Twitter, or whatever, you can take that email list with you, and use that to build up that new community.

Whatever becomes of the next social media platform, or whatever is beyond social - Artificial Intelligence, AI, Virtual Reality? Who knows? The point is that a lot of times as entrepreneurs, we don't think in terms of ownership, and we don't think in terms of assets.

But be clear on this – your email list is an asset.

As an example of the power of the email list, Indiegogo's email list is their strongest asset, and likely the main thing that keeps them in business. All the thousands of creators that use Indiegogo's platform have sent millions of backers to their campaign, and Indiegogo smartly and wisely has captured those backers and given them a good experience on the platform. Then they email them a couple times a week and say "Hey! I know you backed this campaign, you might also like these campaigns."

That simple strategy continues to make Indiegogo hundreds of thousands of dollars every single time that email gets sent out. At **Funded Today**, we're the same way. We have lots of different email lists, with hundreds of thousands of subscribers, and we continue to build our email list because we realize the power of email in the sense that it is an asset that you own. You're not renting it like you are Facebook, and you're not borrowing traffic like you are from Google AdWords on Pay-per-Click. That's a very powerful distinction, and something every entrepreneur needs to do. Email is UNDENIABLY one of the most powerful assets that a company controls.

Your Brand

The other, and perhaps the strongest asset for any company, is their brand. For example, when you can buy two competing shoes, and one's Nike, and one's another brand, you go with Nike. This is because the brand is so strong, and it has trust. That trust means that often we are willing to pay the extra money to get the brand: Nike (or whatever it might be).

As an internet marketer, as a startup, as an entrepreneur, you likely at this point do not have a brand. But, even as a small medium, even a large business, you want to track your marketing (called "Direct Response Marketing") from the beginning. For every dollar you spend, you want to know how much you're raising in revenue. You always want to track your return on your marketing. Branding, historically, is hard to track - how do you gauge that?

So, when you are a start-up, yes, you are building your brand, but that should not be your focus. It's simply not smart to focus on branding without caring about how that's affecting yourselves or your bottom line. In other words, keep the idea in mind that you are, OVER TIME, developing a brand, but your marketing should go directly into increasing your sales, not improving the public's perception of your company.

Even at **Funded Today**, we didn't start really "branding" until pretty recently, and we are a strong company. We were in the Inc. 500, we were the third fastest privately held company in Utah, and number three for advertising and marketing. We did all that without ever focusing on the branding angle. As we said earlier in the book - we can be running successful marketing for a client who says "Hey! I don't like that, that's not my brand!" And we always tell them, "You don't have a brand yet."

So, as you start up your business, realize that you *are* building your brand right now, but your focus needs to be on revenue. Having marketing with this flashy branding does not generate any sales, and is going to get you nowhere.

Generate a lot of revenue and deliver a great product to your earliest adopters. That's how you start to build a brand.

Conclusion

Even though we talked about that fact that this is not as easy as it might look, you can't just throw stuff on your website and hope for the best, don't ever let that discourage you from starting a business. If anything, there's always going to be hurdles to have to figure out, and that's the power of starting a business right, because the greater the barrier to entry to a new product, new offering, the better chances you might have to succeed because other people will have the same issues trying to get into the space.

Key Takeaways

- Entrepreneurs should reject "entreumyopia" to embrace realistic expectations, including the fact that all startups will face challenges, but that greater challenges will precede greater rewards.

- It's good to offer your product or service on your website, but it's better to enhance that website with effective analytics code, optimized sales media that emphasizes your unique selling proposition (USP) to maximize your website's conversion rate (which is typically 1%-4%), and both SEO and persuasive marketing (which will be harder to do profitably for cheaper items) through ads, email, affiliates, et cetera, to help draw paying traffic to itself.

- Collecting customers' email addresses and then remarketing to them via e-mail can help you to build a beneficial, long-term business relationship with them, while obtaining additional sales from them at low cost. All of this can maximize their lifetime revenue to your business.

- Your initial business goal should be to achieve profitability through a breakeven CPA at minimum, which will be worse than it was on Kickstarter and may require you to spend capital at-a-loss for a while to build a sizable-enough customer base—and you should wait until your business is more mature before starting to develop its branding, which yields results that are harder to quantify.

- Your business can grow better by offering multiple products and services through multiple channels, with multiple payment methods, et cetera, as well as offering cross-sells and upsells.

Bonus Section: That Legal Stuff

The obligatory disclaimer: this is for informational purposes only and is not designed to replace an attorney. We recommend you consult with an attorney for any questions, concerns, or specifics related to the legalities of your product or business.

We get asked about legalities a lot because this is something people worry about, so here is some general information based on our perception and experiences.

First and foremost, our goal is not to bash attorneys. In fact, Thomas (co-founder of Funded Today and co-author of this book) is an attorney.

Here it is in a nutshell: your goal as a startup is to start up - not to let potential legal issues paralyze you from even beginning. You need to decide for yourself what time frame, and how much money, is acceptable for you to spend on legal services – as well as if there is an actual need.

Really, the way we see it - just move forward with getting your product out there. If somebody tries to rip you off, who cares? The best product is going to win, and you're going to compete in the marketplace. So, just go - that's our advice. We say this because time and again, seriously, 10 or 15 years later, somebody's still talking about this great idea and they've never done anything about it because they are focused on potential legal issues.

Many people worry about having the patent, trademark, or copyright, and they don't even know if they have a product that people want to buy, or that the community and the market wants to purchase. If you don't have that, it doesn't really matter. So, don't spend all of this time doing legal stuff before you even have a product on the market. (If you feel like you have a good reason to, then do it. Again, we're just giving you our experienced perspective).

Time and time again, we've found that one of the biggest hurdles when people are starting a business is the worry about not being able to afford an attorney, and they believe there are all these legal issues they need to take care of upfront.

Again, as we said above, it's usually not necessary. In fact, most of the time it's better to get product market fit ***and then*** figure all that stuff out. You can always do things like slap a trademark on there.

Thomas is fond of saying, "usage matters the most." That means if you can prove that you were using a product before anybody else, then you can always go back and do things legally, if you create a business that is massively successful. At **Funded Today** we originally registered the "Trademark Funded Today", and we don't even know if we'll renew it when it comes up, because it's just not necessary, even for a company of our size.

Now let's clarify a few of these legal points for your general understanding.

Patent

A patent would be for some type of widget, for how something functions, or a design patent for a design of some product. And a patent would cost you probably around $20,000 to $30,000 - higher or lower depending on the size of the firm. We're in the United States, and you can also get what's called a Provisional Patent. A provisional patent, as the name implies, is not a final patent, just a provisional filing. That's usually around $5,000 with attorney fees, and it's good for one year. So, it doesn't have all the bells and whistles of the patent, but it's basically enough information describing what the patent is. You would need a chat with a patent attorney, but in our experience, that's roughly what your costs would be.

Trademark

The Trademark would be your brand name. So, your brand name could be **Funded Today**, or it could be the name of a product, anything where you want to say, this is my trademark. Once you have the trademark, you would be able to prevent others from using that same name in commerce, to avoid confusion. For instance, none of us can go create a business or an E-commerce business called Amazon, because that would cause confusion in the marketplace.

For anyone on Kickstarter or Indiegogo that wants to transition and be on Amazon, you do need a trademark for being in on Amazon. By having a trademark, you can register with Amazon's brand listing. When you're on Amazon's brand registry, it unlocks a feature called "Enhanced Brand Content" on your Amazon Listing. This enables you to put images, and additional text and really make your listing come alive and substantially boost your conversion rate.

A trademark can take eight months to a year or more to go through the whole process, so you want to start that now. It's not super expensive, like a patent. The filing fees with the trademark office are usually $225 to about $400, depending on what you do, and you can use LegalZoom[75]. You're going be paying $199 for the

---

[75] "LegalZoom." https://www.legalzoom.com/. Accessed 2 Dec. 2019.

LegalZoom service, and then about $225 for the fee. It's not going to cost you an arm and a leg.

Copyright

A copyright is not really going apply to too many of you reading this book, since it applies more to book authors, writers, and related types of work. We're not going to dive into that, but a copyright is more your text, and what you've written, such as this book.

The Law Won't Make You Money

The law never makes your company money. The law is something you simply have to do to operate in a framework that will allow you to move forward.

That's it right? The law doesn't make you money, well, unless you're a lawyer. A caveat to that might be if you have a patent, and then you enforce it against somebody else, and they have to pay you some license fee or you win some lawsuit. Then you'd make some money. Or if you have a patent, and you're preventing somebody else from coming and infringing, then in that case you can maintain some market share - but the law itself doesn't make you money. So, again, you don't want to spend a lot of money or time in the law, because it does not make you money – that's not what creates the value, that's not what actually generates a business.

Yes, we're hammering on that point a bit, because way too many people come to us and want to spend all this upfront time and money on legal issues that don't even exist yet.

And then, there's this: not only will the law not make you money, oftentimes the law will not protect you anyway.

We've seen campaigns that have a patent, and they get in a lawsuit with somebody else saying "Hey, you violated my patent!" and then here they are saying "No, you actually violated my patent, because I actually had this other patent!" The whole thing just becomes a legal war zone.

There's a difference between wanting to be legally protected and wanting to actually move forward with your business. If you're a VC (venture capital) Backed Company, then yes, go and get the patent, go get a few patents and drop $100,000, because it's not that big of a deal with your funding.

But for most of you, the solopreneur, the entrepreneur, who has a small team, who has a limited budget, and can't come up with $20,000, don't worry about it. (Again, that's our perspective, not our legal advice).

A lot of entrepreneurs who are focused on potential legal issues can get kind of stuck in this conundrum where they can't really take action because they don't have the resources to do the legal late work for patent, but they are afraid the big guys will kind of just beat them once they see the product, and imitate it.

Now you might talk with attorneys and tell them what we've said here in this book, and they could say that we are the biggest idiots ever. But we are coming from decades of experience, telling you what we've seen and what we've experienced. Not long ago, at Funded Today, full disclosure, even with Thomas as an in-house attorney, we spent about six figures in legal, and our company is a midsize type company. So, you can really rack up a lot of expenses from attorneys handling fairly simple things.

We had to spend nearly $100,000 just last year to protect our intellectual property, to protect our contracts, to collect on bad debts, and all the other sorts of things that relate to legal. Chances are that you probably don't have $100,000, or more, set aside to go and do these sorts of things. The law can't protect you because you can't pay your attorney. We've hardly found any attorneys whoever willing to work pro bono, particularly in the business side of law.

When you have a patent and then somebody violates your patent, you have to have the money behind you to go and fight. Then when you win, you have to collect, and collecting is an entirely different thing. Chances are, the person who violated your patent was trying to do something shady and dishonest, and so you win. You spent $100,000 and you've stopped them, but now they have no money for you to collect damages. These are all the things you're not going to hear about when you go in and talk to the attorney for the first time.

That's why we're sharing them with you, so you know. So you can make the best decision for you, and your situation.

Yes, the law is important. Yes, the law is valuable. But there's a time and a place in the season, and we think these are the best ways to go about it. When you are a solopreneur start-up, we don't think that's the best time.

We've experienced everything. We've had competitors use our name, and they'll, say, get **Funded Today** on their website. Then we could have Thomas, or another attorney, send them a demand letter telling them to stop using this registered trademark. And then they might say no. And then you have to send another letter, or you have to sue. You might think that your attorney drafted the most amazing letter - it's so scary, so amazing. And it may be. But the other person could simply say, "Who cares?" Then you're faced with a legal battle.

There is a great book titled "Tuesdays with Morrie." In that book, it says, "I can't believe more people don't just get together man-on-man, woman-on-woman, whatever, and talk about the situation and try to resolve it."

That's how we feel. That's the best way to do things pretty much 100% of the time. When people have a disagreement, just get together and talk about it. This could solve so many problems, and reduce the usage of attorneys quite a bit, as well. Sorry, Thomas.

We think that about 99% of the time, if you go about conflicting issues like that (the right way), and you use a little social grace as well as a little social capital, leveraging your experiences to show the other part you're coming to them as another human being who has empathy, you could probably resolve quite a few things. Yes, we know, we're getting a bit philosophical here.

If you start an engagement with somebody and its negative (like a demand letter), how do you think they're going to respond? If you are confrontational, they're going to be confrontational, and if you are both confrontational, how quickly are you going to resolve a dispute? Not quickly.

Yes, in an ongoing successful business there are things you are going to run into, and you just have to figure out how to resolve them. We've found that legal issues are going to be commensurate with the size of your company. Not always, but typically.

So, back to where we started. The goal is to get moving. Once you get moving you might run into situations that will need resolving. You deal with those as they arise. The thing is, there are laws you don't even know about that you might violate. Situations that are impossible to know ahead of time. As an example, "Kuroi Hana"[76] was a knife campaign - a Japanese knife made with Japanese steel. It was a UK company who was creating the product, and this raised tons of money on crowdfunding (7 figures). We were running marketing everywhere, in almost every country.

One of the countries we were marketing to was Germany. And apparently, there is a German law that created issues. Kuroi Hana was saying their knife was made in Japan. When in reality it wasn't made in Japan, it was simply using Japanese steel, but being made in China. Essentially, it was some little nuance about where it's being created, or the material being used. So, because Kuroi Hana was selling and advertising in Germany, or to German people, then they were running afoul of that German law.

Some other knife company saw this and said something to the effect, "Hey, you can't be advertising like this." Then, they sent a letter to Kickstarter saying Kuroi Hana is violating the law. Kuroi Hana had just finished their raise, the campaign was over, and Kickstarter put a freeze on the Kuroi Hana campaign. So, there was no way to get the money, and if the dispute wasn't resolved within 14 days, all of the backers' money was going be refunded. Again, we're talking like $2,000,000 plus.

---

[76] "Kuroi Hana Knife Collection – Japanese Steel by ... - Kickstarter." 29 May. 2017, https://www.kickstarter.com/projects/edgeofbelgravia/kuroi-hana-japanese-knife-collection-edge-of-belgr. Accessed 2 Dec. 2019.

In this case, Thomas was able to work with their attorneys, and the person involved with the German company, and in a period of less than 72 hours or so, work it all out amicably. Kuroi Hana was able to change the wording so it complied with the German law. Everything was good, their campaign was reinstated, and they got the funds.

But, an example like that shows you that even when you go out with the best intentions, you're going run into situations where you might violate the law, or somebody else will say you violated their patent, and they're going to come after you.

This goes back to what we were saying, your legal woes, legal issues, are going to be commensurate with your size. If it happens, you'll get an email from Kickstarter, and we've dealt with this many times because we worked with so many clients. We'd say, on average, one in every few hundred clients run into an issue.

What we recommend that you do:

Incorporate

The first is to incorporate, and that is to show you have limited liability. You don't want to go run a business, get in some lawsuit, become liable under German law, or some port, because your product injured some child, and who knows what bizarre thing could happen, right? You want to limit your liability, so you are not personally liable. By setting up a corporation, or say an LLC, you limit your liability. They won't be able to come after your house or your car. Setting up as a corporation or LLC is different in every state.

LLC is probably the most common, and if you're just a one product company that's going to be bootstrapped, or self-funded, probably an LLC. You can always change your LLC to be taxed as an S-Corporation when you start making yourself an employer, as well.

When you set up an LLC or a Corporation there's two different ways you can specify for how you want to be taxed. You can be taxed as a C-Corp or as S-Corp. A C-Corp means that you pay Corporate Income Tax, so if you make $100,000, the business will pay taxes on that. Let's say your tax rate for that is 15%, you pay $15,000 in taxes on that $100,000. So now you have $85,000 left over. Let's say you're the only owner of that company, so that $85,000 is now going to get distributed to you, and then you actually need to pay your personal income tax on that $85,000 as well.

This is called "Double Taxation." It's another reason why a lot of times, filing as a corporation isn't your best bet, if you're the typical type of business we see on Kickstarter.

An S-Corp basically says the business itself is not going to be taxed. Any of the profits will simply flow through to the owners. So, if you're the only owner, that $100,000 will come all to you and be taxed directly to you. Even if you still had the money held in your business bank account for taxes, you would still be taxed individually on the $100,000. It avoids the double taxation, because there's no Corporate Tax.

That is what's called a Flow Through Entity, so you can't just hold the money in your business. You're going to have to pay taxes on it even if you don't distribute all the money out to your personal account at the end of the year.

To utilize the power of an LLC, you set up a bank account in the LLCs name. You make sure everybody pays the name of the LLC, rather than yourself. You make sure when you sign a check, you sign it as Zach Smith, or **Funded Today**. You make sure you do not sign anything personally, you always sign it acting as an officer, as a CEO, as a managing member, as a partner, whatever it is of your company. This gives you a good paper trail showing that you're using this LLC separately, and distinctly, from your personal self.

If you do this, then you can protect yourself. When you sign contracts, you sign the contract representing your company, you don't sign the contract implicating yourself personally. That's the reason an LLC is so important, because then, as you operate as a business owner, you actually leverage the power of the LLC and the protection, which is called the corporate veil that the LLC affords.

If you have a business, and it's just you, you can set it up as a Holding Group and create a generic name that would apply to anything. As a simple example, Funded Today is not owned by "Zach." **Funded Today** is owned by a Holding Group, and Zach owns his share of the company, and Thomas owns his share of the company, with his Holding Group. So, when **Funded Today** makes a dividend distribution, meaning when **Funded Today** pays the Holding Group, and then the Holding Group pays Zach Smith a salary, and in that Holding Group the only employee is Zach Smith. This is completely legal, and an efficient tax strategy you can do.

To clarify, when we say Holding Group it just means that there is an LLC, that you are the one who owns it, and you're the only one who owns it. So, when you do business, or when you have ownership, your ownership is not direct, it's not Zach Smith owns 50% of Funded Today, it's Agile Holding Group, owns 50% of Funded Today. Zach Smith happens to personally own 100% of Agile

This gives you another layer of protection, but it also allows you to take advantage of some of the good tax laws. It is worth looking into.

Another thing you'll need to do when you set up in LLC is to get an EIN, which is an "Employer Identification Number." Please note, everything we're talking about here relates to U.S. Law. You can get the EIN on the Federal Government's website.

Also, remember if you launch something and it doesn't work, well, now you have that LLC and you can go launch something else. You can continue to use that corporate entity. And once you have something that's going and is working, if you have another venture you want to try, you can still do it out of that same entity.

Think about that when you're naming your corporation. We judiciously did this with **Funded Today**. The name of Funded Today is generic enough that it works really well for crowdfunding, but it also works really well if you want to get your Amazon Listing Funded Today. It also works if you want to get into real estate investing, or in a broad array of industries that we are considering as we continue to grow. It helps us pivot and expand the company.

Do a namecheck to make sure you're not violating somebody else's name. And as a general matter look at the name, it might not be trademark. Just see it is anyone else's using this name, because we could register a business in Utah called Funded Today, and then somebody else could actually go to California and register that same name Funded Today, and it wouldn't necessarily be a violation, or run afoul of the state law. You can also look at the U.S. Trademarks Office website and just do a search to see if anyone else already has this name, or similar name. And if so, then you might want to reconsider the name you'll be using.

Summary

Be judicious with lawyers, don't use them too much, or waste money. Again, legal doesn't make you money, it's just something you have to do. Be judicious and spend some time, not too much, on the legal issues.

Focus primarily on your business, and make it happen!

20

Crowdfunding a Version 2.0 of Your Product and Building a Long-Term Business through Multiple Crowdfunding Campaigns

Business opportunities are like buses, there's always another one coming. **Richard Branson**

After fulfilling a successful project, creating a 2.0 version of your product is one way to improve upon a minimally viable product, which may have been what you offered in your campaign. Utilizing all the feedback you've received, you create a better or more advanced version of your product to launch a new campaign. When you create a 2.0 version, and launch a new campaign, it's important that you don't assume your 2.0 audience is already familiar with your previous campaign.

Whether you want to develop a business strategy utilizing multiple crowdfunding campaigns or Indiegogo InDemand, as discussed below, using what you have learned from your campaign, and continuing to listen to that all important feedback from backers, will allow you to strengthen your product, your ideas, and your business.

Multiple Crowdfunding Campaigns

Inherent in the strategy of doing multiple crowdfunding campaigns, is the idea that you are building loyalty with your backers and building massive email lists. Theoretically, at least, this means that each subsequent launch performs better than the last.

Continually expanding your selection of products is one of the best ways to help your business to grow. Diversification, within limits, is also good for long-term stability. When you do this, you are increasing the customer lifetime value, because you will have new things to sell to each of them.

Crowdfunding as a Business Strategy

When you start to see crowdfunding campaigns as a business strategy, it starts to open up great opportunity. Take for instance, Peak Design. It is a company that has done multiple campaigns with great success.[77]

> "We're a San Francisco based product design company, and we pride ourselves in doing things a bit differently. We're entirely crowdfunded and are live with our 9th Kickstarter project. We have no outside investors, no revenue goals, no PowerPoint presentations. That means it's just us, our backers, and our brilliantly skilled suppliers. We get to focus on what we love to do: designing beautiful, innovative products for likeminded folks. We think crowdfunding is a

---

[77] "All Creator Bio Pages · GitHub." https://gist.github.com/e3753e985ce81f637952c3d2a123fab1. Accessed 9 Jan. 2020.

> better way to bring products to life, for companies, customers, and the world at large."

In fact, Peak Design has done so well using the crowdfunding strategy, it is now the most successful "crowdfunding company"[78] on Kickstarter:

> Peak Design closed its ninth Kickstarter campaign on July 18, 2019, generating $12,142,148 from 27,165 backers, averaging an impressive $447 per backer. Once Peak Design fulfills these orders, it will be the largest fully executed Kickstarter campaign of all time. You may recall that Pebble failed to deliver on its infamous Kickstarter, in which backers pledged over $20 million, but the company never shipped its promised product. To date, Peak Design's nine campaigns have generated $32,375,576 from 122,413 non-unique backers (some people have backed multiple campaigns), making it the most successful company on Kickstarter.

To give you additional ideas of what is possible with crowdfunding, take a look at the following sections from articles also about Peak Design, talking more about how they are using crowdfunding as a business strategy.

A TechCrunch article about Peak Design states[79]:

---

[78] "This Company Just Broke The Record For The Most Money ...." 20 Jul. 2019, https://www.forbes.com/sites/johngreathouse/2019/07/20/this-company-just-broke-the-record-for-the-most-money-raised-on-kickstarter-over-32-4m/. Accessed 9 Jan. 2020.

[79] "Peak Design and building a company on the Kickstarter platform." 8 Sep. 2016, https://techcrunch.com/2016/09/08/peak-design/. Accessed 9 Jan. 2020.

> "Kickstarter has financed the sort of rapid growth that might otherwise elude a young, small company. Before launching the messenger-bag campaign, Peak Design had $350,000 available through a line of credit with Wells Fargo, enough to buy about 5,000 bags. "We went through an exhaustive process to try and get more out of them," says Anhalt, "but they don't lend appropriately to small high-growth companies." (A spokeswoman for Wells Fargo said the bank could not comment on a confidential client relationship but pointed to government figures showing that the bank is the nation's leading lender to small companies."

And Forbes writes[80]:

> Kickstarter and other crowdfunding sites have become hunting grounds for unusually passionate consumers. Typically, companies tap this resource when they start out, but the Everyday Messenger was Peak Design's fifth crowdfunding campaign. The company has introduced all of its new products on the site and along the way has honed a sophisticated strategy not just for raising money efficiently — and at greatly reduced risk — but also for reaching its most enthusiastic customers. "We essentially consider Kickstarter a third sales channel for us," says David Anhalt, the company's financial chief, alongside its own website and the more than a thousand retail stores that stock Peak Design products.

---

[80] "How Peak Design Used Crowdfunding To Kickstart Its ...." 4 Jan. 2016, https://www.forbes.com/sites/robbmandelbaum/2016/01/04/how-peak-design-used-crowdfunding-to-kickstart-its-business-model/. Accessed 9 Jan. 2020.

Note that David Anhalt, the company's financial chief, states that they consider Kickstarter a third sales channel for their products. Crowdfunding is a brave new world in business

One of our serial clients, Steven Elliot Ng, has done well debuting a series of popular wrist watches, wallets, and belts, showing that you certainly don't have to be the most successful company on Kickstarter, like Peak Design, to succeed with this strategy.

Using Indiegogo InDemand

Another avenue in crowdfunding to consider is Indiegogo InDemand. Indiegogo InDemand allows you to continue to raise funds for your campaign after your campaign is over.

Your campaign on Kickstarter has a deadline of 30 or 45 days, or whatever you set, and after that campaign is over, you can't keep raising money on that platform. But, with Indiegogo InDemand you can have a campaign that basically runs in perpetuity. While it's InDemand, you can continue to raise funds.

Kickstarter does not offer this because the company has made a very conscious, purposeful decision, to only be a platform that is for raising money to hitting, or passing, your goal. After that timeframe, it's done - they don't want to be an E-commerce store.

However, Indiegogo InDemand has actually taken the opposite approach, so the beauty and power of InDemand is that you can keep raising funds, you can keep generating sales, even after your campaign is over.

As an example, let's look at Unobrush[81] - the toothbrush that allows you to brush your teeth in 6 seconds. We helped them raise just over $1million on Kickstarter. When the campaign ended, we transitioned them over to Indiegogo InDemand, and they've raised an additional $270,000+ on Indiegogo InDemand. This is money that they are using to be able to get the product to life, and to first ship to their Kickstarter backers, and ultimately ship to their Indiegogo backers.

The strategy behind Indiegogo InDemand is that you keep raising more money. Rather than saying you're going to deliver in a particular month on your Kickstarter campaign, you say, "Hey, because you're a little late, you're going to have to pay a little bit more, and we're going to ship your product in August (or whatever is a couple of months down the road)".

This is a great way to have sustained cash flow, to continue to raise money, and to take advantage of platforms that are much bigger than your website while you get ready and get your business in order.

As we talked about in the last chapter, if you try to transition directly to your website for all your sales, it's a difficult position because very often you're not ready to ship the product, but you still want to raise the capital. Indiegogo InDemand lets you do that. You wouldn't be able to go on Amazon and sell something that isn't done, and you can't even be able to really do it on your own website.

Well, you *can* technically do it, but most people who purchase from a website are expecting to make an

---

[81] "UNOBRUSH - Toothbrushing Reimagined | Indiegogo." https://www.indiegogo.com/projects/unobrush-toothbrushing-reimagined. Accessed 6 Jan. 2020.

immediate purchase of a product, and then receive it quickly (we can thank Amazon for that expectation). So, if you're telling your customers, "Hey, I'm still creating this, it's six months down the road," they're probably not going to accept that like backers in the ecosystem of crowdfunding will.

If you tell people that they can buy and get their product in three months, and then it ends up taking four because of shipping delays, you're going to have a bunch of angry people who are going to call their credit card company and dispute a charge, amongst other things. That's a problem for you and your future business.

Indiegogo InDemand solves that for you because they've done this with hundreds, or thousands, of campaigns, and it gives them a huge advantage to be able to leverage those relationships with credit card providers so that you are protected, and so you can have the cash flow you need to eventually have some product that you can then sell on Amazon as well as your website.

People can still ask for a refund on InDemand if you're too delayed, or they change their mind. A pledger or contributor can actually get a refund through Indiegogo, and no, that's not great, either, but they are set up for it. You won't actually have to deal with those credit card disputes. What is also nice about InDemand, and Indiegogo in general, is that unlike Kickstarter, Indiegogo and Indiegogo InDemand campaigns charge the credit card of the person making a contribution right away, right when they make a pledge. Whereas with Kickstarter, they don't charge peoples' credit cards until the campaign is over, and sometimes, you can have some pledges or charges that don't even go through.

Indiegogo InDemand allows you to continue telling your story and build on your initial crowdfunding campaign page. InDemand gives you the opportunity to engage with new people on the way, and to get new people as part of your tribe, as part of your crowd.

The ability to reach new audiences and receive ongoing exposure on Indiegogo is huge. Indiegogo's audience is very different than Kickstarter's. Indiegogo has a good selection of people, a newsletter, and connections. So, if you meet certain metrics, Indiegogo is amazing at customer support. They're very kind, and they're very helpful. If you meet those certain metrics, they will help you out to reach these new audiences, and that can lead to quite a bit of money and pledges, like we shared with the Unobrush example earlier.

Another important aspect of Indiegogo In Demand, is the "Social proof." When you have sales InDemand, you can show, "Here's how many backers I have, and here is how much I've raised." This can have a huge positive impact on future sales and other opportunities (think a VC, or an Angel, or getting Shark Tank to approach you).

The On-Off Strategy

A powerful tool that on Indiegogo InDemand is the ability to run your campaign for as long, or short a time, as you'd like. There is pretty much no commitment. You turn it off whenever you want, otherwise it just keeps going. You can even turn it off for now, and then turn it back on later.

As an example, the BauBax travel jacket did that - ran it for several months, turned it off, and then turned it back on for a bit and had another run. That's an interesting strategy not a lot of people take advantage of, but it can have a lot of power.

One of the reasons to try Indiegogo InDemand is that when you're coming off of a big campaign and you want to keep that momentum, you want to stay in the crowdfunding community. It's very hard to do that on your own website, if you are a new startup. If you're a big brand and you're launching a new product, then yes, you definitely could just take people over to your social channels where you already have community and engagement. But you most likely don't have that, so really, the momentum is a huge factor and you want to ride that for as long as possible.

Think about all the work and marketing that you put into your crowdfunding campaign. You want to transition your Kickstarter campaign over immediately and take advantage of all of the ad traffic, all of the press, everything that was sending traffic your Kickstarter page. If it had nowhere to go, all of that traffic that was going to your Kickstarter is essentially dead traffic once your campaign is over, because you can't raise money on Kickstarter after that campaign timeframe.

But, if you redirect all that traffic, you capitalize on that momentum and, boom, it all comes over to Indiegogo InDemand – and now that traffic is actually valuable monetarily, because people are seeing your product and actually being able to back your product again, on another platform.

You might land press the last day of your campaign, and it might raise $10,000 on Kickstarter, but what are you going to do when that press was only live for a couple of hours and now your campaign is over? Again, Indiegogo InDemand allows you to capitalize on all the remaining people that haven't read the press yet, haven't received the email, haven't read the Facebook post. Momentum is huge, and it just makes perfect sense to make the transition.

In fact, we even say that it's one of the cardinal sins if you have a big campaign, and you don't have Indiegogo InDemand ready to transition to. From our perspective, you've just literally throwing thousands of dollars out the window.

You don't want to wait a day, or even five hours. You should have had all this setup in the moment your Kickstarter ends, everything should have been simultaneously switched over to Indiegogo InDemand.

That means you usually need to get it set up a week or two beforehand your campaign ends, to make sure everything is in place. You don't want to be placing the finishing touches on your Indiegogo InDemand campaign when there's 30 minutes left on your Kickstarter campaign. That's just not the way to do it. If you don't set it up you could have 1,000 people who are sitting there, and then all of a sudden can't make a pledge. That is money you just lost.

Secret Perks

One thing you can also do in InDemand is utilize a feature that Indiegogo has called "Secret Perks." A Secret Perk is a pledge level that is only available to people who come from a certain link, so you could have a Secret Perk for the prelaunch list from your Kickstarter campaign. You can email that list and say, "Hey, if you didn't have a chance to make a pledge, we have the Secret Perk for you because you were with us before we originally launched!" By utilizing these Secret Perks, you can basically create some exclusivity, "Hey, this is only going to be good for three more days!"

Because in the Indiegogo InDemand campaign you don't have a time limit, so there's not really that pressure to go and make a pledge. A potential pledger can say, "Oh, I'll get around to it later." Surprise, surprise, they never come back and contribute. (This is another reason regular emails are important).

However, using the Secret Perks, you can still put on some of that pressure, where you have time restrictions for when somebody can make a pledge.

Shark Tank & Investors

Yet another reason to choose Indiegogo InDemand is that a lot of people don't know about crowdfunding. But, most people have heard of the show "Shark Tank." If you haven't seen this show, basically, people come on the show and they pitch their idea to these millionaires, and the billionaire Mark Cuban, and they say, "Look, for 50% equity, I'll give you $500,000." Then Mark Cuban says "Great, deal over!" but Mr. Wonderful says, "No, not a deal."

Anyway, the show Shark Tank is a very, very powerful way to leverage your success on Kickstarter and then couple that success with Indiegogo InDemand. For example, Unobrush, which we mentioned earlier, can now say "Look we've raised $1.4 million." They can now approach Shark Tank. In fact, we often see former clients pitching on Shark Tank. We have more clients on Shark Tank than anybody else in the world. Pretty cool.

Now, what you might not know about Shark Tank, and yes, we might be digressing a bit here, but they usually interview the startup for three, four, or five hours, and then they cut the approach down to maybe 15 to 20 minutes for TV.

So, you don't hear a lot of the interview, but Mark Cuban in particular will ask, "Did you do a Crowdfunding campaign?" If you watch the show religiously, you'll see him ask that quite a bit, and the reason he asks that is because he wants to see validation. What better way to show validation than a transparent website like Indiegogo InDemand, that literally shows exactly what you've raised? You can't fudge the numbers - they can Google it, they can look it up right there, "Yep she's raised $1,370,354 United States Dollars as of December of this year."

That is very, very powerful. The other thing to note is that most of our clients and entrepreneurs that use crowdfunding get way better deals than the others who are on the show who don't have sales, who don't have numbers, who don't have this third-party credibility, who don't have the transparency.

The other reason this information is so powerful is that the numbers and social proof matter for investors, Angels, and Venture Capitalists. They see that your campaign is validated, that there are thousands or tens of thousands of people that back the campaign and they say "Well look, this is good." That's a wonderful thing, when you've raised a lot of money and you've proven that your product works. Now you can ask for more, your company is worth more, and when your company is worth more you give a plus equity, long-term that wins for everybody.

If you go on the show Shark Tank, or if you got to a VC or an Angel, or any sort of private equity, the first thing they're going to ask is: "What are your numbers?" If your numbers are not good, they're going to ask for more money, and if your numbers are great, now *you're* in the driver's seat, now you can negotiate, now you have control.

Of course, one of the benefits of Indiegogo InDemand is that you now have a strategy where you don't take investor money. Yes, having good numbers allows you to make a better deal. But avenues like InDemand allow you to continue developing your business, without a Shark Tank or Angel investor.

Key Takeaways

- Using multiple crowdfunding campaigns as a long-term business strategy can be very successful.

- Inherent in the strategy of doing multiple crowdfunding campaigns is the idea that you are building loyalty with your backers, and building massive email lists.

- Indiegogo InDemand is an excellent platform for gleaning additional funds for your project while it's awaiting fulfillment (between Kickstarter phase and E-commerce phase), while leveraging the relatively high "organic" traffic to Indiegogo's website.

- It's best to prepare your Indiegogo InDemand page to debut immediately when your Kickstarter campaign ends, and to redirect traffic from your Kickstarter page through a "Spotlight" button to your Indiegogo page, so that you don't needlessly lose either momentum or pledges.

- It helps to market your Kickstarter campaign through short URLs with adjustable forwarding that can be updated anytime your project transitions from one platform to another.

- While campaigning on Indiegogo, you should use "Secret Perks," negotiate Indiegogo newsletter appearances, and possibly leverage your success to obtain additional funds from Angel investors or venture capitalists, including on "Shark Tank," which can also be very good for publicity.

- You can end your Indiegogo InDemand campaign anytime (and even resume it anytime) until your Kickstarter project is fulfilled, but you shouldn't expect your InDemand campaign to raise more than a fraction of what your Kickstarter campaign raised.

- True success requires you to live outside of your comfort zone.

21

Relaunching Your Campaign if You Don't Hit Your Goal

***The supreme accomplishment is to blur the line between work and play.* Arnold J. Toynbee**

If at First You Don't Succeed...

We'll never succeed if we never try.

Trying hopefully results in success, but, since nobody's perfect, it sometimes results in failure instead. Failure is a natural part of this mortal life, including business ventures. Many newly available products and services - even entire businesses - fail every day.

Although such failures can be stumbling blocks for some entrepreneurs, they can also be stepping-stones for those who choose to nurture the right attitude. That attitude includes humility, faith, and patience.

There's never a valid reason for us to give up on pursuing a dream. We discover ourselves treading the wrong path. Our persistence in trying, learning, and ultimately improving constitutes a vital key to our final success. Yes, that success might require more time than we'd like, and it doesn't always come in the form that we'd originally expected.

There are countless examples of great successful people failing. Thomas Edison, for instance, persistently tested thousands of different incandescent lamp filaments before he finally identified one material that was sufficiently durable (and cost-effective), for residential use.

Although Edison learned exceptionally well from his own mistakes through experimentation, and provides us with a great example in that regard, it's always good for us to learn from others' mistakes as much as possible. So, perhaps we might learn a few things from one of the most spectacular product failures of all time...

The Tragic Tale of the Edsel

Ford's Edsel has become a popular symbol for failed products, and deservedly so.

During the 1950s, Ford had already enjoyed a long series of great successes in both low-priced and high-priced cars, and was interested in extending those successes into the mid-priced car market also. So, its' executives decided to create a perfect premiere car for middle-class Americans.

Uh oh. Unfortunately, their hubris impeded their efforts from the start. For example, although they hired the best market research available, they selectively ignored it (unlike for previous Ford cars) and instead went with their own personal hunches. Also, their refusal to consider failure as a possibility, ultimately resulted in severe overproduction. On top of all that, they generally neglected this car's engineering to focus persistently on its marketing, thereby putting last things first.

The Edsel's marketing is perhaps the only thing that Ford got right about it. Ford skillfully exercised amazing showmanship—perhaps some of the best during that "golden age" of advertising. They generated tremendous "buzz" about the Edsel for an entire year through ads, news, and even a top-rated television special, while persistently teasing the public with fragmented glimpses of its carefully-kept-secret design.

When Ford finally unveiled the Edsel in late 1957 on "E-Day," as Ford's marketers had dubbed it, curious shoppers sometimes lined up around-the-block to see this amazing new "car of the future" that they'd heard so much about. Sadly, those showroom visitors generally felt disappointed as hype finally dissipated into reality, and the REAL Edsel proved to be nothing more than an over-hyped overpriced ugly gas-guzzler that attempted, and failed, to please everyone. The Edsel quickly developed a reputation for unreliability. Additionally, a simultaneous economic recession contributed to a sudden shift in consumer preferences toward compact cars, and that didn't help Edsel sales, either. Ultimately, no vast army of skilled salespeople, advertisers, and PR agents, could polish away the obvious flaws.

For these and other reasons, the infamous Edsel ultimately proved to be "the wrong car for the wrong market at the wrong time." After it lost Ford over $250 million dollars in two years, this car-turned-joke finally drove out of showrooms into history as one of the most spectacular new-product failures EVER.

Ford, as we know, survived this debacle to continue its string of successful new cars, including its renowned Mustang in 1965. And, partly due to such successes, even Ford's Edsel eventually gained some popularity as a collector's item.

What Can We Learn from This?

Unfortunately, the Edsel team seemingly never learned from their $250 million mistakes, or even accepted that they'd made such mistakes. In fact, Edsel marketing manager J. C. Doyle, once even publicly berated car-buyers for refusing to accept what Ford had given them, as he insisted that they should have done. But WE can (and should) learn from such mistakes to avoid repeating them. So, what lessons can we learn from the Edsel project?

- One lesson may be that, whereas pride goes before the fall, humility is key to both learning and progress.
- Another may be that businesses exist to serve customers, not the other way around, and that "the customer is always right."
- A third may be that trying to please everybody may result in pleasing nobody.
- A fourth may be that timing is important, and that consumer preferences change over time.
- A fifth may be that hunches are no substitute for facts (and that, when you've done something right repeatedly before, you should keep doing it).
- A sixth may be that when reality is proving that you're mistaken, then it's good to accept reality quickly - before you've wasted $250,000,000.
- A seventh may be that a superior product-and-price combination is always the single most vital factor in sales, no matter how skillfully presented and promoted it may be — and, similarly, that even the best marketing can only do so much to sell a bad deal.

And perhaps one final overarching lesson from the Edsel project is that even though it failed spectacularly, Ford as a whole kept moving forward, as should we all.

So, if you spend years carefully designing a product until you finally reveal it to the world only to discover that what you thought was a figurative Mustang is (oops!) actually an Edsel... then it'll be alright, as we've said before. If you perceive that your crowdfunding campaign is among those that are failing, then please remember that this is actually normal, because campaigns fail about twice as often as they succeed.

Preparing to Relaunch

When you need to relaunch because you haven't reached your goal, you need to determine what needs improvement and then fix it. Plus, you'll need to prepare your backers to pledge again.

If you did not reach your campaign funding goal, carefully reconsider your project's elements:

- Product
- Price
- Presentation
- Promotion/Marketing
- Funding Goal
- Rewards Structure
- Timing
- Media
- The Platform
- Something else
- A Combination of these factors

You should strive to obtain as much feedback as possible from your backers to attempt to determine why the market isn't responding well enough to what you're offering. Then, learn from that feedback to "pivot" into doing something even better.

In some cases, you can easily solve these problems without needing to re-launch. In other cases, you may need to cancel your original campaign, fix whatever's not-good-enough about it as best as you can (while communicating regularly with your previous backers), and then relaunch your revised campaign.

Relaunching is especially common when making dramatic revisions to your product, prices, goal, timing, platform, or presentation. This is essentially what Coolest Cooler[82] did, as its project initially failed, then eventually thrived after relaunching in a better season with both a finished design and a lower goal.

In other rare cases, you may need to relaunch your campaign, even though it is faring well, due to involuntary cancellation as we talked about in Chapter 17. This is more likely to happen on Kickstarter, which not only imposes higher standards on campaigns, but also tends to err on the side of being overly cautious. In fact, Kickstarter is notorious for wantonly cancelling campaigns (regardless of either how long they've run or how much they've raised). Such involuntary cancellations are rarer on Indiegogo, and the customer service team is also kinder about it, although they still happen. You can minimize any risks of involuntary cancellation by ensuring that you're following all of the platform's rules.

---

[82] "COOLEST COOLER: 21st Century Cooler that's ... - Kickstarter." 12 Mar. 2018, https://www.kickstarter.com/projects/ryangrepper/coolest-cooler-21st-century-cooler-thats-actually. Accessed 7 Jan. 2020.

Or, if you discover significant problems with your campaign after it launches, perhaps with help from your backers, then you may want to cancel it, improve it, and relaunch it. Don't be afraid to take this step if needed. Better to stop, improve and do things right, than to desperately try and keep a sinking ship afloat.

Remobilize Your Backers

You will want to keep in contact with your backers through the process of preparing, and then relaunching. As soon as you have relaunched, contact all your original backers to persuade them to re-pledge. They can help your campaign to gain great momentum quickly, just like pre-launch marketing can do.

If you have all the feedback in front of you and you've reviewed everything, and you still can't figure out why your campaign didn't reach its goal, or you know what's wrong but you don't know how to make it right, don't give up. Hire someone who can help you figure it out, or help you improve the elements that need improving.

Yes, you can hire **Funded Today**. Or you can hire someone else. Just don't give up.

Recommit to Yourself, Your Success

Remember, it's about being committed to your success, not to a singular idea. The commitment to success will carry you across the duration of the life of your product, or your business, your life.

Your crowdfunding campaign is only the beginning. Yes, you might not hit your goal and need to relaunch. Or maybe you do hit your goal. We see campaigns that have a successful raise, and then they're just running an E-commerce campaign and it doesn't work, it doesn't convert, they're not able to drive traffic at a profitable ROI.

Whether you have to pivot and relaunch during your campaign, or after it's failed, or after it's succeeded, just pivot! Take the information you have to move into a more profitable direction.

The most successful people are always watching to see where they can pivot, where they can grow. The biggest companies out there - how do they grow? Typically, the way they grow is through acquisitions. They often don't just stay in whatever they're niche, or their industry is. Well, yeah, they keep doing that to continue that revenue, but the Fortune 100, Fortune 500 companies are often getting the inspiration through the new "Nascent Markets" and tapping into those through acquisitions. Everything is an evolution, always changing, always growing, always morphing. You have to be willing to pivot, and to make those changes.

One failure does not make *you* a failure. There are so many examples of this. One of the most well-known in crowdfunding is Hiral Sanghavi of "BauBax," which raised $9.2 million on Kickstarter. But have you ever heard of the "Wireless Charging Apparel?" Likely not, because guess what? It didn't raise any money, and he had to cancel the campaign. Same exact guy, same exact mindset, same exact everything. His original campaign, which is the 6th or 7th most funded crowdfunding campaign in the history of Crowdfunding, raised $9.1 million - $12 to $13 million raised when you combine it with "Indiegogo InDemand". His next idea - the Wireless Charging Apparel, didn't even raise a dollar.

To repeat: success does not indicate future success, failure does not indicate future failure, and one failure does not mean you're going to fail. Be committed to success not just your idea of success.

You can make more money in business than doing anything else. If you find the right idea it can change not only the world, but it can change your life.

Steve Jobs said it best: when you grow up, you tend to get told the world is the way it is, and your life is just to live your life inside this little world. Try not to bash into the walls too much, try to have a nice family, have fun, save a little money. That's a very limited life.

Life can be much broader once you discover one simple fact: **everything around you that you call life was made-up by people that were no smarter than you**, and you can change it, you can influence it, you can build your own things that other people can use, and once you learn that, your world will never be the same again.

Fun fact:

Did you know that the world-renowned Funded Today podcast, "Get Funded Today," debuted on Wednesday, November 1st, 2018 with its inaugural three episodes?

A Final Note

Everyone has taken a shower, or been in nature, and had that moment of "eureka!" at least once in their life.

If you want to win as an entrepreneur, and as a human being, you need to hop out of that shower, towel off, and take massive action at bringing your idea to life. Doing something about your idea will teach you more in 24 hours than spending another year thinking about it will ever do.

Did you know a goldfish can grow up to 12 inches or more, when in a pond? But, when that same goldfish lives in a fish tank, it stays only a few inches long. That's because it doesn't have the ability to grow when it's in a fish tank. In the TEDx Talk, "Why Comfort Will Ruin Your Life," by Bill Eckstrom," the key takeaway is this:

Growth only occurs in a state of discomfort.

Make this your year. Stop thinking, stop talking, and start doing. It's the doers who win in business, life, and love.

Fun fact:

Did you know that when we ran the marketing for Purple Pillow, just one earned media/PR feature we secured on Sleepopolis.com raised $313,246? Incredible! Right?

Additional Resources

Chapter 1: Intro to Crowdfunding

Investopedia

- What is crowdfunding? fnd.to/investopedia

Funded Today Blog

- How to raise 100m on crowdfunding: fnd.to/raise100m

Funded Today Podcast

- Ultimate crowdfunding prelaunch checklist: fnd.to/prelaunch

Kickstarter

- Kickstarter help: fnd.to/kickstartered

IndieGoGo

- IndiGoGo help: fnd.to/indiegogoed

Chapter 2: Finding a Great Idea that Sells

Funded Today Blog

- Crowdfunding success matrix: fnd.to/fundingmatrix

- 10 proven techniques for raising crowdfunding money – summit presentation: fnd.to/importsummit
- Kinds of projects Kickstarter is most effective at funding: fnd.to/projectypes

Chapter 3: Crowdfunding vs Crowd Validation

Funded Today Blog

- 6 animal instincts for crowdfunding success: fnd.to/animaltypes

Chapter 4: The 7 P's

Funded Today Blog

- The 7 Ps for crowdfunding success: fnd.to/7ps

Chapter 5: Triple F: Friends Family Fools (FFF)

Funded Today Podcast

- Family, friends and fools: fnd.to/fffpod

Funded Today YouTube

- How to leverage your network for crowdfunding success: fnd.to/fffvid

Chapter 6: Setting Up Your Campaign

Funded Today Blog

- Kickstarter vs. IndieGoGo: fnd.to/platforms

Chapter 7: Creating a Video that Converts

Funded Today Blog

- The 1 difference between Kickstarter and IndiGoGo videos: fnd.to/videoblog1
- Do you really need a Kickstarter video for success? fnd.to/videoblog2
- How much money should your Kickstarter video raise? fnd.to/videoblog3
- How to get Kickstarter video help from experts: fnd.to/videoblog4
- 5 tidbits of Kickstarter video advice that could save your campaign: fnd.to/videoblog5
- 4 crucial components of the Kickstarter video formula: fnd.to/videoblog6
- Boost the quality of your video: fnd.to/videoblog7
- 2 steps to creating a Kickstarter prototype video & why you need one: fnd.to/videoblog8
- What to learn from Crowdfunding video awards: fnd.to/videoblog9
- Ideal Kickstarter video length: fnd.to/videobloga
- How to correctly match Kickstarter video format: fnd.to/videoblogb
- When to use humor in video: fnd.to/videoblogc
- 3 key video script elements: fnd.to/videoblogd
- How to choose video background music: fnd.to/videobloge
- How much will a Kickstarter video cost? fnd.to/videoblogf
- 5 crowdfunding video tips: fnd.to/videoblogg

Funded Today Podcast

- Successful presentation video production: fnd.to/videopod

Funded Today YouTube

- Video page optimization: fnd.to/pagevid

Chapter 8: Developing a Compelling Page

Funded Today Blog

- Why use Kickstarter template when you could work with experts? fnd.to/pageblog1
- Ultimate guide to Kickstarter page design: fnd.to/pageblog2
- The power of presentation: fnd.to/pageblog3

Funded Today Podcast

- Successful presentation page design: fnd.to/pagepod

Funded Today YouTube

- Optimizing your campaign page: https://www.youtube.com/watch?v=s2WSzm1RrxY

Chapter 9: Setting You Pledge Levels

Funded Today Blog

- Pricing your crowdfunding rewards: fnd.to/pricingblog
- How goal/rewards structure helps win backers: fnd.to/fundinggoal1
- How to set Kickstarter goal amount: fnd.to/fundinggoal2

- Setting your Crowdfunding goals: fnd.to/fundinggoal3

Funded Today YouTube

- Reward level pricing: fnd.to/pricingvid

Chapter 10: Preparing for Launch Day

Funded Today Blog

- Hiring for crowdfunding – why fewer is more: fnd.to/agencycount

Funded Today YouTube

- Prelaunch outreach training: fnd.to/outreach

Chapter 13: Marketing Your Campaign – Press

Funded Today Blog

- Understanding PR in crowdfunding: fnd.to/prblog

Chapter 14: Marketing Your Campaign – Other Traffic Methods

Funded Today Blog

- The power of promotion: fnd.to/promotion

Chapter 15: Prelaunch Community Building and Email Lead Generation

Funded Today YouTube

- Email lead generation: fnd.to/leadgenvid

Chapter 17: Creating a Campaign that Won't Get Banned

Kickstarter

- What happens when project is suspended? fnd.to/suspensions

Reddit_

- Kickstarter suspended our project – help! fnd.to/suspensionpost

Chapter 18: Delivering on Your Campaign

Funded Today Blog

- 4 essential steps to manufacturing crowdfunding campaigns fnd.to/manufacturing
- Customer service for crowdfunding campaigns fnd.to/backerservice

Chapter 19: Building a Company Post Campaign

Funded Today YouTube

- Messaging and reengaging with cancelled backers: fnd.to/cancelsvid

Chapter 21: Relaunching Your Campaign if You Didn't Hit Your Goal

Funded Today Blog

- Your campaign might fail and that's okay: fnd.to/failure
- Crowdfunding suspension and/or relaunch: fnd.to/relaunches

Don't' be afraid to give up the good to go for great.

-John D. Rockefeller

About the Authors

Thomas Alvord – Funded Today Co-Founder & Chairman

Thomas Alvord lives in Lee's Summit, MO with his wife Melanie and their three sons. He graduated from Brigham Young University with a law degree and a Master's Degree in Public Administration.
He has run marketing for many online digital campaigns, including for multiple United States Presidential campaigns, and multi-million dollar political committees. He has also consulted with Fortune 500 companies on how to improve their digital marketing and strategy. Thomas has raised $329,030,216 for thousands of inventors using the crowdfunding platforms Kickstarter and IndieGoGo. He is an attorney with the Utah Bar, and in 2019 founded LawHQ.com.

Zach Smith – Funded Today Co-Founder, CEO & COO

Zach Smith is a serial entrepreneur. A primary passion is helping others turn their dreams, ideas, and inspirations into successful companies. This led to his creation of Funded Today, LLC, the world's most successful crowdfunding firm and largest provider of crowdfunding marketing services worldwide. In 2018, Funded Today finished 27th on the prestigious Inc. 5000 list of America's fastest-growing companies and #2 for fastest-growing privately held companies in Utah and #3 in the "Advertising and Marketing" category. Chances are, if you've seen a successful campaign on Kickstarter or IndieGoGo, Zach Smith and Funded Today have been the driving factor behind its success!

Zach speaks fluent Mandarin and graduated Summa Cum Laude as the valedictorian from Weber State University's Goddard School of Business and Economics with a business degree. He craves knowledge and whenever he has spare time, enjoys real estate investing, angel investing, private lending, playing competitive indoor soccer and other sports, as well as reading business biographies and autobiographies, listening to podcasts and audiobooks, traveling the world, and working with young entrepreneurs and start-ups.

FUNDED TODAY
KICKSTARTER INDIEGOGO

Made in the USA
Monee, IL
23 February 2021

61204183R00226